About the Author

Brian Thomas was born into a working class family. In the era of post-war austerity many young people felt obliged to contribute to the family income and for their own wellbeing. Money was short and pay was poor but at least work was plentiful and a secure career was possible. The future was bright and, often, fun.

Dedication

"Ah, why should all life labour be?"
Alfred, Lord Tennyson

Brian Thomas

THAT'S IT

AUSTIN MACAULEY
PUBLISHERS LTD.

A CIP catalogue record for this title is available from the British Library.

ISBN 9781785543999 (Paperback)
ISBN 9781785544002 (Hardback)
ISBN 9781785544019 (E-Book)

www.austinmacauley.com

First Published (2016)
Austin Macauley Publishers Ltd.
25 Canada Square
Canary Wharf
London
E14 5LQ

Contents

Chapter 1

THE PAPER BOY

The Paper Boy reached the crest of the hill a few seconds ahead of the homicidal maniac! He stopped to breathe and to hear his heart hammering. "Done it," he said slowly and soundlessly to himself, "Done it again".

There was a time when every working class boy, and some girls, wanted to be a paper boy, or paper girl. It wasn't just the money. That was important, although it was only a few shillings a week and it gave kids, for such they were nearly always called in ordinary homes in those days, what mums and dads used to call a chance to learn the value of money. It was also the feeling that you were doing something useful, that you were a working person and that you actually could get a bit of money to spend on yourself, and maybe others, without the embarrassment of having to ask your mum or — worse — your dad for some. Actually, a lot of ordinary kids never asked their mums and dads for money, either because they knew they wouldn't get it or because they knew that their parents didn't have it. There were several drawbacks attached to paper rounds. In the first place, except for the very few compact rounds near the shop and near to your house, a bike was essential. It didn't have to be a new one, but it had to be reasonably serviceable, and not all families could afford to furnish their children with bikes. A bike was a big thing, even for Christmas, but a second hand one would do. And, of course, you had to be able to ride it, which was by no means certain. Many children are unable to identify how or when they learned to ride a bike – or swim for that matter. Mind you, swimming was easy if you lived near the coast because the sea was there and entry to it was free. All you needed was a bit of courage and maybe an older sibling or friends to encourage you. Riding a bike was much the same, except that bikes didn't appear in front of you for nothing. Having got the bike and learned to ride it, another drawback was that you had to turn up at the paper shop every weekday at about half past four in the afternoon and — far harder — half past six in the morning if you were lucky enough to get a coveted morning round! These restrictions meant an awful lot. In the case of an evening round, you had to miss anything that took place after school even if you liked it very much, and even if it meant that you couldn't join in the football trials or whatever else it was that you thought that you were brilliant at. In the case of a morning round, you arrived at school any, or all, of sweaty, tired and late!

In spite of these hardships, there was always a waiting list of such length that some boys and girls grew up before they ever got a paper round! The way to do it was to go to your local newsagent and ask. That in itself took a bit of doing if you were not very forward or lacked confidence. You could also spread your net wider, especially if you already had your bike and didn't mind going a mile or two to alternative newsagents' shops. Notwithstanding the waiting list, if you were lucky, or if you kept pestering the proprietors, you got your first employment and began work.

Now, the evening round was easy and straightforward. A child could, and often did, do it. The age limit specified that you had to be at least twelve years old, or thereabouts. It was advisable that you be able to read because the newsagent would provide a list of streets and house numbers indicating where the papers had to be delivered. The newsagent also supplied a large white canvas bag, just the right size, and specifically manufactured for carrying the newspapers. These bags grew grey with age of course but they were a mark of your status as a paper boy and the possession of such an item was a source of pride and an object of envy, at least for some. The simple bit was that all the evening papers were the same — "The Daily Echo" — and all you had to do was fold each of them a couple of times, so that you could push them through the letter boxes — not always as straightforward as it sounds, as any postman or postwoman will testify. Then you would go through your list of numbers for each of your streets until the task was complete and you had no papers left or — horror of horrors — you did have a paper left and must have missed a house out!

All paper boys and girls, postmen and women, and indeed, anyone who has tried to deliver things to people's houses — such as political leaflets, church circulars, adverts for local Indian restaurants and so on — must have reflected upon how much easier the task would be if all letter boxes were of the same dimensions and the same height from the ground! And if there were no fierce dogs trying to bite your hand off as you pushed the items through the letter box and into the house!

The Paper Boy, having safely reached the top of the hill or, rather, the gentle rise, was able to pause and reflect for a moment, draw breath and even smile at his good fortune at not only evading the maniac, a deranged killer if ever there was one, but also upon having reached his target! He had had the bad luck to be sacked from his first round, an evening round at his local newsagent, for persistent cheek to the proprietor's son, who, it has to be said, was an adult with a rather exaggerated sense of his own importance. "It's time you realised that you *work* here!" was what the proprietor's son had, quite reasonably, averred following the final bout of impertinence. Actually, the Paper Boy was what certain social scientists called an introvert and atoned for this by feigned over-confidence, frequently amounting to downright rudeness. This was something the Paper Boy invariably regretted, but could do little to stop. Nonetheless, the Paper Boy had served for some time and he felt that his loyalty should have been given some consideration. Especially since a kind word and a gentle voice was something to which the Paper Boy was susceptible, as a young primary school teacher could have attested to, if she had ever realised that quietly calling the Paper Boy by his first name in a friendly and solicitous manner was what had transformed him from a cheeky, uncooperative pupil into her willing slave. She was also quite pretty and that, too, may have had something to do with it. The loss of his evening round was probably for the best because the paper boy had, by the time of his dismissal, the good fortune to get a morning round and getting up early for this *and* doing an evening round was, albeit quite enriching, proving too exhausting. In common with many other working class kids, who often had to do some work to get the 'pocket money' that their parents' couldn't afford to give them, the Paper Boy's school work had begun to be a victim of his herculean efforts to deliver newspapers at all hours! The early morning round involving rising at some ungodly hour, biking several miles, missing breakfast, getting soaked and shivering with cold was much less coveted by classmates, notably those from families who could afford for their offspring to stay in bed, have breakfast and buy a weekly bus ticket to school.

One of the methods of gaining the elevated and, perhaps, exalted status of 'morning paper boy' in those times was to cross the county boundary. This was something the Paper Boy had learned from his friend Jim, who had already done it. The fact was that some local authorities had different rules regarding child labour, so that the minimum age at which youngsters could begin to do morning paper rounds varied from town to town and shire to shire. The downside of this, in the case of the Paper Boy, was that crossing the county line involved a lengthy cycle ride and an even more impossibly early getting up time! It was almost like getting up in the middle of the night. And that first morning round was a 'killer' too!

It involved loading up at the shop, cycling a short distance to the Avenue, a long, long tree-lined road leading down to one of the chines — wooded ravines leading down to the sea and beaches — and commencing work, most of which was restricted to the houses on the Avenue itself. This wouldn't have mattered, but nearly all the houses were large early twentieth century buildings standing in their own capacious grounds with lengthy driveways. On top of that, most of them had been converted into flats, so that every house involved clambering up interminable winding staircases delivering to the flats on several floors. Jim, on the other hand, enjoyed a small compact round in the same area close to his base shop, that involved easily reached shops and offices packed closely together. The only one of these which involved walking upstairs had — what fun — a lift! On the occasions that the Paper Boy covered his friend's round, a regular occurrence since paper boys and girls often helped one another out in that way, it took him several attempts and time wasted returning to the stairs before he realised that the outer lift door had to be firmly closed for the lift to work. On his own round, the Paper Boy, naturally, soon got fed up with the stairs in the elderly dwellings without lifts and he began to get a bit nonchalant about the deliveries. He began by tossing the papers from near the top of the final flight of stairs to fairly close to the entrance doors of the top flats, then to leaving them near the bottom of the stairs, then to doing the same with all the deliveries above the ground floor and, finally, to throwing opening the main entrance door of the building on the ground floor and launching each delivery roughly in the direction of its recipient's domicile! Not unexpectedly, this drew some justifiable complaints from the customers to the newsagent, who promptly relayed them in no uncertain terms to the Paper Boy! On one occasion, a customer, lying in wait for the

Paper Boy behind his front door, burst out and confronted the startled deliverer by shouting down the stairwell, "Do you call that delivering the papers?"

It wasn't, but the Paper Boy, far from being contrite as he should have been, was greatly annoyed by this and got his revenge shortly afterwards by delivering to the first flat the papers ordered by the second, the second flat's order to the third and so on all down the avenue, until the very last and topmost flat in the very last house got the papers intended for the first flat, that the Paper Boy had quite deliberately missed out. This was a spiteful and silly thing to do and the Paper Boy later regretted it very much. He was sacked again for this indiscretion and quite right too!

So, there he was at the top of the gentle rise with a somewhat blemished employment record, but at least safe and well into his third paper round. He'd been able to get this one for at least two reasons. The first was that newspaper shop owners didn't ask for references or check with previous employers and the second was that competition amongst young people for paper rounds had begun to ease. One can only speculate as to the reasons for this phenomenon, but it was likely to be that, as families became better off financially and recognised the harm early mornings and evening work was doing to their children's' health, education and life chances, they either started to replace the paper round with pocket money or increased the amount of the latter that their children already received each week. Thus, the Paper Boy was seamlessly able to get another position, albeit one that was even worse than the last!

Worse it most certainly was! The boss was a sour old curmudgeon, the round began with a hill — the gentle rise — continued along roads of palatial dwellings with long drives, but at least no flats, and wound around apparently interminable tree-lined avenues, tennis courts and woods inhabited, surely, by the wealthiest of people living in the what was then called 'the lap of luxury'. It seemed to go on forever! And the papers! One bag was not enough and, on certain days, even two was barely sufficient! "That's why," the Paper Boy thought, "he provides these big black old-fashioned bikes with carriers on the front." Just like his dad's Gas Company bike. "Why on earth do people need two or three daily newspapers and armloads of these shiny magazines, and what's this thing called 'The Financial Times'? There seems to be an awful lot of them!" He learned later that the FT was an essential element in the lives of rich people, who needed to track the worth of their stocks and shares and that is why, or so the tart old newsagent informed him, it was absolutely essential to deliver these things swiftly and promptly and unfailingly! It was hard work. So hard, that the Paper Boy soon decided to set himself some targets, the first of which was to get to the top of the first hill ahead of the homicidal maniac! He wasn't really a homicidal maniac of course; he was a milkman. But he bore a striking resemblance to pictures the Paper Boy had seen — in the papers he delivered, of course — of an insane killer who'd destroyed an entire family on a picnic in the Forest! No matter that the milkman was, in all probability, a decent enough fellow and, from time to time, actually greeted the Paper Boy quite warmly as he, the Paper Boy that is, sped by intent on getting to the top of the hill. The Paper Boy never responded, for it suited him to imagine the worst and what might happen if he stopped or if the crazy killer cornered him in one of the driveways. Besides, it gave added impetus to his urgent race to the top of the hill! So, here he was again at the crest, wet with sweat but ahead of schedule!

Another target the Paper Boy devised was even more preposterous than the idea of being hounded by a mad milkman. It must have been winter when he first set himself the ridiculous target of reaching a certain point on the round before it got light! Winter is always the worst time for doing paper rounds. It's cold, it's wet, it's dark and your hands can freeze to the handlebars and your fingers hurt so much that you cry out with the pain! So, why set yourself a target that got progressively harder to attain as each day passed in the winter months and then deceive yourself that you were getting quicker as the mornings lightened towards the spring? The evidence strongly suggested that the Paper Boy may have been a bit short of common sense.

It was astonishing how quickly paper boys and girls learned the addresses on their rounds and which papers went into the letter boxes of which houses even in roads and avenues — nothing so common as streets on the Paper Boy's round — that had house names instead of numbers. One elderly customer remarked to the Paper Boy early one morning, that the people who delivered his every need such as milk, coal and newspapers were useless! "But most of the houses aren't numbered, mister," replied the Paper Boy, quite reasonably. "Of course they aren't!" the elderly pedant shouted, "They have names! My postman manages it easily enough, why can't everyone else?" "What if it's a new postman?"

asked the Paper Boy; again quite a reasonable question, or so he thought. "Don't you be rude to me young man," the old buffer said, frowning. "I'll be down to that shop later!" And he was. To complain about the cheek of the Paper Boy, who was threatened with the sack by the equally irascible shop owner. A third sacking was something the Paper Boy could ill afford, so he hung his head and contented himself with muttering obscenities in the certain knowledge that the senescent newsagent couldn't hear.

Houses without numbers only made life difficult until you got used to them. The days on which the glossy magazines came out were particularly irksome, especially in the winter. A minimum of two fully-laden bags were required, the first full of newspapers arranged in order of delivery and the second crammed with the magazines and journals. It made life really arduous because the bags were inordinately heavy, making it difficult to keep the bike upright whenever you stopped or leaned it against a lamppost, or a wall, and the magazines had to be delivered only to those who'd ordered them. Every house on the round had at least one newspaper, and often several, but not every house had a magazine. Some magazines would be missed, especially on dark cold mornings, with the result that much backtracking became necessary, accompanied by much swearing and cursing! Add to this inclement weather, cold, wet hands and seemingly incessant rain and some papers and magazines were barely readable by the time they reached the hallway floor, the porch or the garden path. The Paper Boy hated 'magazine days'!

Matters were exacerbated if you couldn't afford proper clothing to protect against the cold and the wet. The Paper Boy's friend — the one who'd had the superior paper round, but had moved on following the Paper Boy's second firing to a rather similar round in the same area as the Paper Boy himself — had a rather irritating habit of disappearing for weeks at a time. That is to say that, although he lived next door, he was never seen! These were the periods when he was 'saving up' for something. 'Saving up' required a level of self-denial that was not within the compass of the Paper Boy until many years later in adulthood. On one evening, Jim, having not been seen for some time, except occasionally doing his paper round at points where it intersected with Paper Boy's route, suddenly re-appeared. It was a dark, wet and windy morning and the Paper Boy, notwithstanding the council mackintosh his mum had persuaded 'Uncle Bert' to part with one night after the Speedway, was soaked to the skin and feeling particularly miserable as he approached the midway point of his round. Suddenly, out of the sleet and mist an apparition emerged, clad from head to toe in bright yellow oilskins — leggings, a jacket that could have sheltered a family of badgers and a voluminous hat familiarly known as a sou'wester! The Paper Boy, already frozen to the marrow, froze even more — with fear! "What?" gasped the Paper Boy unconvincingly! The wraith in yellow stared back but said nothing, at which point the Paper Boy engaged his pedals and fled, only to learn later from his perplexed pal that it was he. The Paper Boy was very jealous of his friend's oilskins.

Worse still was the ever present threat from dogs. The chances of getting your fingers bitten off as you thrust the papers through the letter box were pretty high and a wary eye had to be kept out at all times for loose animals in the gardens and driveways of the well-heeled clientele. Careful inspection before entering, however, soon translated into a cursory glance and once the Paper Boy made an assumption that almost cost him his council jacket and maybe even a lot more than that. A large German Shepherd dog — then called an Alsatian – that appeared to be secure on its lead, turned out not to be. Cunningly, it remained lying down, stared balefully at the paper Boy, allowed him to deliver the papers and turn to go before emitting a howl that would have frightened General Gordon and rose on to its legs to give chase. The Paper Boy pedaled furiously towards the gate he had quite deliberately left-open, reached it faster than he ever had before or ever would again and, with a dexterity that would have made a trick cyclist in Chipperfield's envious, leaned over, holding tightly on to the desperately swerving, swaying bike with his right hand, to thrash his free left arm wildly at the open gate, eventually striking it so that it swung violently, struck the onrushing dog on the snout with a comforting thump and clanged into place — shut. The dog was quite cross, that much could be discerned from its growling and fang baring, but the Paper Boy was safe again and this time from a genuine danger!

If being hounded by dogs, berated by customers, harassed by bosses and worked to the point of exhaustion — well, almost — was not enough humiliation, there was one other that the Paper Boy would, upon reflection, have to concede was entirely self-inflicted. Getting up so early in the morning and being so short of time and with the facilities at his home being fairly limited, the Paper Boy nearly always neglected matters of toilet and cleanliness. This resulted in additional difficulties at school, where even some of the other boys, most of whom did no paid work at all, began to notice the Paper Boy's lack of hygiene. The haste with which getting up and dressed was accomplished also meant that the Paper Boy often needed what is now politely described as a 'comfort break' halfway through his round. Perhaps more than once, and it was at these junctures that the Paper Boy was relieved, in both senses of that word, in the long drives and copses that normally annoyed him so much, but for which he was then so very grateful. It was during the school holidays that the Paper Boy was most negligent, particularly in the winter. He would struggle out of bed into the cold of his minuscule bedroom — working class homes were always freezing cold in the winter in those days and many are still — and throw on whatever came to hand in the way of clothing whilst, significantly, neglecting to remove his pyjamas first! One day, after leaving the house in the darkness of a December morning, cycling the several miles to the newsagent's shop and getting going on his round, the Paper Boy realised that he would have to pause quite soon and began to regret whatever it was he had overindulged in during the previous day! Well, it was the Christmas holidays! "Thank goodness for the woods," he thought, for once, as he diverted from his itinerary into the first available copse. As is always the case, the urgency to urinate and defecate increased in direct proportion to the closeness of the place it could be safely and modestly done and this time, to his eternal shame, the Paper Boy didn't quite make it and was compelled to cast away his soiled pyjama trousers amongst the trees where, as far as is known, they remain to this day and the never to be recounted incident indelibly inscribed in the psyche of the Paper Boy!

At least at Christmas there might be a tip or two. Not often though! One night, close to Christmas, the Paper Boy went carol singing with his two sisters in the area of his paper round. "They're really well off," he told his siblings, "we'll get loads of money." They sang and sang until they were almost hoarse. "The Lights are on so they must be in," the Paper Boy's younger sister ingenuously observed at one point. Eventually, they gave up having got next to nothing and decided to go home. On the way home, the oldest of the three, a determined girl, suggested they get off the bus and walk through the council estate. "It's not all that late," she said, "we may as well try a few houses here." The other two looked doubtful, but went along with it, and they collected more money, sweets and kind words in twenty minutes of pretty indifferent carol singing and premature knocking on council house doors than they had in several hours of trudging up and down drives in leafy lanes! And they arrived at home contented. The Paper Boy never forgot that lesson and this was one reason why the Paper Boy was not all that hopeful about tips. Some paper boys and girls pushed little envelopes through the doors with "a Happy Christmas from your paper boy" — or "girl" — written or even printed on each one. That must have been quite an onerous task and one the Paper Boy was far too idle to undertake. Besides, he was, and remained, too reticent to be so bold as to confront the customers with a dilemma or their meanness. However, one day he got a surprise. As he pushed the papers through a letter box, the door swung open and a tall man in a dressing gown gave him two half-crowns! Two half-crowns! Five shillings! A fortune! It was his lack of confidence that made the Paper Boy step back and mutter something approaching gratitude as he simultaneously held out his hand for the coins. Unsure where to put the money, because his pockets, especially his trouser pockets, were worn and unreliable containers for reasons best left unsaid, he popped both of the half-crowns into his mouth for safe keeping. Half-crowns were large coins, so that it was unlikely that he would swallow them, but it did make breathing more difficult during the remainder of his round that morning. Speaking was next to impossible, which mattered only when he returned to the shop and his boss attempted to engage him in conversation. The Paper Boy never recalled what the shopkeeper was trying to evince that Christmas, but he never forgot how awful it was trying to produce sensible and coherent responses with a mouthful of large silver coins!

Sometimes, the papers arrived late. They came by train in those days and occasionally the trains were delayed. The Paper Boy never thought about how the papers and magazines got from the railway stations to the shops but he did get very agitated if they were late, especially on schooldays, because the proprietor would announce that those deliverers that had to get to work had to have their papers sorted and prepared to go before those who merely had to get to school by nine o'clock. The Paper Boy wasn't entirely clear about this at first and found it hard to believe that someone doing an early morning paper round then had to go on to another job of work. "What does he mean, those who've got to go to work must be served first," thought the Paper Boy. "It's grownups that have to go to work; adults! Eventually, he realised that one or two of them were, in fact, adults — albeit young ones! Years later the Paper Boy appreciated that some people had to do two jobs to make ends meet. This was a fact which should already have occurred to him, since his mother had worked in school canteens and then as a waitress in cafes in the evenings for many years and his father was forever doing 'over-time' or other bits and pieces of paid employment, but at the time, it irritated him to have to wait in the certain knowledge that he'd be late for school — again! He knew that the teachers, who called themselves 'masters' in those days, would have no patience with boys arriving at a grammar school after the appointed time for the day to commence, no matter what the excuse. One of the Paper Boy's mates became a 'master' too — of feasible excuses! He was especially clever because he didn't live on the far side of the harbour and saying, "The Bridge was up, sir," — even if it wasn't — was not available to him. His best effort, in the Paper Boy's opinion, was when he apologised for being late, but claimed that it wasn't his fault because the bus had arrived early. When challenged on the apparent weakness of this account, he said with stunning cunning, "It was early sir, so I missed it! "The Paper Boy enjoyed no such ingenuity and, whilst habitual lateness didn't attract canings, which the Paper Boy was often subject to for other, not always adequate, reasons he had to suffer many detentions after school or things called 'impositions' — a fancy term for writing reams of nonsense about nonsense for the satisfaction of the 'masters', some of whom bordered on sadistic. They didn't really have any conception of what working class homes and lives were like. One warm afternoon in the Latin class, close to the end of his time as a morning paper boy, and not for the first time, the Paper Boy was startled out of his reverie by, "Wake up you lazy fellow!"

So, some people needed two jobs and the Paper Boy's dad was one of them. He worked five days a week — it was, at one time, five and a half — as a Gas Fitter. In those days, there were proper apprenticeships for skilled jobs such as gas fitting, and whilst — as is still the case today — young people learning a trade got exploited in terms of conditions of service and pay, after seven years the apprentice emerged with qualifications and recognised and respected skills. Even so, the pay was still not good, and like the Paper Boy's mum, men such as the Paper Boy's dad took on other work. Either what were called 'foreigners' — private jobs for individual customers, relations or friends paid for privately with payment agreed between the practitioner and his client — or other menial jobs such as evening work or deliveries of anything from circulars, advertising leaflets or newspapers. Adults who delivered newspapers were almost invariably men and most did the work on Sunday mornings. Thus, Sunday mornings were always broken by the cry of the paper man calling, "PA-PERS! PA-PERS!" in a barely intelligible bellow as he progressed on his way. The Paper Boy and his younger sister puzzled for many years over what it was the Sunday paper man on their street shouted, and The Paper Boy became convinced that the paper man quite deliberately slurred the words to add to his mystique. The Paper Boy's sister, ever self-obsessed, convinced herself and nobody else that it was her name being called out — goodness knows how she came to that conclusion! Even when they knew what the Sunday paper man shouted, they never understood why. Sunday morning paper rounds were, like weekday morning rounds for schoolchildren, prized and sought after in their day as a useful source of additional income for working males and, somehow, the Paper Boy's dad got one.

The Paper Boy and his dad did the Sunday round together. Not at first, but once they started, it was something that probably brought them closer than they'd been since the Paper Boy was a little boy and had first met his father after the war. They generally got up together except when the older man, on purpose in the Paper Boy's view, left the younger one to sleep and then accused him of, "Not playing the game" — one of the father's many tired old clichés. Mostly it was all right though and the younger 'man' more than pulled his weight.

Just like the arrangements on weekdays, the Sunday papers arrived by train, but they had to be collected by each of the Sunday paper men who, acting almost as freelance small businessmen, bought the papers from the wholesaler at the railway station and sold them on to their customers at a modest profit of a penny or two for each paper. How the rounds were established and passed from hand to hand was to remain a complete mystery to the Paper Boy, but it was possible to build up a round, trade parts of it with others and add to it by canvassing or other means. Perhaps that is why the Sunday paper men shouted. The Paper Boy and his dad didn't shout, partly because it was a bit embarrassing, but also because they didn't need to. Their round was big enough and it wasn't long before an old friend offered the Paper

Boy's dad a chunk of his round on a council estate. This the Paper Boy then did as a sort of additional job, whilst his father carried on with the main round. The Paper Boy liked that. He struck up a good relationship with the people on the estate, who were often outside during clement weather, cleaning their windows or their doorsteps for, in those days, people took a pride in their homes. The few who owned cars would almost certainly be outside on the road. There weren't many drives in places where the design of the streets and houses reflected the fact that people weren't supposed to have very much and the handful, who'd managed to buy a car, however modest, would be cleaning it with enormous love and care as a prized possession. Sometimes, the Paper Boy would stop and talk to customers, and to others, for people were also very friendly in those days. Pausing to chat to people on the estates wasn't that easy on a Sunday morning, when everyone listened to 'Family Favourites' at full volume! There were other stopping points too, some of which became regular halts for both father and son. At one such halt, on another street of council properties, the intrepid pair was provided with a plate of the most delicious cold sausages and cups of tea. The householder here was an ebullient, plump, balding chap, who was full of fun and entertained his Sunday paper men partly out of genuine kindness, but also because he loved to talk. It was he who told the Paper Boy, that early on every Friday and Saturday evening, his wife would draw a large blue cross across his stomach with a crayon. "If that cross isn't there when I get home," he said, "I'm in big trouble!" The Paper Boy and his dad always laughed at this jolly fellow's jokes. Given the kind of toilet humour they delighted in, it was a curious coincidence that this cheerful old chap lived quite close to another customer, whose daughter — greatly admired by the Paper Boy from afar — was not that long afterwards crowned 'Miss World'!

Ultimately, their round grew to the point where it was necessary for the Paper Boy's dad to build a little trailer to carry the papers, but it was the nature, or perhaps the culture, of the estates and the streets of houses that made up the greater part of the Paper Boy and his dad's round that determined the kind of papers that they sold from the trailer. One hundred and nine copies of the 'News of the World' for example and only three copies of the 'Sunday Times!' The rest fell between those two extremes with lots of 'Sunday Peoples' and 'Pictorials' and a few 'Sunday Telegraphs'. Years later, the Paper Boy looked on this as an indication of working class preferences with the distaste that was temporarily imbibed by his educational indoctrination following selection for the boys' grammar school at eleven years of age, something he eventually grew out of once he realised that selection had much more to do with social class than equality of opportunity. Although he never forgot, as a very young boy, his dad sending him to their own local newsagent — the one where the Paper Boy began his career as a paper boy and the one from which he was first sacked — with the stunningly sexist and contradictory instruction to fetch, "A 'News of the World' for me and a 'picture paper' for your mother."

They started to take the dog. There always seemed to be a dog in the house. Years later, the Paper Boy came to believe that it wasn't so much the smell of the dog or the inconvenience of having a dog that he minded, but the chore of walking it and, far worse, the job of cleaning up the piles of mess and pools of urine in the kitchen when he got back from school! No wonder his sisters always managed to find some reason, or excuse, for arriving home a little later than he did. What *was* a wonder was the fact that he didn't seem to realise this! In the end, the Paper Boy concluded that nobody should own dogs unless they were prepared to look after them themselves and unless they didn't have to leave the dog alone for long spells, while they were at work or elsewhere. This would, in the opinion of the Paper Boy, have ruled out most working people and all children!

It would also have meant that, apart from the vile task of clearing up faeces and urine in the kitchen, he would also have been spared the embarrassment of dragging a bitch 'on heat' home from the fields on one never-to-be-forgotten occasion, followed by a pack of male dogs trying to mount it. Or the awful realisation that the stray dog he had befriended on another day and was busily protecting his frightened cousin from, far from being over-friendly, was actually trying to satisfy itself against his leg. In those days, dogs were often left to roam and foul the streets when and wherever they felt the need to. It was a nuisance, but not, of course, the fault of the animals. And especially not the fault of the poor creature that was carried off in the front carrier of the Paper Boy's father's gas company bike just because it had become more trouble than it was worth. Only later did the Paper Boy and his sisters realise their father must have been on the way to a vet. However, the resourceful dog escaped after about five miles on the gas company bike just as it reached the vet's, and after a full week had elapsed, turned up again — asleep in a doll's pram in the back yard. Perhaps not an 'incredible journey' but certainly quite a surprising one, after which the dog was spared.

That wasn't the dog that joined them on the Sunday paper round. The paper round dog was a small black dog of indeterminate strain and friendly disposition. It was easy to control and never went far from the Paper Boy or, especially, the Paper Boy's dad and, therefore, it didn't need to be on a lead on quiet Sunday mornings. Not, that is, until, entirely unpredictably and totally of character, it walked into the road. There were never many cars about early on Sundays in those days, but there was one then and the Paper Boy watched in horror as the dog was run over by a black car. To his credit, the driver stopped and got out. It wasn't his fault, but he crouched over the dog, which lay prone in the road and felt for its heart announcing, "There's still a little beat there." He looked up hopefully at the Paper Boy and his dad, neither of whom blamed him. The dog never made a sound. It died and the Paper Boy and his father, not knowing what to do, carried its body, which struck the Paper Boy as astonishingly limp, back to their house in the little cart behind the father's bicycle. Still unsure what to do, they took the dead animal, its tongue lolling from its head, into the rear garden, dug a hole and buried it quietly and solemnly. They were very late that day, and upon finally returning to the house and accepting a welcome cup of tea from the Paper Boy's mum, they sat in silence. "Where have you been?" she enquired. The Paper Boy's dad, a regular if unconvincing liar, made some excuse about a late train and the woman said, "Where's the dog?"

At least Christmas was better on Sunday paper rounds. Nearly everybody accepted that Sunday paper men had to be rewarded with a tip during the season of goodwill, so the Paper Boy and his dad did pretty well. All tips were scrupulously collected and shared equally. Getting up early to deliver newspapers on a Sunday at that time of year was to be assailed with offers of drinks, food and what the French call 'bonhomie'. If he hadn't been in the company of his father, the Paper Boy could easily have been drunk by the end of the round. He accepted whatever he could without irritating his dad and without testing his bladder overmuch. At least he didn't have to discard any clothing; he'd grown out of that by then and the clothing too probably.

The Paper Boy could never remember when his dad started the Sunday morning round, or when it ended. Nor could he recall when his dad had asked him to join him and do the round together, but he did remember that he was delighted, because that was the moment at which the Paper Boy became a Paper Man!

Chapter 2

THE KITCHEN HAND

The Commander stood on the door step, tight lipped and legs astride. "I'll pay you two and six an hour," he said, as though he was offering the Crown Jewels. Based upon this presumptive and insubstantial offer, the Paper Boy became a Kitchen Hand in a posh hotel.

How the Kitchen Hand longed to be a commis waiter! One or two of the boys he knew at school were commis waiters. The hotel normally supplied the short white jacket, but you had to have your own black trousers, a crisp white shirt and a black tie of your own, none of which the Kitchen Hand possessed. They were paid more as well and they hurried back and forth between the dining rooms and the kitchens past the still rooms and the washing up rooms, feeling important and looking essential, like doctors in a hospital. And they got tips! And they had access to the food! All those who worked at the menial tasks like washing dishes and cleaning glasses could hope for was to grab a handful as the hors d'oevres or the dessert trolley went by between the kitchen and dining room. This had to be achieved away from the watchful eye of the maître d'hôtel which wasn't easy. Not once did the Kitchen Hand see one of the well-to-do persons whose dishes, and sometimes glasses, he assiduously scoured and dried. That was for the commis waiters, the real waiters, the maître d'hôtel and the Commander.

The Commander was the hotel's owner, or so the Kitchen Hand believed. Quite what it was that the Commander had ever commanded, apart from the waiters, the chefs, the cooks and the hands in the kitchen and the washing up rooms, the Kitchen Hand never found out and it never troubled his mind very much either. He just assumed that the Commander must have had some important role in the war.

There were a number of personnel in the washing up room. There was a young Hungarian, whose name the Kitchen Hand never knew, but who was always smiling and always friendly. The Hungarian was fascinated with the exigencies of the English Language and was forever rolling little phrases around his tongue like "oops-a-daisy" and "never mind"! "Never mind," he would say repeatedly whilst smiling with his wide, naive eyes sparkling. He worked hard too. Years later, the Kitchen Hand concluded that the Hungarian must have arrived in England following the abortive Hungarian revolution in 1956, but he was never sure of that. Then there was the French Speaker, another one whose name the Kitchen Hand never knew. The French Speaker, a middle aged man, was always saying how he could have been in rather superior employment and had told them so at the Labour Exchange – later to go through several metamorphoses to end up as the Job Centre. "Mind you," he'd say, "I did tell them I'd do anything — interpreter if they like!" This meant that he felt that he should have been doing something a bit more edifying than washing dishes for the Commander, but that he'd had the grace to accept what was offered to him. "Passez moi les assiettes de salads", The French Speaker would say in much the same accent and with much the same stress as a twelve year old schoolboy in a French class or a semi-literate labourer on a building site. Nonetheless, he *could* speak French, if not fluently, then grammatically accurately at least as far as the kitchen Hand, whose French was somewhat stilted, could ascertain. The French Speaker confused the Kitchen Hand because the former, notwithstanding his accent, spoke a foreign language, which was a rare achievement for the middle and upper classes in England, never mind a working class washer-up! As usual, the Kitchen Hand's insights came later in life, when it dawned upon him that the French Speaker probably picked up French during the war years. Mac was, as you'd expect, a Scot. His principle skill in the washing up room was to beat rhythmically on large empty tins — goodness knows where they came from — whilst loudly whistling rousing and patriotic Scottish melodies such as 'Loch Lomond' and 'Scotland the Brave.' Mac was a kindly and helpful soul, but he longed for a certain role in the washing up room that was simply unattainable as long as the Old Gentleman was there. The Old Gentleman had somehow, before the Kitchen Hand's time, secured the sole right to the enviable task of washing and polishing all the wine glasses, tumblers, brandy glasses, champagne flutes and so on. Head bowed, he would retreat to the sinks on the far side of the washing up room, where he would slowly and methodically wash, dry and buff the glasses with what seemed like the optimum in care and devotion. The Old Gentleman rarely spoke and never crossed anyone. In truth, the glasses job was an easier one and much less demeaning and Mac dearly would have loved a break from cleaning and drying of plates, tureens, bowls, assorted dishes, cups, saucers and all the other detritus of the wealthy diners, but he couldn't bring himself to do more than whisper from time to time that someone else should have an opportunity to do the glasses. The Kitchen Hand didn't care and certainly didn't want to upset the order of things in the washing up room, so he kept quiet and never responded to Mac's sullen asides. It was the Brainy Kiddie who did. "Extraordinary," thought the Kitchen Hand in later life that he never learned a single name of his fellow workers in the washing up room! The Brainy Kiddie – so-called with the utmost contempt by the Maître D' who would sidle up to the Kitchen Hand from time to time and say, "Make sure that *Brainy Kiddie* does his share!" — challenged the Old Gentleman to share the glasses job. The result was a sharp rejoinder from the Old Gentleman, who wasn't used to what he considered to be his inalienable right to a superior role in the hotel being questioned, albeit only in the washing up room, some unpleasantness and a lasting feeling that the ambience 'below stairs' had soured somewhat. The Brainy Kiddie, although "a bit posh" — another of the Maître D's saws — was brainy enough to recognise a bêtise, so soon withdrew and never mentioned it again. And he never raised the other suggestions he had confided to the Kitchen Hand about improving the organisation, as he saw it, of his fellow workers. He did, however, suggest that he record some of Mac's whistling and tin box hammering, but he never did that either. He was, after all, only a student and a temporary member of the washing up room squad.

The washing up room staff worked in shifts. The Kitchen Hand usually did a shift, which started fairly early, for the breakfast pots and pans and terminated late in the afternoon when all the lunch and tea-time stuff had been cleared, cleaned and put back in all the right places. The whole process was something of a treadmill. Sometimes, the Kitchen Hand worked the later shift covering Evening Dinner. This went on forever and was akin to slavery! The thing about jobs such as this one is that they never end. Once everything is clean and tidy and once everything is in its place, it all starts again and it all has to come out again, be used again, get dirty again, be cleared again, washed again, put away again and so on... On top of that, there was another mystery. From time to time, a woman would appear at the washing room door and plead with the Kitchen Hand to, "Help out next door." This mostly occurred towards the end of the early shift, when the Kitchen Hand was either alone or with one other companion and things were winding down in the washing up room. The Kitchen Hand was happy to "help out" next door and quickly discovered, to his surprise, that there existed a second sort of 'still room' adjacent to the washing up room, where the woman and others sweated as much or more than he, the Hungarian and all the others. One day, the Kitchen Hand saw the woman from the 'still room' on the bus on his way to work. She was accompanied by a child of about ten years of age, who appeared to be severely handicapped. 'Handicapped' was the term for what is now called 'disabled'. The woman was struggling to keep the child quiet and in his seat and the Kitchen Hand felt a wave of sympathy for her. He wasn't yet capable of empathy and, indeed, wasn't even familiar with the term. From that point on, the Kitchen Hand worked hard to finish his work in the washing up room, so that he could go next door and help in the 'still room'.

It didn't bother the Kitchen Hand, that in all his weeks working for the Commander, he had not set eyes upon a hotel guest. He recognised, even then, that they would have no interest in his kind. The Kitchen Hand derived just one abiding skill from his experiences in the hotel trade; he learned how to make Melba toast. Quite why, or how, and who taught him, he forgot very quickly afterwards but he never forgot how to do it and was at great pains to share the secret with as many others as would deign to listen and to learn. He also loved to explain, to anyone prepared to listen, the connection between wafer thin crispy toast and an Australian opera singer who once sang at the Empire Theatre in Bacup, Lancashire and, to boot, had a dessert named in her honour as well! The Kitchen Hand often mused in later life upon why on earth someone should bother to unlock the secret of Melba toast to such as him but he didn't worry about it overmuch.

In any case, that summer came to an end and the Kitchen Hand's dad said, "How'd you like to do the sticking up at the Conservative Club son? It'll be worth a few bob." The Kitchen Hand had no idea what that meant but heard himself say, "Yes dad, when do I start?"

Chapter 3

THE STICKER UP

Getting from the gents back to the top of the alley without being seen was impossible. Nevertheless, The Sticker Up had to try because he'd wet his trousers! He didn't get away with it.

In those days, there were a lot of pubs and working men's clubs and many of the clubs still had a political label from the days when it was considered appropriate to form social clubs to promote the ideas and offer a focus for those men, and it always was — and generally still is — men, that supported the beliefs and policies of such organisations and, therefore, frequented such establishments. Most of these were, originally, either Liberal or Conservative clubs but following the establishment of the Independent Labour Party in the early twentieth century, many Labour Clubs sprang up. What surprised the newly appointed Sticker Up was that it didn't seem to matter anymore what the political label was. The men went to their clubs for other reasons including cheap beer, 'men only' bars, and the opportunity to fraternise with friends and work mates and to enjoy access to sports. That's if you can describe darts, snooker, dominoes and skittles as 'sports'! It did occur to him later that, if these had been Olympic sports, then Great Britain would have won a lot more gold medals. Meanwhile, it was the last of these, skittles, which involved the Sticker up.

A good number of the clubs and pubs had skittle alleys. A skittle alley was a long, narrow section of the room with laminated wooden flooring, often in outside buildings, that looked like long sheds and were erected especially for the purpose or in extensions similarly provided by the brewery now in ownership of the pub or club, political affiliation having long since either disappeared or become subservient to the other purposes of the clubs. Some alleys simply formed the edge of a larger 'function room' where dances, meetings and other social events were held. The alleys varied in size and shape quite a bit, but were generally four or five feet wide and about three or four times the length of an average living room. They usually had low side boundaries of wood, some of which could be removed to afford greater space in the room for the dances or meetings. At one end of the alley, nine skittles, or 'pins', as they were sometimes called, were set up forming a diamond shape. These were always made of wood and, although they were all somewhat similar in that they nearly all were wider at the base than at the top, they varied a lot in size and shape. Some were squat and bulbous, some wide-bottomed and tapering to the top and others like large cylinders, slightly bulging at the waist. Some were much heavier than others and one infamous set was much bigger than any others. The central 'pin', the one at the middle of the diamond, was called 'The Landlord' and was always noticeably bigger than the rest. It was these differences in the skittles and slight variations in the length, width and style of the alleys that gave the host club or pub what was called 'home advantage'. The game of skittles was a competition between teams in leagues.

The game of skittles bore, or rather, bears, for some alleys still exist today, no resemblance whatsoever to American ten pin bowling! There were only nine pins, the alleys were less smooth and polished, a chalkboard was used to record the scores, rather than an automated scoreboard. There were no fancy lights or noises, no music, no poor quality food at exorbitant prices, no fee for playing other than annual membership if it was a club rather than a pub and, above all, no machine to reset the skittles after they had fallen. That was the job of the sticker up for which he was paid a few 'bob' (shillings, each worth ten pence) and a couple of pints.

The teams were made up of six men and some pubs and clubs fielded several teams. No women played skittles, at least not to the knowledge of the Sticker Up. Few women frequented the clubs anyway. Each member of the team took it in turns to roll three wooden balls down the alley with the purpose of knocking down as many of the skittles as he could. The first ball was quite large and heavy, the second of medium size and the third about the size of an athletics shot but, of course, not nearly as heavy. Should a player knock down all nine skittles with his first ball, or with the first two (a 'stick-up'), then all the fallen skittles would be re-erected by the sticker up. So, theoretically, it was possible to score twenty-seven at each turn. In practice, this never happened and a decent score would be in the order of eight or nine a 'stick-up' being a fairly rare occurrence. All fallen skittles were cleared by the sticker up, not just for 'stick-ups', but also between each roll of the balls so that the sticker ups were kept pretty busy. When each player on both sides had rolled his three balls, the scores were totted up for that 'leg' of the game and the whole process began again until the proscribed number of 'legs' had been completed, when the winners were those members of the team with the highest total score.

It has to be said that 'roll' is something of a misnomer for the manner in which the balls were propelled down the alley. If a score of eight or nine was a good one, then it is clear that it was quite difficult to knock the skittles down and certainly far less straightforward than in ten pin bowling. Considerable skill was needed and the best players could strike the front 'pin' at an angle sufficient to get it to go in one direction, whilst the ball went in the other, taking out as many of the following skittles as possible. Although there was, inevitably, some luck involved at times, the leading skittle had to be hit in exactly the right place to do the most damage behind it and knock over the most skittles. As stated, the skittles and the alleys varied and it was not impossible to put a ball through the skittles without hitting any of them. Although it was mostly the quickest balls that did the most damage and resulted in the highest scores, this was not always the case and a skilful skitter could vary the pace and use accuracy rather than strength to good effect. All players used the same basic technique to propel the balls down the alley. They crouched behind the 'start' line at the head of the alley with the ball in both hands between their legs and thrust themselves forward with some vigour to release the ball from both hands simultaneously with as much force and accuracy as they could muster, or considered appropriate for the situation the 'pins' were in for that go. This resulted in the player ending up at full length on the alley floor and, in some cases, sliding down the alley after delivery for several feet (a metre or two). Some players wore waistcoats (still fashionable for older men in those days) which became shiny with repeated buffing on the alley floor!

The Sticker Up sometimes regretted his ready response to his dad's request, particularly when he was struck on the leg by a wayward skittle. This didn't happen often, but it was one of the hazards of the job and could be quite painful and sometimes embarrassing. But not as embarrassing as the occasion when he was forced to hold up the game to go the gents for a wee — a weak bladder was to be a lifelong problem for the Sticker Up – and in his haste to return, urine splashed down his light grey trousers. The Sticker Up tried to sidle back into the alley and sneak unseen along the side wall, only for one

of the team to call out, "Had an accident then mate?" Or

when a misplaced skittle fell over just as an opposition player was on the point of launching himself at the alley floor, but managed to hold onto the ball, turn away and roll over before coming to rest in an ungainly heap against the side of the alley. "What's your game, mate?" he cried, "I could've been badly hurt." It was his pride, like the Sticker Up's, that was injured. In fact, a Sticker Up had to be pretty slick to clear the 'dead wood' as the fallen skittles were called and get out of the way of the next ball to keep the game moving. Also, it was a difficult task to re-erect the skittles at the close of each player's turn, ready for the following man who'd be 'champing at the bit' at the top of the alley. It was hard work.

The Sticker Up's father was no Conservative. The Club just happened to be a convenient venue for his skittles and for his snooker. It's unlikely that any of his team were conservative either. Charlie, the captain, was a working man in his fifties, who would announce the opening of the match with, "Right lads, off we go to war." He was probably a war veteran, as was the Sticker Up's dad and some of the others. Charlie was never ever critical of his side, preferring to encourage and urge them on rather than to shout or to be hostile in any way. A lot of present day managers and leaders could have learned a lot from Charlie. Frank, who must have been an old age pensioner and looked ancient to the Sticker Up, always went first, probably because he was the worst member of the team. No surprise really, because he could barely get to the line and crouch to deliver the balls. When he did so, he would flop to the floor inelegantly and the ball would bobble along the alley and, if it reached the pins with any pace left, it normally knocked over one or two, unless Frank got a lucky bounce and the ball would get amongst the skittles and they would help by knocking each other over! Peter came next. He was a chain smoker who, when offered a 'fag', would say, "Thanks mate, I eat 'em!" Peter was a lot livelier than Frank and a lot younger, but he was also a bit erratic and could get any score between four or five and thirteen or fourteen. The following two team members would normally get reasonable scores, say seven or eight. Then came the Sticker Up's dad, who could also be relied upon for a reasonable total from his three balls and Charlie would finish off the turn with a fairly decent average. Thus, the team normally finished in a respectable position in whatever division it was they were in of the many divisions that made up the District Skittles League.

From time to time, one or other member of the six regulars would be ill or unable to turn out for one reason or another, and on these occasions, the Sticker Up would be called upon. The Sticker Up was quite good and certainly no worse than the other, more senior, team members. Eventually, something drastic happened to one of the older men and the Sticker Up was asked to become a full participant and colleague — one of the prouder moments in his mundane life up to that point!

The good thing about skittles was that it brought a father and son together in a mutual interest. In most other circumstances, they shared little except football and snooker. One day, towards the end of a match and close to the end of the skittles season, which concluded in the spring, the Sticker Up's dad said, "Son, I've got a job for you." "What's that, dad?" asked the Sticker Up. His father replied, "I want you to paint the house! I'll see you alright!" The Sticker up realised that this meant that his dad was proposing to pay him. If so, he knew that it wouldn't amount to very much, but that is how the Sticker Up became a house painter.

Chapter 4

THE HOUSE PAINTER

It's no joke being forty or fifty feet up a swaying, fully extended double ladder, juggling with a heavy tin of oil based paint and a paintbrush! Especially if you've never done it before!

The House Painter had no training or education in the art of house painting whatsoever! He was utterly ignorant of the niceties involved in scraping off the old and peeling paint, preparing the surface, applying a base coat of primer, then a coat of undercoat and, finally, putting on one, or even two, fresh coats of gloss. The House Painter's father was no better and provided his son only with an enormous tin of blue gloss paint, which he'd probably come by illicitly, and a large paintbrush — and the ladders. Goodness only knows where he'd got the ladders from! He certainly couldn't afford to buy any. Armed with this equipment, and with this paucity of information, the House Painter set about his task.

The upside of the affair was that the House Painter wasn't afraid of heights. Well, that is to say that he was, but not very much! A double ladder tends to bounce up and down in a most alarming manner when ascended. Imagine that; a bit of wind, a large and heavy tin of paint in one hand and a paintbrush held between the teeth, whilst the free hand moved from rung to rung followed by a right and then a left foot with both knees akimbo! After a short period, the feet begin to exhibit painful stress, the tension in the body begins to cause aches and pains and stretching to reach the highest point to apply paint tires the painting arm and hand. The other hand struggles to keep the paint pot where it can be reached and, of course, once the painting begins it is a case of, "Look, no hands!" No hands on the ladder, that is. It took some time for the House Painter to realise that not only was it safer to ascend and descend with an upright, vertical body away from the ladder, but it was also better to work in this position, rather than leaning towards, or even on, the ladder with knees either jammed against it or gripping it so tightly that they became sore and bruised! Having decided to begin the job at the top, the gable end of the house, the House Painter was doing the most risky part of the work first and there were many times when he thought, "This is a very dangerous game." Often the House Painter would be standing on one leg with the other leg fully extended to counter-balance the weight of his outstretched arm and body, as he leaned over to reach the furthest extremities of the gable end without having to move the ladder too often. Almost equally dangerous, was man-handling extending ladders with no training and not that much physical strength. On the only day that his father was there to help to move and adjust the ladders, the House Painter managed to stretch, reach and shift the upper ladder, so that it slid down the lower ladder until it reached his father's arms holding on further down near the base and striking them with considerable force and with a fearsome thud! The House Painter's father's reaction to this was to look at his son, wide-eyed, and say plaintively, "You let it go." The House Painter, for reasons he never would or could understand, found this incident exceedingly funny and had to turn away, clutching his mouth and struggling to retain his composure. When it became clear that his father's arms weren't broken, which they might well have been, the House Painter's condition worsened to the point where he was forced to disappear around the corner of the house choking to contain himself. Nor was there any way of anchoring the ladders at their base except on that one occasion when his father was present and the work was cut short by the incident described above. Several times, the bottom of the lower ladder began to shift alarmingly with the House Painter at or near the top of the upper ladder. He was fortunate to complete the job uninjured. Health and Safety and 'risk assessment' were certainly not on the agenda.

The House Painter had, by this time in his life, a healthy interest in the opposite sex. His problem was that he was absolutely hopeless at communicating with them — or anyone come to that — approaching them, and particularly at speaking to them. Thus, he generally admired them from afar and the period of the house painting was no exception to this. One day, a few yards up the road towards the little church, there emerged from a perfectly ordinary semi-detached dwelling a vision of such striking beauty that the House Painter struggled to stay on the ladder! It was a girl so lovely that the House

Painter simply had to stop work to watch. She was tall and slim and wore her golden hair in what was then called a "French Pleat" — combed towards the back and curled into a sort of spiral at the back of her lovely head. The House Painter descended to stand at the front of his parent's house, staring fixedly with eyes like a cow. The third or fourth time that he saw the girl, who must have been staying with relatives for a few days that summer, the House Painter acted purely instinctively and hurried down his ladder, put away his brush and paint for the day and set out to follow her. His difficulty was that, by the time he'd done all this and put away the ladders, the girl had disappeared in the direction of the main road. He hurried after her. Assuming that she had caught a bus and gone into the town centre, he did the same albeit he had no idea where she was intending to go, apart from the clues in her summer attire of pale blue 'ski pants' and white blouse and the large towelling bag slung from her shoulder. The House Painter boarded the next bus, roamed around the shops in the town centre, walked up and down the Gardens and along the promenade above the beaches, spending most of the rest of the day in so doing. Not unusually, he never saw the girl again.

He did, however, see one of his aunties and he did complete the job. These two events occurred at about the same time. The House Painter was embarrassed by the unexpected arrival of his aunt, especially since it was an aunt that he was not particularly fond of. He'd reached the ground floor windows and was busily slapping blue paint over the cracked and peeling existing paint on the frames. His aunt suggested quite strongly that the painting job would have benefitted from a modicum of proper preparation and would not last any length of time before requiring some extensive remediation. Her husband, the House Painter's uncle, was a practical man so she knew what she was talking about and the House Painter was confronted, not for the first time and certainly not for the last, with a clear sense of his own inadequacies. The uncle was also a very kind and gentle man and became one of those most remembered by those who benefitted from his generosity over the years, including the House Painter. The aunt departed without saying much else, so that the House Painter had no idea why she had arrived or what she wanted. He was glad to see her go.

Left with only the front door to do, the House Painter ran out of blue paint. Whilst he'd no conception of why or how, he did, however, have a small tin of pink paint. Accordingly, he made the decision to paint the front door, which unlike the windows, was sheltered by the porch and still in reasonable condition, with two coats of pink gloss. He wouldn't have considered doing two coats, but found that one was insufficient to cover the remains of the existing green paint adequately. At this point, an uncle arrived. This relative was, for some long forgotten reason, to be taken home by the House Painter. 'Home' was not far away, but this particular uncle was what in those days was described as 'a bit slow' or — in the words of the House Painter's father — "A little bit diddle-o"! The uncle was also eager to get home because his tea, an early evening meal taken at about six o'clock, or as soon as they got home from work, as was usual in those days, was overdue and one of his favourite pastimes was eating. Consequently, the uncle kept urging the House Painter to finish off the job and get going! Now, the House Painter's grandfather, his uncle's father, had been a builder's merchant and his building company had been bequeathed to two of his sons. Neither of these were the uncle present at that time, but in line with his habit of misjudging people and what they told him, the House Painter got the notion that he, the uncle who was anxious to get home for tea, had some knowledge of painting. "Is it dry enough for the second coat?" asked the House Painter, "or is it still a bit tacky?" "It's okay," replied the uncle, "get it on and let's go!" The House Painter went ahead and found his brushful of pink paint for the second coat, dragging the first coat along the surface of the door. He persisted. The job got finished quickly but it was a bit of a mess and the pink paint looked awful anyway. They left and it was many years before the House Painter's skills, or lack of them, were called upon again. When they were, he did a rather better job but he wasn't paid for it. Meanwhile, he was growing up and he needed proper paid employment like delivering the nation's mail.

Chapter 5

THE POSTMAN

The Postman was arrested just as he was about to board the bus.

This was in the days before electronic communication and before the Post Office was raped and cherry picked by piratical delivery companies anxious for quick easy money in return for a service that was not only inferior but placed commercial gain over public benefit. It was also before the whole shebang was sold off by a right-wing government at a knock-down price to their rich friends in the finance houses. So, in those days, the Post Office took on loads of extra hands at busy times such as the days and weeks preceding Christmas. Many of these were plucked from the dole queues, but such was the need for additional help to maintain its excellent service, that the Post Office had to recruit from sources of humanity other than what later became known as the 'work shy' and 'benefit scroungers', namely, students! Although they were also generally regarded as 'layabouts', students became essential to the proper functioning of the delivery of Christmas cards and parcels during the 'festive period'.

Thus it was that The House Painter morphed into The Postman. Given that the Post Office needed all the help it could get, it wasn't difficult to get 'taken on'. For The Postman, this meant rising earlier than he really liked and catching a bus — in those days, public transport was also run in the interests of the public rather than brigands and profiteers — which carried him to the Central Post Office Sorting Office. There he was in common with the legion of other temporary staff, instructed in the rudiments of letter, card and small package delivery, given a uniform comprising of an official Post Office armband of which he was rather proud and then dispatched to what was — and still is — called a 'walk' to deliver enormous, heavy and awkward bags of mail to residents eager to receive their post, particularly since Christmas was the time when people got nice things like greetings and gifts, rather than bills, abuse and threats.

The Sorting Office was a huge, sweaty, scruffy, but imposing hall of a building full of postmen and post women moving purposefully about, emptying bags and stuffing letters, cards and packets into little slots called 'pigeon holes', without pigeons, according to the area in which the addresses placed each item. It was noisy because of the constant buzz of conversation and chatter, and because of the music blaring out of speakers fixed high upon the walls, which also meant that the workers had to shout to make themselves heard, especially if the person addressed was some distance away. It has to be said that the channels selected by the most forthright of the staff were not offering quality music and, as the days neared the end of December, it was mostly bawdy songs interspersed with contrasting religious stuff, mostly Christmas carols. However, the carols were nice. This was mainly because they were always traditional carols before the times when they were modernised and often ruined with updated tunes and words! As often as The Postman left the Sorting Office to begin his 'walk' with his enormous and weighty canvas bag, uplifted by the strains of a carol, the song he remembered years later was an oft-repeated and vulgar old jazz song of which the refrain was "Don't Touch My Tomatoes" with the 'a' of 'tomatoes' sounded like the 'a' in 'cake' — like Americans do.

Each 'walk' comprised a number of streets, buildings and addresses and there were usually particular routes and shortcuts, which made it easier and quicker. That doesn't mean it was easy to carry a huge bag weighing what seemed like half an elephant, or to follow the route whilst plucking the cards and letters from the bag at the time and place needed for accurate delivery. One of the most galling experiences was missing an address or an item and having to go back and deliver it. Most postmen were often affectionately referred to as 'Posties' in those days, and most Christmas recruits soon learned not to bother going back and the offending item would be taken back to the sorting office and delivered the following day, or worse, posted! The delay didn't matter, after all, it was Christmas! On the plus side, The Postman, like The Paper Boy before him, discovered that as he progressed around a 'walk', the going got easier as the bag got lighter. It was also good exercise. As the manager of the youth football team The Postman played for at the time remarked, "You'll play some blinders after this!" which meant that he thought the work was good fitness training for young footballers. It was, but it made little difference to The Postman! Sometimes, if The Postman was lucky, his supervising 'Postie' would wangle him a Post Office bike. In limited supply, and therefore not easy to come by, a bike made the whole thing a lot less arduous by taking the weight of the bag and making the, largely downhill, return journey to the Sorting Office a pleasure. What joy! The downside — and there always is one — was that The Postman got back a lot earlier and therefore 'clocked off' sooner and served rather less hours, thereby getting slightly less in his pay packet. In those days, working people were paid in cash in a little buff envelope with holes in it, so that they could check the contents before opening. Unbelievable, but true!

The arrest occurred on a day when The Postman had been fortunate enough to acquire a bike, had checked back in to the Sorting Office by late afternoon and was about to return home. The bus had stopped and he had one foot on the platform and the other still on the pavement, when a police car pulled in behind the bus. In those days, most buses were double-deckers with open platforms, so that intending passengers were able to leap on and off more or less as they liked, and often did, until the increasing number of 'platform accidents' persuaded bus companies to get bus designers to design, and bus builders to build, buses with enclosed platforms and doors that opened and closed only at the bus stops! Thus, The Postman was able to get off again, when an eager policewoman leapt from the passenger seat of the police vehicle, approached him and grabbed him quite determinedly by the arm. "Just a moment, sir," she said, "can I have a word with you?" "Why? What for?" said The Postman, astonished! "I must ask you to accompany me to the station," she replied in time honoured fashion. "You look a lot like someone we want to speak to." "But I'll miss the bus," said The Postman, lamely. "Never mind that, sir," she said, "we can give you a lift." The Postman had never been addressed as "sir" before. Nor had he ever been detained by the police in full view of the public and, therefore, come under suspicion as a miscreant. It was embarrassing. The Postman's thoughts returned to his only court appearance some years earlier aged about thirteen. Having been stopped by a policeman and 'done' for riding a bike after dark without lights, his dad accompanied him to the juvenile court where his father's presence and his own contrition and meekness rescued him from anything worse than a reprimand and a modest fine which, it hardly need be added, he had had to stump up himself. It just wouldn't happen these days! This was far worse however and The Postman was a bit worried. As it turned out, he needn't have been, for it was simply a case of mistaken identity and soon put right with an apology from the over-zealous policewoman to boot! That didn't erase the embarrassment though.

One day, The Postman was labouring up the hill that formed an arduous part of his 'walk,' when he walked into a lamp post. Still reeling from this calamity, and with his head spinning, he trudged into the sweet factory at the top of the hill next to the laundry. It was close to Christmas and some sort of social function appeared to be in full swing as The Postman entered the building to be greeted by a sweet and pretty young woman receptionist. "Would you like a beer?" she asked with a smile that almost made The Postman faint — or it may have been the effects of the lamp post. "Yes, thanks," he replied before handing over the handful of mail and swigging back the bottle of beer she handed to him. "If you want another, you'll have to give me a kiss," said the receptionist with another stunning smile. The Postman was thrown into total confusion by this, stammered some barely audible response and hastened from the building to immediately regret his gaucheness and his witless inadequacy. It was a wasted opportunity and one of many yet to come as he grew older. Occurrences such as this one would be in his daydreams forever and he'd wonder whatever became of the pretty young receptionist. He never saw her again.

But things decidedly looked up the very next day when The Postman was approached again, this time by a senior management person in the sorting office. He was looking for temporary staff willing to do large parcels delivery. This involved a group of temporary workers called a 'team' working under a regular 'postie' with a hired van and driver to deliver parcels. Having got used to his 'walk' The Postman wasn't sure about this but he agreed to do it and, as it turned out, it was wonderful! On parcel delivery, the hired vans were not Post Office vans and, therefore, could not be easily identified as being on Post Office work. The drivers were anybody without a job, but in possession of a heavy goods vehicle driving licence and the 'Posties' in charge were looking for the chance to make as much overtime as they could. This particular van was a furniture removal lorry and therefore available for hire during the Christmas holidays when not many people moved house. The 'team' consisted of the 'Postie' in charge, The Postman, several other temporary postmen and the driver. The capacious wagon had plenty of room for all the workers and all the parcels and there was plenty of time to trundle around the roads delivering the packages which, whilst sometimes quite large, were never, ever as heavy as the letter bags. Each day, under the watchful direction of its 'postie', whose principal role was to make sure that nobody worked too hard, even working at snail's pace, the 'team' eventually got all the parcels delivered and then looked to the leader, the 'postie', for further instructions. The 'postie' never let them down, and each day, the van was driven to the edge of town to a stretch of common land to wait out several hours of gathering gloom while the 'team' chatted and smoked in the back. With Christmas getting closer, sometimes they even drank beer.

The leader and some of the other younger members of the 'team' were likely to talk about their activities of the previous night or their prospects for the coming evening. The 'postie' appeared to know more than most about women and their needs and was by no means shy in detailing his successes with the opposite sex. In fact, it was the main topic of conversation. On one such occasion, after the usual salacious details of his activities of the previous night, he concluded expansively, "Everyone knows about women." There was pause as members of the 'team' glanced at one another, suspecting that the 'postie' couldn't possibly be equal to his stories, but not daring to say so, and certainly not daring to interpose with tales of their own. "I don't," ventured The Postman. "Then we'll teach you," said the 'postie' generously, "that'll be our Christmas box for you." He didn't really mean 'we'll' and 'our' but 'I'll and 'my'. The Postman was right not to expect too much for nothing was ever forthcoming, the self-styled sex expert never invited The Postman to accompany him on his nights of joy and, by Boxing Day, The Postman had given up and put it down as just another missed opportunity or, in this instance, no opportunity at all. But the long summer vacations from late June until early October, including the entire months of July, August and September, brought even better opportunities for gainful employment and The Postman surrendered his Post Office armband in favour of the fuller regalia of the bus company.

Chapter 6

THE BUS CONDUCTOR

In the days when employers provided proper equipment and clothing for their workers, and bar-room bouncers looked like they'd just come from the enclosure at Epsom Downs, a bus conductor's uniform could pass for that of a South American admiral!

A very handsome outfit it was too, for in those days, public service companies were remarkably fastidious in equipping their employees with appropriate uniforms and accoutrements. It comprised a light brown or beige cotton jacket with green cuffs and facings — the summer uniform as far as the regular drivers and conductors were concerned but for the temporary staff, a clear sign of role identity — a large lapel badge with KK followed by an identifying number and even a peaked cap emblazoned with the company badge and logo — additional emblems of corporate pride, or maybe not!

Even nowadays, some firms take on extra staff for the summer months and then, in the times before all-inclusive trips to Spain and Greece became compulsory, it was very common for bus companies, particularly those in coastal holiday locations, or in tourist centres, to hire quite considerable numbers of people. These were mostly students to help man, or 'person', the extra services necessary to carry the increased numbers of 'holiday makers' as they were called back and forth to beaches, castles, country mansions, gardens, zoos, show-grounds and so on. The requirements for entry to the rank of temporary bus conductor, it has to be conceded, were not terribly demanding, consisting, as they did, of filling in a form and a brief chat with a personnel officer. What followed was, however, a bit more rigorous – Conductor School! Conductor School was run by Inspector Gummack, who must have been at least a regimental sergeant major in the war and behaved just like one ever afterwards! Impeccably attired in his dark blue Inspector's uniform, he strutted up and down before his class of would be conductors and instructed them in the art of bus conducting. First, he distributed each candidate with a leather shoulder bag with several overlapping pockets in which to keep varying denominations of coinage, a ticket machine which looked fiercely complex having two rotatable dials on the top, one for pounds and the other for pence up to ninety-nine pence, and a handle on the side which, when turned three hundred and sixty degrees, issued streams of paper tickets through an aperture at the front. Also, a roll of plane ticket paper to go with the ticket machine, a bus timetable for all the company's routes and a fare chart like an encyclopedia! It was fortunate that the learner conductors were seated at what looked like canteen tables for, had they not been, they would certainly have been unable to carry all this stuff!

From his position at the front of the room, Inspector Gummack showed everyone how to drape their leather bag across the shoulder from left to right, how to do the same with their ticket machine, but from right to left and how to load their ticket machine with the roll of ticket paper. The last of these tasks had some class members struggling, but not nearly as much as reading the timetable and fare chart. Fortunately, the tome of a fare chart could be dissembled, so that small sections for each number bus could be extracted according to what route was required. Even so, reading the chart wasn't easy. The print was very small for one thing and identifying a particular fare from one place to another by locating the boarding stage — bus stops from which the fares were calculated were called stages, and still are, probably — down the left hand side of the page and running one's finger across the grid of adult single fares below the list of destinations across the top, until one reached the required destination was not easy! Secondly, it wasn't always a single fare for one passenger that was wanted. "A man does board your bus," Inspector Gummack would boom, "at the Town terminus with his wife, two children and a pushchair. He does want returns for the beach at Sandhill's and he offers you a pound note. How much change will you give him?" The eager would-be-conductors had to find the adult fares, then calculate the child fares — usually, but not always, half the adult fare — work out the return fares which, in order to encourage the taking of return tickets, weren't always twice the single fare, add the fee for the pushchair, turn and re-turn the dials on the ticket machine to the correct points, issue the tickets by rotating the handle on the side a full turn for each ticket, add the total fares to be charged and calculate how much change the passenger was entitled to from his pound note. Inspector Gummack didn't even begin with simple straightforward single fare journeys for one person and the challenges got ever more complex, for not only were there pushchairs, but also dogs, not only returns, but also weekly and period tickets for regular passengers and commuters, and not only children, but also old people and blind persons and, worst of all, there were special tickets that had to be issued to passengers boarding and alighting within the area of the rival corporation trolley bus company. Inspector Gummack introduced these by giving each member of the class a little wooden clip board with a row of old-fashioned looking trolley bus tickets of different values kept in place by springs, a bit like those on mouse traps, which had to be pulled out by hand and clipped at the appropriate point by a little punch built into the top of the ticket machine. Not only did the conductor have to remember where the corporation bus area began and ended, but also never forget to issue the special corporation tickets of the correct value, so that the share of the corporation bus company could be remitted to it later. Issuing the wrong tickets was tantamount to committing a serious felony! And, one more serious matter, if a conductor issued a ticket, usually a return, costing more than one pound, which was rare but possible, he or she had to take care to return the pound dial on top of the ticket machine to zero or, as a consequence, issue numerous following tickets for one pound something! The money in every conductor's pouch had to be reconciled with the total recorded amount on the ticket machine at the conclusion of each shift and this also had to coincide with the figures recorded by the conductor on his 'waybill', the latter being a kind of log of numbers entered from the ticket machine at the beginning and the end of the day. All this was difficult enough without forgetting to return the pound dial to zero and it was open to question whether a modern mathematics graduate would grasp it nowadays! In fact, old hands advised deliberately issuing a few tickets printed with fares below the cost charged to the passenger to get ahead early in the day — never returns of course which might be picked up by inspectors later, or even queried by alert passengers, in which case a second ticket to make up the difference was the answer. 'Two star' tickets — so-called because the machines printed a star symbol rather than a zero when not turned at all, were not recommended as a way of dealing with the money problem because the machine recorded everything and indiscretions could, in theory at least, be picked up by vigilant office staff. In any case, the idea of 'getting ahead' with one's cash was not to defraud the company, but to get ahead and stay ahead in case of errors, so there were no arrears upon reconciliation of the cash in the bag with the evidence of the ticket machine at the end of the day.

If all this sounds complicated, it was. Some learners simply could not cope with it and had to give up. And the inspector had his favourites, mostly those who shared his enthusiasm for cricket and gaped at the TV in the canteen during breaks and then spent the first twenty minutes of the following session discussing the nuances of it all with Gummack, whilst the rest of the class sat around fiddling with their machines or reading the newspaper. The most astonishing thing of all was that Conductor School lasted an entire week of these excruciating and repetitive exercises covering many routes and situations, whilst every few minutes, the inspector would remind his charges of the necessity to maintain a clean and tidy appearance, to always wear the company apparel, to keep a sharp lookout for intending passengers, to assist young mums, children and old persons to board and get off the bus, to be polite and courteous at all times, never to accidentally touch the person of women passengers on a crowded bus, or one that lurched at an opportune moment — "Oops! Sorry madam," as Inspector Gummack put it — and to keep a wary eye out for those blind people who bought concessionary tickets and then went upstairs on the rural routes to get the best views! There were also lengthy, and even more boring, sessions on health and safety and study of the latest laws and wisdom from the Health and Safety Executive. These included establishing a good relationship with drivers and knowing the correct signals to inform them of what was going on behind them in the bus. One ring to stop at a 'request stop' — it may seem a little strange, but the bus was supposed to stop at all stops other than 'request stops', whether or not anyone wanted to get on or off — and two clear rings to set off again, when everyone was safely on board and only the conductor was on the platform. Two clear rings when the bus was in motion and approaching a bus stop told the driver that no-one wished to alight, so he could carry on without stopping, assuming there was no-one waiting to get on. That was entirely unofficial, because all bus stops were supposed to be observed in all circumstances and Gummack made it crystal clear that the practice of missing out passenger-free stops was frowned upon! Incidentally, passengers never rang the bell themselves; that was ipso facto part of the conductor's job and no passenger would dream of doing so! In spite of all this, and the fact that he was a remarkable pedant who demanded perfection and precision, Inspector Gummack was well-liked by all who encountered him. In an odd way, he had a sense of humour and, although no-one ever wanted to meet him in his role of inspector out on the road for fear that he would, inevitably, find something wrong – Inspector Gummack did get on the Bus Conductor's bus on once — he cared about his classes and he wished them well. Perhaps the most astonishing thing was the fact that he, and the bus company, took training so seriously and offered such a thorough grounding in the realities of conducting a bus.

Some of the regular drivers and conductors didn't like temporary staff, especially 'smart Alec' students, so it was wise to keep one's head down, to behave with all due deference to all the permanent staff and not just the inspectors. Also, to act, as far as possible, like they did. This would include joining in the canteen card games, buying one's driver tea, treating the cooks and cleaners like human beings, never missing a shift and being ready to do overtime when asked. The drivers, invariably men in those days, were usually decent blokes, but they varied a lot in personality and needs so that the Bus Conductor reacted in different ways to different drivers. Albert, for example, liked a drink between trips and began by getting the Bus Conductor to run up to the canteen and order what sounded like, "Two cuts o' tee," but was, in fact, "Two cups of tea." This soon graduated to, "Two pints!" Mild for Albert and bitter for the Bus Conductor, a task which put the Bus Conductor in serious jeopardy, because it involved leaping from the platform as the bus hurtled around the final bend into the bus station and dashing across the road into the public bar of the now long gone Alston Arms, where Albert would join him to describe the performance during the lunch break with his wife. Albert's axiom was, according to Albert, "You make it hard and I'll make it soft!" The Bus Conductor always listened, but secretly marvelled at the very possibility of a man of Albert's age doing anything other than nap during the dinner hour. Actually, Albert wasn't all that old and also, of course, the Bus Conductor was secretly jealous! Then, there was Saint John. That was his surname, rather than his calling, and anyone less like a saint would be hard to find. No-one seemed to know Saint John's first name and he was generally known as 'Johnnie'. He was prone to foul language and bad tempered abuse, especially concerning the police, and would probably have been diagnosed as suffering from Tourette's Syndrome had he had the benefit of psychiatric help. It was probably all to do with an inferiority complex for on one occasion, having been accosted by a police motorcyclist concerning a minor traffic transgression and having responded with great humility, he said, when asked by the Bus Conductor who'd heard it all and was only engaging in what used to be called 'passing the time of day', what had happened, responded with, "I told him to go and piss up his helmet!" Arthur was, on the other hand, not only a working class gentleman of the old fashioned kind, whose wife worked with the Bus Conductor's mum in local school kitchens, but also a gentle and kind person with a sweet and generous nature. He taught the Bus Conductor quite a lot about how to behave towards friends, fellow workers and the public. Not that the Bus Conductor applied Arthur's unwritten code of conduct with any consistency in the succeeding years, but at least he was aware of how it should be done. There were others that the Bus Conductor remembered in later life. One, during a torrential downpour at Sandhill's, when the Bus Conductor poured scorn upon the locals fishing in the harbour nearby, expressed the view that he'd be with them, if only he hadn't to drive an empty open top bus back to the depot. The Bus Conductor made a mental note to be less opinionated and didactic in future, an undertaking he failed to keep for any length of time. Another, who was a trifle cocksure, showed the Bus Conductor how it was possible to believe that you were popular with your workmates, whilst actually being disliked by most of them. A lesson that the Bus Conductor did take to heart. Yet another encouraged the Bus Conductor to drop sixpence after sixpence from his conductor bag, that had to be made good later, into the slot machines appropriately named 'one-armed bandits' in a local resort-type place, whilst awaiting the hour to set off back to the depot. Another lesson well learned for later life! And the Bus Conductor never forgot the elderly driver, who barked at him to, "Brag the worth of your hand!" This was during one of the card games in the depot, when the Bus Conductor, holding a prial of kings, was actually trying to be kind by 'calling' the elderly driver, so as not to fleece him too much. "How ungrateful," he thought! The softness in this gesture became a part of the Bus Conductor's personality and the reason that the Bus Conductor remembered it had less to do with his success in the card game, which was rare, than with the doe-eyed look one of the conductresses gave him for doing it. Another chance spurned. And then there was Sam. The Bus Conductor, for whom everyone over about twenty-five years of age was old, was surprised when Sam approached him one day with a smile that would have lit up heaven and said,

"I'm a family man now!" The Bus Conductor wasn't sure what Sam meant, or how to react, but quickly concluded that Sam's wife had given birth to their first child. The lesson here, totally missed at the time, was that becoming a parent is a wonderful and unique experience.

Apart from the odd generally unpopular character, some of the drivers didn't like each other and especially disliked those who hung back behind other drivers to minimise their load and, of course, their conductor's workload. It's a truism now, and was then, that the irritation associated with waiting for a bus can be worsened when two arrive together and this practice exacerbated the likelihood of this. Some drivers, when spotting a close following bus, would go around a roundabout in order to let the following vehicle through, rather than take their route exit first time. This worked unless the following bus followed the leading bus around the roundabout. In which case, the first bus would sometimes circumnavigate the roundabout a second time, sometimes followed by the second bus doing a second circuit! This caused confusion bordering upon panic amongst passengers and occasionally led to serious disagreements in the canteen later — maybe even fisticuffs! What all this shows is that bus drivers were a mixture of all sorts of characteristics such as kindness, unpleasantness, generosity, wisdom, foolishness, and so on. They were typical of any group of people anywhere.

There were three basic shifts on the buses. The early shifts began at five or six o'clock in the morning and the drawback of those was that you had to get yourself to the depot on foot or by bike and then ride it home again after work. The Bus Conductor frequently left his bike propped up against the wall at the bus station and got a bus home so that, notwithstanding its indifferent condition, the bike was eventually stolen and, thereafter, he had to walk to work for the early shift! That was something of a pain, but there were some nice things about 'earlies' once you'd got out of bed, made it to the depot and clocked in. It was pleasing to be up and about when so few other people were around and by mid-afternoon you were free again. The middle shift was a bit like a normal eight to six working day and 'lates' could last until about eleven or twelve at night, when the last buses were being shunted back to their starting points, ready for the following day, except on a Sunday, of course, when everything finished early because, unlike today, there was a pretence that people observed it with something approaching reverence. If only! Late shifts had the disadvantage of putting the Bus Conductor's social life, already severely limited by resources and his inadequate personality, on hold. He discovered a way to make the best of it on a Sunday night at the end of a week of 'earlies', by going through the usual Ritz-style dance hall torture and choosing the plainest girls imaginable, notably at 'last waltz' time, in the knowledge that he would be unavailable the following week for dating. This worked up to a point, but whilst it may have enhanced the egos of some rather unfortunate young women, it did nothing to further the love life of the introspective Bus Conductor.

There were, also, three basic kinds of route. These were the rural rides, the town routes and the extras. In some ways, the first of these was the best and the Bus

Conductor particularly enjoyed lounging across the back seat, whilst the early bus to the 'middle of nowhere' took him and his driver into the countryside to begin transporting the relatively well-off country dwellers to their destinations in the town. He could also sing or whistle — in the days when he still could whistle, that is — at the top of his voice because no-one would hear and, even if the odd rustic and a few goats or chickens were frightened, few would care! One of his colleagues sang opera greats, even on busy routes, so the Bus Conductor thought it best to stick to something approaching classical hits, such as those from Gilbert and Sullivan or 'Beethoven's Greatest Hits!' The vicar was a typical country passenger, often present when the Bus Conductor felt bold enough to whistle or sing, and whilst he would occasionally join in with the Bus Conductor's warbling, he was also likely to complain bitterly about being dropped near the Butcher's Arms, rather than outside the vicarage. The bus stop was outside the Butcher's Arms. On the whole, the country routes were the easiest and most pleasant.

Unlike the town routes, which, even in the early mornings and late at night were busy not to say frenetic! A twenty-five minute journey on a number four between the town centres could be absolute hell for the conductor with fifty-odd seated passengers, plus those standing. And there'd be seven such return trips in a shift! There were, and are, regulations about how many cows or sheep can be carried in a given truck and the same thing applied and applies to humans in buses and coaches — but not trains, oddly enough! Thus, when every seat was taken on a busy bus, eight more passengers could stand. This made conducting hugely more difficult, especially when standing passengers ignored the Bus Conductor's calls to, "Move right down the bus please!" and he had to push his way past them and try to ensure that he was back on the platform and in control of the situation as each stop approached and it may have been necessary to shout, "Full up, sorry!", to repel boarders — not always easy — and bang on the bell to get the bus in motion again as soon as possible. Of course, fares had to be collected from all these passengers as well. Singles, returns, weekly tickets, concession tickets, those special corporation tickets from the little clip board. And the money had to be taken. Oh, how the Bus Conductor longed for all customers to have the exact money! Few did and he was forever fumbling in the bag for change, whilst holding onto the most recently proffered ten bob note or even one pound note!

It could be just as bad on the extra routes; those that ran to the beaches and places of interest during the summer months only, or were put on as 'specials' to serve some event or other, or as a 'relief' bus to ease overcrowding on the regular services. The most exciting of these were, and it is supposed still are, the open top double-deckers running to the popular seaside spots. They could be just as busy as the commuter routes into the towns with the added problem of how to hang on to the ten bob notes, whilst issuing tickets and giving change on the upper deck. "Between your teeth," was the advice the Bus Conductor got from experienced colleagues. They didn't say how you were supposed to communicate whilst doing so, but it did, on the whole, ensure the safe keeping of the 'paper money'. Wise hands also advised looking out for low bridges and large banners strung across the roads advertising summer fetes, steam 'fayres' or agricultural shows. There were also tales, most likely apocryphal, of young conductors falling over the side or being blown off the top deck, to sustain, at best, undignified embarrassment or, at worst, horrific injuries. By the time the Bus Conductor made his maiden journey on an open top bus, he was close to petrification. But he soon got used to it, and of all the experiences on the buses, the open tops were the most fun.

If signs are an indication of the standard of a society's civilisation and sophistication, then public transport vehicles are a good place to look. The messages haven't changed much either and they still tend to be in the form of orders and warnings rather than helpful suggestions. There are a few exceptions to this general rule, for example, the advice offered in the lower compartments of double deck buses; "Please lower your head when leaving your seat." This was actually very helpful, because the roof of the bottom decks was lower on one side to accommodate the passageway alongside the seats in the upper deck compartment of the older vehicles. Most of these signs were changed by scratching out certain of the letters and adding or amending others, so as to read "fleas over your head!" This was the work of artful youths and was probably a better reflection of the standards of the times. Other signs included, "Do not distract the driver," which was next to impossible anyway and "Please do not put your feet on the seats" to which ought to have been added, "or your dog either!" But the best indicator of the culture of the times was the bald statement, "No spitting!"

Collecting the fares could not only include the fumbling with bag, machine and money but also be downright hard. Transactions to be negotiated with considerable tact and forbearance. It was a skill, maybe even an art! An art that was aggravated by the bus company regularly 'revising' the fares, which meant, of course, increasing them, by difficult passengers and by inspectors. On one occasion of a general fare increase by the bus company, a fare from the depot on a busy route went up from seven pence to eight pence and conductors received a notice to that effect. However, the fare from the depot to the boundary of the trolley bus company was four pence and the trolley bus fare from there remained at three pence, so that wily passengers could, in theory, book a four penny ticket on the company bus and then a three penny trolley bus ticket in the trolley bus area, a total of seven pence! Thus, the eight penny fare had to be revised again — back to seven pence. The fact that no passenger ever did book two separate tickets, or would have ever have dreamed of doing so, didn't matter. What did matter was that Inspector Gummack boarded the Bus Conductor's bus at that time and challenged him over the issue of a seven penny ticket based upon the original fare, and after the second revision, still the correct fare. The Bus Conductor explained how the fare had been increased by the company and then decreased almost immediately to take account of the possibility that someone might book two tickets to avoid the penny fare increase! Inspector Gummack, realising he had not kept up with the pace of change, and not able to find any other errors on a full and busy bus, took his humbling in good part. It was a triumph for the Bus Conductor and also the last time he ever saw Inspector Gummack.

Less of a triumph was the day the Bus Conductor issued a man and woman with two returns and a half fare single. The half fare single was for their dog. All children, dogs, and pushchairs being charged at half the adult fare and no returns permitted for the second and third of these! The reasoning underpinning this was never clear, but it was a source of annoyance, and passengers often asked whether the company thought that people should leave their dogs and pushchairs at their destinations. On this occasion, it wasn't the principle that bothered the man and his companion. "What's the single for?" asked the man. "It's for the dog," replied the Bus Conductor. The man smiled and said, "That's not a dog, it's my wife's fur bag! "But on the whole, the Bus Conductor managed very nicely. It was one of the things he was good at and there weren't all that many of them. He supported the elderly, supervised the children, guided the blind, dealt with the abusive and disciplined the yobs! All of which indicated a possible future career.

There was a species that the vast majority of the regular drivers and conductors disliked. The bus company was introducing 'one-man' operated buses — single-deckers with the entrance at the front and a ticket machine mounted next to the driver. Whilst the company saw this as the future, correctly as it turned out, most of the regulars saw this, also correctly, as a threat to their livelihoods and as the beginning of the end of the bus conductor. It was. Because of this, most of them didn't like the drivers who volunteered for the extra pay attached to the 'one-man' operated buses. As far as local authority bus company employees were concerned, this may have been an unexpected, if inexorable, development, but if someone had told coachmen in the eighteenth century that the day would come when the highwaymen would be running the stagecoaches, then the former would have found it quite hard to believe too! The conductors of the twentieth century, and their union, could do little and the Bus Conductor had, in the end, to move on to alternative employment in manufacturing.

Chapter 7

THE FACTORY HAND

The Factory Hand was one of a number of young men —
it was considered by the factory employers that most of
the work that they had on offer was entirely unsuitable
for females, something they wouldn't get away with
today — who decided to spend the summer processing
all kinds of fruit and vegetables.

In spite of the decline of bus conductors, before the
demise of the bulk of the manufacturing industries in
favour of an emphasis upon de-regulated financial
hucksters, prior to the wholesale exploitation of
desperate immigrants and up to the advent of zero hour
contracts and casual labour, it was still quite possible to
get temporary full-time work, especially during the
months of high summer from June to the end of
September. That was when the fruits of the soil were
harvested and when much of them were still 'home
grown' and that was when the Bus Conductor became,
for one long, languid summer, the Factory Hand.

The jobs were almost as varied as the produce and, whilst the work was to some degree subject to the vagaries of the unpredictable English summer weather, so that if the quantities of food to be dealt with fell into short supply, hands might be laid off at a moment's notice at any time, pay was reasonable, accommodation was included and smart white boiler suits to protect one's clothing were provided. If the weather was wet and the work dried up, the young men withdrew to a nearby public house to waste their time and the wages earned thus far by drinking what passed in those times for bitter beer and by indulging in bar-room games, such as darts and dominoes. The two 'double tops' with which the Factory Hand clinched one unforgettable game remained in his memory, when much else had long been forgotten. Such was the mind-set of the typical twenty year old that the Factory Hand's father's oft repeated verdict, "The youth of today; they don't know they're born", was closer to the truth than the Factory Hand or any of his friends cared to concede.

The living quarters for the temporary summer workforce consisted of an enormous barn-like building that had, at one time, been a factory of some kind. There was a complete absence of heating of any kind — well, it was summer, albeit an English one — so it was freezing cold most of the time! There were a few stone basins at one end with running water, also freezing cold, and close by, some ancient toilets that resembled those in the school yards of nineteenth and many twentieth century state schools with huge stone urinals from which it was possible to piss over the walls onto anyone foolish enough to stand too close. The cubicles enjoyed old stone bowls and some still had doors. Where these existed, and it was the exception rather than the rule, they'd been broken so often that privacy depended upon long enough legs to wedge a foot against the door, or to employ a co-operative companion prepared to physically hold the door in place, or to share guard duty outside with his back turned — of course! The floor of this enormous 'hall' of an edifice was filled with crude bunks lined up in rows close enough to reach out and touch the person in the next bunk. The few nails driven into the mortar between the brickwork of the walls soon filled with coats, jackets and even suits but, there being no other storage and no chairs, the whole scene quickly degenerated into a chaotic mess of discarded clothing, nightwear and assorted possessions. No-one tidied or cleaned and no-one seemed to care. The prevailing stench was a mixture of 'Old Spice' after shave, faeces and sweat. It became a veritable Hogarthian scene of utter squalor!

Work in the factory and, sometimes, outside in the yard, consisted of keeping a number of different 'lines' in motion. The worst of these, and by far the most modern, was the 'Baked Bean Line'. It consisted of a huge, towering machine mysteriously producing tins of labelled baked beans. The only thing that changed appeared to be the labels. Two hands were detailed to sit and watch the cans of beans as they progressed through the machine from one end to the other, their job being to intervene if anything went wrong. None of the hands knew what was likely to go wrong, or what to do other than shout for the foreman and, as far as is known, nothing ever did go wrong and this is why watching the 'Baked Bean Line' was the worst of the tasks. There was actually nothing to do except stare at the machine. As a result, nearly everyone assigned to that 'line' fell asleep. It was hard enough to stay awake after a good night's rest which, in any case, wasn't remotely possible in the so-called dormitory, but add a few pints and a late night to the equation and it became utterly impossible. Anyone falling asleep was punished by being removed from the 'Baked Bean Line' to more arduous work, which resulted in a regular succession of hands being ordered to the 'Baked Bean Line' and promptly being taken off it again. Some even made no effort to stay alert, preferring to be occupied in something less boring. Such as the 'Broad Bean Line', which started outside in the yard with insatiable machines that had to be fed with broad beans and where it could get so cold that the workforce wore overcoats. There was scant regard for safety, so the Factory Hand was not surprised to see one of his companions being dragged into one of the broad bean shelling machines by the hem of his overcoat. "Help!" he shrieked, rather understating the urgency and with little chance of being heard above the din. The Factory Hand dropped his share of broad beans and made towards his stricken workmate. He was too far away to be of assistance and could have done nothing anyway, when the young man being dragged into the whirring machine, with commendable presence of mind, undid the toggles of his coat and slipped quickly out of it just as it began to become shredded in the teeth of the mechanism. In the words of the Duke of Wellington at Waterloo, "It was a close run thing!"

The "Strawberry Line" began with the sorting and grading of the fruit as it passed before the workers on a moving conveyor belt. This was one of the tasks, along with making up boxes and packing them, that the company allowed females to do and, it has to be said, you needed to be pretty nifty to keep pace with the number of strawberries passing by. The good, large ones had to be left alone to pass on for putting in little card 'baskets' for the posher supermarkets. Small, bruised or imperfect strawberries had to have any bad bits plucked out with the thumb before going on to be tinned and the bits plucked out went into containers to make into strawberry jam. Quality control was something for the future! Strawberries and raspberries, whilst hardly likely to excite fear in the normal run of things, could also expose hands to danger when, having been tinned, went on to being cooked in enormous rotary ovens that were scalding to the touch. As the ovens went round and round, a number of the workers had to stand upon little wooden plinths and lift the lids from time to time to make sure that the rotating tins of boiling fruit were not getting jammed against the metal bars at the top of each oven. This was a frequent occurrence and, when spotted, the offending tin had to be rapidly removed, lest it dented every following tin rendering them unsalable. This job, often one engaged in by the Factory Hand and one of his closest friends, was made more unpalatable because the·tins often split open when they jammed and squirted hot strawberry or raspberry juice in all directions, which was not just dangerous but fairly unpleasant too! On one memorable occasion, immediately following the weekly issue of fresh overalls, the Factory Hand was on duty on a rotary oven of the "Strawberry Line". His friend, on a later shift, had charged the Factory Hand with the collection of his overalls and the Factory Hand had done so and placed them with his own on one of the plinths adjacent to the point where he was on duty. Routinely checking for blockages, the Factory Hand raised the lid of the oven to be greeted by a shower of blistering red liquid. The rule was to unblock as quickly as possible and summon help. As it happened, a supervisor was nearby and as was the usual response of such persons, he panicked, tossed the clean overalls to one side, seized the handle of the oven lid from the Factory Hand, got drenched in strawberry juice, removed the blocked and broken tin of strawberries and roundly cursed the Factory Hand for not doing his job properly! Instead of protesting, as he ought to have done, the Factory Hand accepted the abuse and, in the words of the Second World War slogan, kept calm and carried on. The trouble began when his dear friend accused him of deliberating smearing bright red strawberry juice around the crotch of his, the friend's that is, fresh clean, white boiler suit. The hurt felt by his friend was worsened by the fact that the Factory Hand's boiler suit had, amazingly and quite by chance, been totally unaffected.

As the tins of cooked fruits and vegetables came off the 'lines', they had to be stacked for cooling and this was done in various ways. Automatically, as in the case of baked beans, or by a curious use of a large paddle shaped tool to sweep them from rows emanating from the ovens and into large drums ready for immersion in cold water as part of the cooling process. If these ingenious methods failed, as they often did, then 'hot take off' was the order of the day, whereby the temporary workers, in pairs and suitably gloved, grabbed the rapidly accumulating red hot tins of cooked food as they tumbled from the ovens and stacked them by hand into the drums. 'Hot take off' was the hardest job of all! It meant bending almost double, seizing two tins, rising to almost full height clutching them, bending double again to deposit them in the drums and repeating this again and again and again. In theory, this could only be sustained for a few minutes before another pair of workers took over. Unless, as happened when the Factory Hand and his equally stupid friend had been engaged in 'hot take off' for some time and a foreman approached to offer them a break, the pair insisted that they were okay and could carry on. The foreman, realising that they were being brash and cocky decided to give them a lesson and left them to it for a lengthy period, after which they readily agreed to a break and came away gasping for breath and barely able to stand. Foolish youths, "… They don't know they're born."

The final part of the processing was the packaging. This was by far the easiest job and by far the most peaceful, because it was done in a separate room away from the buzz of the factory floor. There, amidst the noise and bustle, it was possible to sing at the top of one's voice to shout and to swear and, in order to be understood, learn to read lips. By contrast, in the packaging room the workers were able to relax and to chat whilst folding cardboard cases, filling them with tins of fruit or vegetables and sealing them ready for being moved around on forklift trucks and, ultimately, transported in lorries to shops and supermarkets. And here the factory bosses, in line with their sexist approach, did allow women and girls to be employed! And it was here that the Factory Hand was again humiliated by the supervisory staff, when he was moved into the packaging room when all the female staff had left for some sort of protest meeting and a smoke and a cuppa, leaving him totally alone to cope with several conveyor belts shunting boxes of tinned foodstuffs at him, that all required sealing and moving at the same time. The Factory Hand dashed from belt to belt, frantically trying to prevent boxes from falling off the end of the belts on to the floor. He summoned a foreman, who said with thinly disguised contempt, "Listen, son. We have teenage girls to do this job if you can't manage it." The Factory Hand blushed as he often did and carried on.

Nights in the dormitory were not a good preparation for a day's work. Those who went to bed early often awoke still in their beds, but out in the street, whence their silly, and often bibulous, workmates had carried them, which was, perhaps, an improvement on waking up amongst a haze of acrid cigarette smoke and a hubbub of conversation, noises and worse. The neighbours, having the great misfortune to dwell close to the factory, occasionally felt bold enough to intervene to protest about the noise. In those days, there was a lot less 'light pollution' so that on clear nights many of the workers went outside to marvel at the night sky. The locals didn't mind that as much as the language with which the young men expressed their appreciation of it all! And often they went into the city to spend their money on booze and, if they could persuade them, women. The Factory Hand could easily manage the former as the time when he nearly fell out of the back of a van attested to, but was not nearly as good at the latter. Most young ladies were intransigent and indifferent to the charms, such as they were, of these young men, such that The Factory Hand was compelled to put it all down to experience and was left carrying a reel of negatives recording life at the factory that he promised to return to a Scottish boy called Hamish. He never did.

What he did do was to become an Ice Cream Man.

Chapter 8

THE ICE CREAM MAN

If you've ever been tempted to try to sell ice cream on a wet afternoon on a council estate in a northern city — don't! The Ice Cream Man tried the following summer. It was another transient manual job.

Whilst not necessarily being an improvement upon factory labour, it was most certainly less arduous than the job he had applied for first, been interviewed for and been turned down! The bluff railway manager just could not believe that an apparently gentle and quiet spoken young man could possibly work on the railway alongside such hardened creatures as ballast diggers, permanent way maintenance men and rolling stock shunters. Neither could his experience in the canning factory or on the buses convince him. Mr Whip Easy had no such reservations, so instead of becoming a railway shunter, the Factory Hand became an Ice Cream Man, which may have been just as well, especially since the Factory Hand wasn't at all clear what was involved in railway shunting.

There were certain other differences, one of which was that the Ice Cream Man had nowhere to live and was forced to accept temporary lodgings on a living room floor. This rather unsatisfactory arrangement was the outcome of a liaison with a young woman — at least there was one at this stage! Regrettably, the young lady's parents didn't share her enthusiasm for this state of affairs, or her generosity, and the Ice Cream Man very soon had to take a dingy room with worn out furniture, a grotty bed and a money-in-the-slot black and white telly. It wasn't ideal but it gave him a measure of independence — and freedom.

Meanwhile, his career as an Ice Cream Man began to blossom — in a way! At first, he was assigned a small van with side access. Every morning, he went to the depot, loaded the back of the van with an assortment of ice creams and ice lollies on sticks, in tubs or wrapped, packed the contents with 'dry ice' and spent much of each day touring the streets and estates of the city, sounding the strident van horn and attempting to sell his wares. It wasn't easy. The van wasn't especially noticeable, it was very small and the inclement weather gave little encouragement to the population to buy freezing and not very good quality ice creams. The Ice Cream Man was reduced to selling Chocolate Hearts to his girlfriend's mother! But he persisted and spent long hours searching out customers, before returning to the depot with his 'dry ice' almost gone and a reasonable proportion of his load sold. At the end of a week or two, he was called into the manager's office. "You've proved yourself as a salesman," the manager told him, "One of the big vans has become available and I'm giving it to you." The manager beamed as he said it, expecting the Ice Cream Man to be overjoyed at this rapid promotion and transformation into a fully-fledged Mr Whip Easy! The Ice Cream Man couldn't help but smile. He didn't really care, but the manager was so obviously pleased with himself, that he had to pretend to be delighted at the prospect of getting a Mr Whip Easy van with the soft ice cream machine that produced the whipped up rubbish that every child and many adults loved *and* plenty of storage for all the other things including the genuinely popular Chocolate Hearts.

Serving whipped ice cream isn't as simple as it looks. When the tap is turned on, the whipped-up soft ice cream pours out quite quickly and the receiving cone has to be held beneath the tap and moved rapidly around and carefully lowered, so that the descending ice cream forms a spiral as it builds up into a peak and tails off with a sharp point when the tap is closed again. Training is required or, rather, a bit of practice. "You'll need training," said the manager with some emphasis on the "training". The Ice Cream Man smiled again, not, as the manager thought, at the prospect of the Mr Whip Easy van and the increased status, but at the idea that training was needed to serve ice cream. The manager was right though! Serving whipped ice cream took a bit of doing and the Ice Cream Man wasted a fair amount of the stuff before he perfected the technique and was ready to go out onto the road in his capacity as a Mr Whip Easy.

The fleet of Mr Whip Easy vans were the elite vehicles of the firm, they were large and colourful, they were decked out in the company livery of blue and yellow and they had loud musical chimes ringing out

'Greensleeves' to all and sundry. As a Mr Whip Easy, the Ice Cream Man could develop his round and compete effectively with the other ice cream sellers in the city — or so he thought. The Ice Cream Man's new round began with a series of terraced streets close to the city centre. It was fairly densely populated and many of the small dwellings housed families with children and elderly persons. Both of these are well known categories of ice cream lovers, so the going was likely to be good for purveyors of soft ice cream — or so it seemed.

The Ice Cream Man expected fierce competition from what he saw as his main rivals — the Mr Creamy's of the ice cream world. The Ice Cream Man was under no illusions that his ice cream was any better than Mr Creamy's, so the technique, when the opposition was sighted, was to nip ahead of them by a street or two and then stay ahead. This strategy worked for both sides, so if sales were poor on a particular day, it usually meant that Mr Creamy had done the spotting first and gone ahead. In this situation, it was necessary to re-overtake so that scenarios occurred where ice cream vans were leapfrogging one another all over the city! However, it was all done in a competitive but good-natured way in those days and it wasn't until years later that 'ice cream wars' developed into something far more sinister, dangerous and even life threatening!

There were instances when the normal rules of the game didn't apply; when something different happened and these were occasions upon which that the Ice Cream Man learned a bit more about ice cream. One day, quite early in the morning, he came across an old man riding a tricycle a few yards ahead of his own Mr Whip Easy van. The tricycle was, to the Ice Cream Man, unusual in that it had one large rear wheel and two rather tiny front wheels, between which rode an enormous box-like structure on the side of which he could just make out the words "Brown's Traditional Ices". Intrigued by the wording, the Ice Cream Man pulled over and watched. The tricycle paused at the kerbside and, to the astonishment of the Ice Cream Man, several people, including children, mums and dads and several elderly men and women immediately gathered and formed quite a significant queue in response to which the old man lifted the box lid and procceded to load ice cream cones with generous scoops of what looked remarkably like ice cream which, of course, it was and dish them out to his customers in exchange for money. The old man on the Brown's bike was doing a lively trade! The Ice Cream Man laughed aloud at the thought of competition from an old codger on a tricycle! "No problem," he thought, "these people have no loyalty! They'll take anything if Whip Easy isn't there first. I'll overtake this old guy and leave him for dead. It'll take him ages to realise what's happened and he'll never catch up on that contraption!" And, without more ado, the Ice Cream Man drove into the next-but-one street listening to the jangling chimes of "Greensleeves" and chuckling to himself with glee. He stopped to await the hordes of true ice cream aficionados. They didn't come. One old lady did, eventually, appear at the counter on the side of his van to request her daily Chocolate Heart. "Where is everyone?" asked the ice Cream Man breezily as he handed her the precious concoction of ice cream and chocolate on a stick. "Oh," she replied, "it's Tuesday, they'll be waiting for Sid." "Sid? Who's Sid?" said the Ice Cream Man. Sid, it transpired was the old man on the tricycle, who, the old lady bluntly informed the ice Cream Man, sold Brown's "proper" ice cream, by which she meant ice cream made with proper ingredients like real cream. The Ice Cream Man learned to fear Sid and to avoid him and his "traditional ices" like a plague of flies!

Other incidents taught the Ice Cream Man a little about human behaviour and how to respond to it. How does one react, for example, to a woman with some sort of trembling affliction whom, upon being handed two cones laden with ice cream promptly shakes the ice cream off and whom, thanks to the Ice Cream Man's basic humanity, upon being handed two replacements, promptly repeats the exercise? And what should one do when approached by a potential customer at nine-thirty in the evening whom, upon being graciously asked his requirements, becomes very abusive and threatens legal action should the Ice Cream Man ring his chimes in that street after nine o'clock ever again! And how should one respond when a little child on the council estate leaves her toy bike in the gutter for Mr Whip Easy to inadvertently crush with his van and her mum, for whom the Ice Cream Man had a secret passion, explodes with unreasonable and uncontrollable rage? And what does one do when, horror of horrors, a woman comes up and says, "Your ice cream tastes sour!"

The last of these was a matter for the manager. "Either you plug your van in overnight or you clean out the ice cream vat and refill it the following day," explained the manager, "then you've always got a nice fresh product." "But there's nowhere to plug in," said the Ice Cream Man with astonishing logic, "what then?" "We'll get the sockets fixed," said the manager with a frown. There was no answer to that, so the whipped ice cream vat in the van had to be cleaned every night. What the manager or any of his colleagues failed to tell the Ice Cream Man was that, before removing the lid, clearing out the last dregs of the day's ice cream from the vat and doing the cleaning job, it was necessary to relieve the pressure by opening the tap. Otherwise, when the lid was removed, the ice cream would explode through the top of the vat and smother the roof and the interior of the van with a sticky white mess. This wouldn't have mattered quite so much if the Ice Cream Man hadn't been accompanied by his girlfriend on the occasion when he first performed this task and staggered from the van looking like he'd just emerged from a rubbish container in a chicken factory or was starring in a horror film about zombies rising from a slimy underground vault. She laughed! He went red as much with annoyance as shame but, fortunately, his embarrassment was masked by the ice cream running down his face!

Many people wonder how on earth ice cream men and women, or any workers stuck in a lorry or a van all day selling things, manage to get through the day without needing a toilet. The truth is, of course, that they don't. It may well be that more modern vehicles have built in toilets like caravans do, or follow routes that offer opportunities for itinerants to stop and use public facilities, but years ago, when the Ice Cream Man went forth, the vans were pretty basic and the council lavatories few and far between. Peddling his wares in the midst of terrace after terrace of nineteenth century 'back-to-backs' or on soulless post-war housing estates, short of requesting access to the back yard loo or the upstairs lavatory of customers who were complete strangers —

which was unthinkable — the Ice Cream man had either to hold on or find some alternative arrangement to relieve himself. Having suffered since childhood from what he regarded as a weak bladder, arising from a congenital physical shortcoming neglected by his feckless parents, or from what his mother and, later, his teachers regarded as congenital laziness, in the end it became a question of risking his health, wetting himself or finding another option. This, he did with admirable resourcefulness — for once! It was quite simple too. A commodious saffron coloured plastic bucket was all that was needed! It should be noted that the colour was determined not by a wish to disguise the contents in any way but by what was available when he called at his local Co-op shop. In any event, the bucket served admirably. In the fairly frequent circumstances when the Ice Cream Man needed to urinate, especially if the day followed one of the his increasingly regular evenings of indulgence in bitter beers, he would crouch low in the back of the ice cream van, out of sight of passing pedestrians and potential customers, undo his trousers and use the yellow bucket. The absence of hand washing facilities in the van meant that there was a downside to this practice and an element of risk to the general public, but that was limited, and in the mind of the Ice Cream Man, it was preferable to that of embarrassing accidents and dry cleaning bills. There were mishaps of other sorts involving spillages and van cleaning at the end of the day, but the bucket idea, besides being very re-assuring was, clearly, better than nothing! Even when the occasional client, having approached the ice cream van and finding it, apparently, untenanted called out, "Hello – it's empty!" or "Where's the Ice Cream Man then?" and turning to companions with curious glances and suspicious frowns, would be surprised by the sudden appearance of the Ice Cream Man from below the level of the counter. "Yes, madam, what can I get you?" the Ice Cream Man would say, appearing suddenly like Punch in a seaside show, wearing a sly smile concealing his secret as though it was perfectly normal to be lurking on the floor. It was just as well that no one ever discovered the true nature of the Ice Cream Man's solution to the toilet dilemma. Who knows what scandal it might have caused in the local press by petty journalists ever on the lookout to conflate a minor incident into a full blown heath scare or, better still but far less likely, expose the disgraceful conditions of service endured by ice cream men and women along with many other working people?

Ultimately, the health issue didn't matter because, as far as is known, nobody was harmed by the Ice Cream Man's lack of hygiene and the Ice Cream Man gave up his career in retail selling in order to visit his sister abroad. When he returned, he enlisted in the National Health Service.

Chapter 9

THE NURSE

Quite how the post of Assistant Nurse in an enormous Victorian mental hospital became available remains something of a mystery, but it did, and the manual worker became a professional, albeit a rather poorly qualified one. That is to say, poorly qualified in terms of the knowledge and skills likely to be useful in such a post; medicine and psychiatry.

At almost the same time as getting his new job, The Nurse acquired a bicycle, which was just as well, because the hospital was some six or seven miles outside the city. Riding this elderly velocipede back and forth didn't bother The Nurse because he was young and strong then, but a particularly bitter winter had set in and the freezing cold hurt his hands. This was the only thing that really troubled him and for only a short time for, once he'd begged a pair of gargantuan stoker's mittens from one of the workers who toiled in the hospital boiler room, things improved no end! The bike had been obtained through the good offices of The Nurse's girlfriend's father, who knew a family wanting to dispose of it. In those days, people didn't take perfectly usable items to the local tip or simply dump them. They re-cycled them, in this case literally, often by passing them on to others who did have a use for them. Happily, this practice of free re-use of unwanted, but still serviceable, items has become more commonplace.

On his first journey to the hospital, The Nurse pondered the irony of becoming a nurse himself some years after having been hospitalised with appendicitis. He'd been rushed from the sixth form common room to the operating theatre and thence to a ward where he'd spent a week or two recuperating in times when patients were looked after properly, and hospitals were full of nurses and doctors feeding and cosseting inmates until fully recovered, and where nasty infections didn't lurk in every corridor because the whole place was cleaned for cleanliness, rather than for profit. And where he'd fallen in love with the nurses and become entranced with the nobility of nursing the sick. He wanted to do it! He had a vocation! This romantic nonsense lasted for some time, even to the point of obtaining a volume from the 'Careers Master' at school, whose only task associated with careers seemed to be to wordlessly loan out books about the professions, in this case, a tome on job opportunities in the National Health Service. Thereafter, it faded away — the desire to nurse that is — partly because nursing was considered a woman's job, and also, because most such ethereal things tended to fade until they became just ideas entertained in the past, but not to be taken seriously. Until now!

On his first day, to his delight, The Nurse was issued with a white coat. In those days, qualified nurses were dressed in clearly identifiable uniforms such as are only seen in old films nowadays. Females wore blue dresses with white nurse's hats, aprons with a watch pinned upside down, so that it could be consulted readily for taking pulse rates and temperatures, a black belt and a red cape to wear to and from work. Male nurses and doctors of course wore a white coat, "Proper order!" as The Nurse's dad would have said. And all this in stark contrast to the modern nurse's loose fitting pyjama-like outfits and doctors looking like they'd be more appropriately placed either in a bank or a bar, usually according to how old they were.

Those were the days before the cost cutting exercise, euphemistically called 'care in the community', and all psychiatric patients were then treated in hospitals instead of being dumped in houses to fend for themselves. Thus, the wards at the mental hospitals were full of people who were mentally ill in some way or another and the first task assigned to The Nurse was to watch over a patient. Reporting to the Charge Nurse, also resplendent in a clean white coat, on his first day, The Nurse was told brusquely, "Watch that fellow there." Accordingly, The Nurse settled himself in a chair next to the bed indicated and watched. After about an hour of this rather boring job, a tall distinguished looking man, also wearing a white coat, entered the ward and approached The Nurse." He must be a doctor," thought The Nurse, "he looks important." The doctor, for such he was, addressed The Nurse. "What are you doing?" he asked. "I'm watching him," replied The Nurse indicating the prone figure in the adjacent bed. The doctor looked surprised,

"Don't you think it would be a good idea to talk to him?" he said. The Nurse stood up, thinking that was the respectful thing to do. He hadn't been told to do anything other than watch the patient and, in any case, he thought the man in the bed, whom The Nurse had considered relatively young to be a patient in a mental hospital, was asleep. The Nurse didn't choose a response, but the one that emerged was to look bewildered and stare silently back at the doctor, who must have thought that The Nurse was another patient who'd somehow got hold of a staff coat. The Nurse learned later that this particular doctor was a senior clinician called Mr Backhouse, who was as remarkable for his big, shiny, leather boots — which looked like they'd just been liberated from the High Street 'Army and Navy Store' — as he was for his undoubted professional expertise! On this occasion, Mr Backhouse looked puzzled rather than irritated and moved away to talk earnestly to the Charge Nurse, whilst glancing back at The Nurse and the patient in the bed. The Nurse never found out for certain what was wrong with the patient, why he'd been asked to watch over him, or what Mr Backhouse made of it. He concluded that the man in the bed must have been somehow at risk or was likely to try to escape. The Charge Nurse, in all likelihood, told the doctor something that made it appear that he — the Charge Nurse that is — gave appropriate and full instructions to new and inexperienced staff. It wasn't a good start and, as far as The Nurse was concerned, it was made worse by the fact that at the other end of the ward, a young man of about his own age seemed to think the whole episode was inordinately funny! The Nurse was later able to restore the balance with Mr Backhouse to some extent, when the latter burst into the ward one day ahead of a posse of his subalterns. As he, Backhouse, approached the cringing Charge Nurse, The Nurse looked up from feeding a patient and, surreptitiously drew the great man's attention to the fact that his, Backhouse's, trouser flies were unfastened, an act that earned him, The Nurse, a warm appreciation and a more cordial relationship from then on.

The young man who'd found The Nurse's initial discomfort so amusing was called Jacques and he was French. Jacques was, in fact, a year or two older than The Nurse and had fled his native land to avoid military service. Jacque's pacifist and left wing beliefs were, at that time, new and rather puzzling to The Nurse, who had few ideals beyond getting a smoke, a pint, a game of football and sex in decreasing order of frequency. Nonetheless, they became very good friends. Jacques was higher in the pecking order in the health service, but not by much. He was a qualified mental nurse, below the doctors and charge nurses but above an assistant nurse, which was as low as one could get unless the cleaners, boiler men and maintenance men were included and even they were often more helpful in promoting patient wellbeing than a lowly assistant nurse! And Jacques had a sense of humour too. He remorselessly taunted The Nurse's vague right wing and frankly racist notions and his crude, underdeveloped ideas about the world. Upon spotting the 'Made in Germany' sticker on the frame of The Nurse's bike, Jacques derided it with heavy irony as "A wog bike! "And noticing The Nurse's clumpy boots he took to calling them "Backhouse boots" much to the annoyance of The Nurse. Jacques could play chess and since The Nurse had learned to pay chess at school, where he employed younger boys who had just enough sleight of hand to steal his opponents' rooks at the same time as feigning interest whilst spectating — which demonstrates rather clearly the level of the game in sixth form common rooms in those days — they, Jacques and The Nurse, spent many an hour poring over a chess board during visiting hours or when things were slack on the wards. Surprisingly, The Nurse proved victorious in most of these encounters. Even so, years later, Jacques presented his friend with a gift of a boxed set of carved chess figures upon the occasion of his marriage, which Jacques attended. The Nurse kept the chess set as a cherished memento of his time as a mental nurse. Jacques would surely have been pleased had he known of the influence he'd had upon later developments in The Nurse's political outlook. The latter never knew what became of his young French friend.

Although The Nurse encountered patients who were seriously mentally ill, "manic" as many of the regular nurses offhandedly put it, most of the inmates were geriatrics and GPIs. GPI, The Nurse learned, stood for General Paralysis of the Insane. One of the male nurses, the sexes were strictly segregated then and each was always cared for and treated by staff of the same sex, told The Nurse that cases of GPI always became prolific approximately fifteen years after a war because of the link between GPI and sexually transmitted diseases and the time it took for the illness to develop and manifest itself. Thus, the work was, mostly, looking after men who were demented and disorientated arising from age, or men aged about forty upwards who'd been in a war zone some ten to fifteen years beforehand.

The Nurse's duties included many menial tasks such as assisting with feeding, bed making and changing soiled patients bedding. At appointed times, the meals had to be collected from a central distribution point close to the kitchens, where a queue of staff and trusted patients would form. A burly charge nurse would stride up shouting, "Make way for an ex naval officer!" much to the delight of the patients and accompanied by much eye-rolling and head shaking by those of the staff in the line who'd heard this routine every day for about twenty years! Feeding could be a difficult and time-consuming, but essential, task and The Nurse soon learned to keep the patient focused upon the job of eating, whether it was at the bedside, or at the table. The tables were set out in all the wards, rather after the fashion of a small cafe, and some patients liked to think, or genuinely did think, that they were enjoying their meal in a restaurant and that the nurses were waiters. This was an illusion that The Nurse and some of his colleagues were happy to encourage, except when things went wrong, such as the occasion when The Nurse, busy assisting one old gentleman at one side of a table for two, noticed the one on the opposite side beginning to fall sideways as his eyelids drooped and his laden soup spoon slid into his lap. Unable to reach him, The Nurse shouted, "Mr Jenkinson!" The charge nurse, at another table, jumped with alarm and swung around with a frown and a gasp, looking as though he'd been stabbed in the back, rather than been alerted to a possible emergency. Mr Jenkinson woke up, sat up, grabbed his soup spoon and called to The Nurse for a glass of brandy. The Nurse replied, "Right away Sir," and handed him a small plastic tumbler of medicine, before moving to the adjoining table to dish out pills and medicines there.

Bed wetting and soiling was a frequent occurrence despite the efforts of some, but by no means all, of the nurses, The Nurse himself included, to anticipate it and forestall the worst of it. Some patients had little or no control over their bodily functions and one in particular, an ex-Grenadier guardsman, would call out just before or as it happened. "Nurse!" he'd shout, "It's coming out my ass!" Too late, but an effective way of drawing attention to his predicament and being washed and changed. Bedridden patients were entitled to a change of pyjamas now and again and, out of sympathy, The Nurse would offer them a choice of pyjamas, the alternatives being red or blue striped night gowns. A typical exchange would go as follows; "Well, Charlie, which do you want, red or blue?" To which Charlie would yell in stentorian tones, "Blue!" Or sometimes, "Red!" Which demonstrated that The Nurse could be kind and that some of the patients were sufficiently alert to know the difference. One of the consequences of soiled beds was the deleterious effect they had upon the scourge of the medical wards — bed sores! Nearly all the bedridden patients were subject to this dreadful affliction and Bill was one of these. Bill always looked bewildered and appeared confused. "What's that, Bill?" enquired The Nurse one day when changing him. Without looking down, Bill responded, "I think it's a piece of carrot." A reply which convinced The Nurse that Bill might be a bit more alert than he was given credit for! In practice, The Nurse became more fastidious than most of his colleagues in frequently oiling and massaging the rumps of his charges in attempting to stave off the advent of bed sores, or at least to mitigate their worst and rather unpleasant effects. Once they'd broken out, however, it was almost impossible to prevent them deteriorating, until it was possible to insert a fist into the raw, bloody and cavernous holes exploding on the unfortunate bodies!

A lot of the inmates had been valuable members of their communities prior to the onset of their illnesses and included ex bank managers, teachers, stevedores, sailors, footballers, rugby league players and so on. Whatever they had been, they were all deemed to be in need of occupational therapy. The Nurse was occasionally required to assist and supervise this activity, which was, notwithstanding whatever counselling and psychotherapy that preceded it, pretty abysmal. At one end of a long room, down the centre of which there was a line of tables and chairs, a number of patients were introduced to a collection of empty metal containers including baked beans, chopped tomatoes and other processed food tins, which had been washed for the purpose. Next came pots with glue, scissors and decorative paper such as rolls of wallpaper all graciously donated by local firms. The tins passed along the lines of patients and labels were removed, paper was measured and trimmed and cut, glue was applied to the outside of the tins and colourful new coverings stuck on the outside of each tin. The final activity, at the bottom of the line of tables, was the removal of the new decoration, before the supervisory staff carried the bare tins back to the top of the line for the process to begin all over again. If this was a trifle counter-productive, the patients never seemed to notice it and many hours were passed in what The Nurse considered to be utterly useless and, in spite of some submissions from his superiors suggesting that the nature of the mental and physical stimulation was therapeutic, he remained unconvinced. At least they weren't "Roaming the streets" as The Nurse's father might have put it!

There were often, however, some very important things that The Nurse was asked, as opposed to required, to undertake. First, and maybe foremost, of these was to assist with laying out the dead. When a patient died, he had to be carefully laid out on his back, washed, all of his orifices blocked or tied off and his nightwear removed in favour of a white shroud through which his arms went and which tied at the back. Tasks such as this were not fun and had to be performed with as much reverence as possible, although, as some of the regular staff averred, it didn't matter much to the dead person. It mattered to the dead person's relatives though and it mattered to The Nurse, who took it all very seriously indeed. The first dead body that The Nurse ever confronted occurred quite early on during his time at the hospital and it was rendered a rather worse experience through the fact that it was unexpected. The Nurse, having approached a bedridden patient that he knew well with a bowl of easily digestible soup and addressed him congenially by name, discovered that the said patient had expired. The Nurse was taken aback but, with commendable calm in such circumstances, he slowly put down the food and — being not totally certain — asked the charge nurse to come over and have a look. "He's gone," said the charge nurse matter-of-factly, evoking recollections of The Nurse's dad's expression, "Gone on." No fuss ensued and the body remained where it was until later, when at a time least disruptive to all the other inhabitants of the ward and to the routines of life therein, it was covered and removed to the mortuary. The Nurse was shocked and the charge nurse was sufficiently perceptive of this to be kind and helpful. He offered to allow The Nurse to leave early; a generous gesture for there was still much to be done on the shift. The Nurse declined and carried on and, whilst he always behaved in an appropriate manner, by the time he'd seen his ninth or tenth death he was happy to contribute at the bedside. It is astonishing how rapidly humanity becomes impervious to death.

Then there were the injections. The Medical Ward was so-called because the inmates there were medically impaired as well as mentally sick. A good proportion of them needed injections of various medicaments on top of the more usual oral medicines, many of which were used to maintain the patients in a state of calm resignation, or even apathetic bewilderment — or so it seemed to The Nurse. "If I show you how to do it, can you do the injections when it gets really busy?" enquired a friendly charge nurse one night on the Medical Ward. "What, are you sure?" responded The Nurse with almost equal measures of surprise and trepidation. "Oh yes," said the charge nurse, "come on, I'll show you." The charge nurse on this occasion was one of those in whom The Nurse had considerable trust, because he'd been assiduous in helping The Nurse with the intricacies of nursing and confided in The Nurse when his first wife — the charge nurse's that is — had run away to become a prostitute in London. At least, that's what the charge nurse had told him and The Nurse believed him implicitly. Besides, the charge nurse was the goalkeeper for the Hospital staff football team and had helped The Nurse get into the side, so he just *had* to be a reliable friend. On the first night, following The Nurse's hesitant agreement to participate, the charge nurse proceeded to demonstrate the techniques associated with injecting fluids into the buttocks of adult males, whilst The Nurse observed closely how it was done. On the second night, the friendly Charge cleaned the first buttock, handed the first syringe to The Nurse and said, "Hold it like a dart, aim for the top right hand quarter of his backside then you'll be sure to miss the main nerve, throw it slowly and firmly but don't let go. "That's right," he went on as The Nurse did as he'd been told, "push it gently and squeeze the top with your thumb." No one else ever knew it, but in no time, The Nurse was proficient and did the injections with some panache more than a few times thereafter.

Finally, there was ECT! ECT stands for Electro-Therapy and without it there were, according to the professionals, loads of ordinary people walking the streets of towns and cities who would otherwise have been locked away for treatment as psychopaths! The Nurse assumed, although it was never confirmed by anyone, that patients had to agree to undergo ECT. Having been counselled, and they and their families convinced of the beneficial outcomes of ECT by the doctors and mental health consultants, patients, supported by nurses and assistant nurses, prepared by arraigning themselves in the usual hospital shroud-like attire considered suitable for such practices. They would be helped on to one of a row of beds and administered a muscle relaxing sedative drug by injection. These were far too important to be done by The Nurse, whose role in ECT never got beyond help with undressing and dressing, helping patients get on to the beds, holding on to them whilst they were on the beds if it became necessary, which it often did, and generally looking on aghast as what looked like crude headphones attached to wires were placed on each patient's head and something rather like a hard piece of wood or metal covered in white cloth was placed in each patient's mouth. The latter was to prevent injury as an electric current of indeterminate voltage was switched on and passed through the 'headphones', with the effect of causing the patients to clamp their teeth together with sudden and ferocious violence and thrash about so much that they were in severe danger of falling on the floor, had The Nurse and others not been on hand to prevent it. To make matters worse, treatment was meted out to one patient at a time, so that it was just as well that those following were barely aware of what was happening as their turn approached, the process was carried out and they were wheeled back to their wards to recover slowly and, eventually, to wake up under the watchful gaze of people like The Nurse. Only then did The Nurse wonder if the man he'd been asked to keep an eye on six months or so previously had been for ECT. ECT was a controversial treatment that some authorities in mental health believed had no place in the humane care and rehabilitation of patients, whilst others were convinced of its effectiveness.

On a lighter note, the Nurse was enjoying his introduction to the hospital football team. For one thing it was possible to be released early from a shift to get to a match, to get out of a late shift or even to get time off; almost like being paid to play! For another, it led to other things. Amongst these was a place in the mixed staff-patient rugby union team. The Nurse had played rugby at school, but never had he experienced rugby as played by mentally sick men! Some, having pleaded to be on the team, would stand around, as though they were watching a game of bowls, others would, on the rare occasions that they managed to catch a pass, would throw the ball anywhere at all in any direction, as though the ball was red hot, just so long as they got rid of it soon enough to avoid being tackled by an opponent. Most of them appeared not even to be remotely capable themselves of tackling the opposition and those that could were as likely to pull their own players down as those of the other side. Indeed, some seemed to have so little idea of what was happening, that the games became a constant wave of opposition attacks interspersed with sporadic struggles to hold onto the ball, whilst dragging several young men along until buried by sheer weight of numbers. Scrums and rucks were like trying to push several rhinoceroses aside and line outs were a bit like trying to out jump a flock of large birds! "Like playing with a lead ball," observed one nurse as the defeated hospital team trooped off. Or like swimming in treacle! Much to be preferred was the squash team, where the contest was one against one and could be enjoyed, but best of all by far was the women's staff hockey team. The women only played friendly games against other female teams, or mixed sides, and nobody wanted to play in goal. Quite how, or why, The Nurse came to be offered this position remains a mystery, but the good things about being the goalkeeper for a women's hockey eleven included the protective helmet and padding, the lack of a requirement to be nimble and the fact of spending over an hour and a quarter behind a crowd of young women running around in short skirts, who with some notable exceptions, were both shapely and pretty. Someone had once told The Nurse that there are three kinds of women; "tasty", "tidy" and "tawdry"! Those in the first of these categories were young and attractive, those in the second were older, but had looked after themselves, and those in the third had not. Anyway, The Nurse had a good time throwing himself about on behalf of the hockey team and he became something of an icon amongst the female staff because of it. What a shame that he was so useless at taking advantage of this!

Members of large institutions become institutionalised. That is to say that they suffer the deleterious long-term effects of residence in an institution. This is as true for members of hospitals as for any other kind of institution and, whilst many people manage to retain the bulk of their commitment and their vocation, it affects everyone to a greater or lesser degree. Often people, in this case both staff and patients, become dependent upon the institution and are unable to face leaving it. In these circumstances, patients declared well again will refuse to accept the diagnosis and staff, when offered the opportunity to move or get a promotion, or when confronted with change, will turn it down. Some of the worst effects of institutionalisation, however, occur when staff have been in place for too long, have stagnated and become cynical. This can have fairly harmless outcomes, such as bored and restless nurses acting out their roles in a routine and hapless way, but sometimes it can result in something less innocuous and even downright harmful. The Nurse tried to devote at least some of his time when things were slow, apart from playing chess with Jacques that is, to productive occupational therapy, such as perambulating around the ward with old men in Zimmer frames, talking to the bedridden in the faint hope that they'd stay awake during the day and checking for bed sores and soiled sheets. These were things that many staff just didn't do, in some cases because they didn't have time, but in others, because they couldn't be bothered. The Nurse tried hard, tempting though it was at times, not to ridicule or humiliate patients, things which some staff found amusing and seemed to see as part of the job and The Nurse refused to be involved in sending geriatrics on nonsensical errands with meaningless messages or unattainable goals. However, it's relatively easy to stay focused and dedicated in the knowledge that what you are doing is not a career and it is not forever. When the time came, The Nurse simply gave up nursing.

Chapter 10

THE WAITER

From time to time, one job is not enough. Or even two!

Somewhere along the way between being a Bus Conductor and becoming a Factory Hand, and before morphing into an Ice Cream Man and a Nurse, a student and then a student teacher had emerged. Being a student, of course, is not a job and didn't involve much of what could be described as work, but it does normally lead to a qualification called a degree which, in those days, actually indicated a reasonable level of intelligence and meant that the holder was one of a small percentage of the general population to have attended a university. Failure to complete a postgraduate education course was then no bar to becoming a teacher and, eventually, The Ice Cream Man and The Nurse became one. But teachers were not well paid, so being a teacher didn't necessarily generate sufficient income, especially when surprises in the form of unexpected bills came along. It is surely oxymoronic to suggest that a council rates bill was unexpected. Or simply that the recipient of the bill, notwithstanding his degree in history, was semi-moronic for not realising that when you live in a house as a grown up, you can expect the local council to exact rates. Also, by this time, there was a wife and a baby, so a second job had to be found, and since occupations in public houses were plentiful at that time, a post as a waiter was sought and obtained.

English pubs were once thriving and exciting places, where people met frequently to chat, debate, pontificate, smoke and drink. Later, to eat was to be added to that list and, in some cases, to listen to music. There were all kinds of pubs from old-fashioned rural inns with thatched roofs to enormous city establishments that had once served railway stations and large urban conurbations. A lot of these were noisy, dirty, acrid places with labyrinthine rooms running into one another and many had rooms big enough to hold meetings, concerts or wedding feasts. It was in one of these that The Waiter began his successful, if fairly short-lived, spell in the licensed trade, The Brougham; an enormous nineteenth century building in a suburb halfway between his home and the city centre. Work in such public houses could be great fun, but it was also hard, and the hours tended to be long and finish late in the evening. There may have been loads of friendly, and often not so friendly, people and there may have been loads of banter and laughs, but at the end of a shift in a busy bar, most of the staff would be tired out. The Waiter included!

There are many skills involved in working in bars and The Waiter was quick to learn most of them. Within a short time, he was able to listen to and take in an order from a table of five or six raucous individuals in a noisy concert room, hold the order in his head, whilst waiting at the 'waiters only' hatch at the bar, and simultaneously shout for attention from the frenetic bar staff, remember the price of each drink, calculate the total cost, find his way back to the table through a lively and constantly moving crowd of drinkers with the drinks, take the money and give the correct change to whoever's round it happened to be. And it wasn't long before he became adept at carrying a tray of drinks, including pints of beer, shorts and soft drinks on a tray one-handed above head height, whilst ducking and weaving between the tables and customers and he became equally adroit at unloading the drinks one at a time, without unbalancing or spilling those remaining on the tray. This required expertise that a circus juggler would have been proud of! Another essential requisite was to be able to smile and cope with the gentle, and sometimes not so gentle, derision and repartee of the clientele. Waiters that were able to do so became notably popular with the 'regulars' and, whilst that usually meant scurrying back and forth with greater regularity and swiftness, it also meant more tips. As one of the habitual frequenters of the saloon bar said, "I've taken a shine to you, young man, I don't know why, but I have. You're good and you're quick. Keep the change!" Occasionally, The Waiter was given an opportunity to work in the hallowed concert room, where the noise was deafening and a pall of cigarette fumes hung in the air, but where the tipping was even more generous. There were different events in the concert room for every night of the week except Tuesdays. Early one evening, a good looking young man approached The Waiter just as both were entering the imposing double front doors of The Brougham. The Young man enquired if it was 'Singers Night', a regular midweek occasion in which absolutely anyone who felt that they could sing was able to do so in a competition with a cash prize for the singer judged to be the best. The Waiter never knew what the cash award amounted to, it couldn't have been much, or who did the judging, but he did see the young man again towards the end of his shift. "How did you get on?" asked The Waiter. The young man looked nonchalant and replied impassively, "Oh, I won it. Do you know where The Cheshire Cheese is?" To his astonishment, The Waiter learned that there were men and, less frequently, women, who toured pubs like The Brougham nearly every night just to enter these talent contests. It was like an early form of reality show, but without the fame and fortune for the winner. However, according to the young winner at The Brougham that night, there was money to be made by decent singers and, again in his own account, the young man did okay and usually won. What puzzled The Waiter was that the young man didn't appear to have any ambition beyond winning local pub singing competitions. The Waiter hadn't heard him sing, but he did wonder later what became of the young man and whether it was an encounter with a future star of stage or television. By this time, Christmas was approaching and The Waiter's performance had improved to the point where he was becoming a very polished and effective operator. However, when the landlord approached him one night late in the evening to offer him a permanent 'promotion' to the concert room, he resigned.

What had not improved, and the festive season hadn't helped, was The Waiter's financial position and he was obliged to continue his career in the pub trade, but this time at a hostelry called The Seven Moons within walking distance of his house. Responding to an advertisement in the local newspaper, The Waiter telephoned and arranged to call at the Seven Moons early one evening. "I did three months at The Brougham in the city," said The Waiter in response to the landlord's query concerning experience. It was fairly clear from his expression that the landlord was not familiar with The Brougham, but he said, "Well, that's good enough for me, can you start tonight?" The Waiter could and he did start that very night and, thereafter, did six nights a week with hours from eight in the evening until closing time at eleven. The Waiter was interested in pub names, their history and local associations and he'd wondered about the name of The Brougham. "From some sort of nineteenth century carriage," he supposed, "maybe it was a starting point for services in to the city centre." The Seven Moons occasioned similar musing at the end of which The Waiter concluded that it must have some connection with a planet having seven major satellites – Saturn perhaps. But if so, why should a little post-industrial township have a connection with Saturn? None of those he asked, and there were quite a few, could answer this question, but many seemed puzzled or slightly amused that The Waiter should ask it!

The Seven Moons had been built in the recent past, probably in the early 1960s, of red brick with a blue slate pitched roof, a most unprepossessing edifice! It was situated towards one end of the town between a huge 'overspill' council estate of houses and tower-block flats and a series of traditional streets of brick terraced houses. It was like The Brougham in only one respect. It had an enormous concert room with a stage at one end, in front of which was an open area surrounded by low tables with groups of four or five chairs. It was always dark for the lighting was, with the exception of the spotlights throwing illumination on the stage, deliberately dimmed. The curtains were never opened, so that even on summer nights, the room was dingy with the usual haze of cigarette smoke hanging in the air. Nonetheless, the Seven Moons – The Waiter never heard it referred to by any diminutive – was *the* place to be on any night of the week and 'de rigueur' at the weekends. That was because it was the only venue offering non-stop entertainment of the kind that attracted everyone of 'drinking age', some under 'drinking age' who could get past the bouncers, lots of 'thirty-somethings', some trendy over forties and even the odd 'oldie'! Other public houses had music, sometimes live music, but nothing like the non-stop battering of pop and rock that reverberated in and around The Seven Moons!

Every single night, there was music so loud that it was impossible to conduct a normal conversation. There were 'Disco Nights' of continuous chart-topping pop records, live rock and tribute bands on other nights, singers of every sort, including rock, pop, country and western, crooners and so on, and on some nights, there were dancers, exotic and otherwise and talent contests involving all kinds of young local hopefuls. Small wonder, then, that at eleven o'clock, The Waiter and his colleagues stopped dead and slumped into the first available seat to await their free half pint of beer — anymore had to be paid for — and rested until it was time to clear the tables, stack the chairs and go home. The Waiter was never in bed before midnight — often a good deal later — and during the months of his internship at the Seven Moons, his job, his marriage, his football, probably his hearing and his life all suffered. Only his drinking and smoking improved! He also became quite proficient at lip-reading!

There were normally three waiters, one called John, another called Pete and The Waiter himself and they were at full stretch for most of the hours the bar was open. There were unpredictable lulls, however, and the three took advantage of these to sit and rest. At least John and The Waiter did. Pete's idea of a rest was to gyrate in front of the stage after the fashion of Mick Jagger with the Rolling Stones echoing around the room like a thunderstorm. This parody became so popular amongst the younger clientele of both sexes that Pete was called upon to do it regularly and so often that The Waiter advised him to negotiate a fee with the landlord. Pete would giggle at the prospect of being paid for his antics, but he never was for he never asked. He was good though and the Disc Jockey loved it as much as the youngsters. So did John and The Waiter, because with the entire room transfixed upon Pete, they got a brief respite and a chance to smoke and chat. John was a little older than The Waiter and a good bit older than Pete and he was there because he was poor and he had a numerous and very young family to support. "We're struggling now," he confided in The Waiter, "but we'll be okay later on and the kids can grow up with us, like friends. "The Waiter sympathised, but secretly felt sorry for John, whom he knew would never realise his dream of prosperity, surrounded by his grown-up children, who would be his 'mates' as well as his offspring. Still, The Waiter saw no harm in indulging John's wistful hopes. After all, he had some of his own that he cherished just as much.

One of The Waiter's tricks was to get the DJ to play obscure tracks, his favourite being "Burundi Black", a piece purporting to be by an African drum ensemble. It was loud, extremely so, but it cleared the floor of twisting bodies for a while, so that the staff could go about their jobs rather more easily, in spite of the continuing din. Rock and roll was still extant but glam rock was the "in" thing and the melody and the lyrics of "Ride a White Swan" remained with The Waiter for the rest of his life. So did the image of the elderly gentleman who came in most nights and sat on the edge of the stage, where the din was at its most cacophonous. He smoked a panatela and sipped a gin and tonic, and every now and again, waved vigorously to attract the attention of a waiter to recharge his glass. "Why on earth does that old chap come in here every night?" The Waiter asked at the bar. The young woman behind it merely shrugged and said nothing. It remained a mystery.

There were singers and dancers too. On one memorable occasion, two local teenagers in matching "hot pants" — then "all the rage" — danced on stage. Some performers could be jeered and cat-called, but the girls' act was one of many that were well received by the indulgent crowd, except when the plumper of the pair, who really was a bit too obese for her outfit, began to dance a little too outrageously, at which point, the audience lurched from adulation to ridicule and the whole thing became embarrassing for anyone with a modicum of sensitivity. The Waiter most certainly had. And he was as susceptible to flattery as the next person. He'd nearly had enough of the noise and the smoke and the weariness, when one of the landlord's daughters said,

"You *know* you're our best waiter by miles!" All men like The Waiter are easily won over by a soft word; a pretty face and a voluptuous body, so The Waiter stayed on at The Seven Moons rather longer than intended. The last time he saw The Seven Moons it was boarded up and surrounded by litter and fragments of broken glass. A portent of things to come for many public houses of all kinds all over the country.

Chapter 11

THE REFEREE

"Or even two!" Two jobs not being enough, that is, was sometimes the case. Refereeing often follows when the playing of football has finally been abandoned and when another useful, if not very substantial, source of money is still called for.

There was, in fact, something of a gap between The Waiter and The Referee but the money earned by the latter was very handy, more for the Referee's daughter than for himself. Not many people can remember the very last time they engaged in a particular activity, such as a sport, or a hobby, or sex, but The Referee could recall his final outing as a competitor before his transformation into an arbitrator. He'd been what used to be described as a 'full back', then a 'wing half' or 'centre half'; how modern aficionados would chuckle at those terms! Ultimately, following an injury to a team mate, the future referee volunteered to go into goal and so became a 'goalkeeper', which proved to be something he turned out to be quite good at and could, perhaps, have performed at a rather higher level than he ever did. But his final outing was as an 'outside left' in a friendly match and the final act occurred when the ball was crossed from the right. "Easy," he thought and prepared to strike, only to discover that the ball had gone. "Time to stop?" he asked himself and enrolled on a training course for referees. "I want to put something back into the game," he told his father, who responded by saying, that in his day, having played at a somewhat more accomplished level than his son, he'd had to give up playing to earn a bit of money. "Every penny counted in those days," he said disdainfully, dismissing The Referee's pseudo-altruism at a stroke.

Training courses for budding referees were, and probably still are, a combination of theory and practice. There'd be a number of weekly sessions at which the laws — not 'rules' — were discussed and analysed; experts such as experienced ex-refs gave the class the benefit of their wisdom or lack of it and films of astonishingly gruesome tackles and equally astonishingly bad refereeing were gasped and laughed at by future referees, many of whom would turn out to be just as bad, if not worse, themselves. At the end of these sessions, there was a written test, which could not be too difficult or the supply of new recruits to the Referees Associations up and down the country would have dried up pretty rapidly. Moreover, there were three grades, and subject to passing more tests and successful practical observations, it was possible to progress to the top grade – Grade Three. The Referee was quite content to reach Grade Two.

Experience of referees also suggested that they varied a great deal in ability and personality. In his past life as a footballer, The Referee recalled one, known as "The Big Fisherman", who wore an enormous roll neck Guernsey type sweater, sailed around the pitch like a galleon with an impassive, unsmiling face and never, ever spoke. Another wore a typically shiny outfit in the then traditional black refereeing colour with a large County Football Association badge on the breast pocket and was best remembered for urinating in the centre circle at half-time! A third, having taken the names of several players, decided to storm off waving his arms in the air and shouting obscenities. Better role models, if only slightly, were those officials that The Referee accompanied to games as a voluntary extra dimension to his training prior to his qualification. These were referees who had been chosen for this purpose or had volunteered for it. Either way, they tended to be obsessives, whose view of their own ability far outstripped the reality so that The Referee learned more about how to irritate club officers and players, how to waste time with finicky application of the minutiae of procedures and about the mentality of the martinet, than he did about how to conduct an orderly process from introductions and preamble to the start, the conduct and the completion of a minor league football match. This, he did learn, however, from several good and well respected refs and from his own common sense.

There are several basic techniques underpinning good refereeing. One is to look the part. To wear a clean, black outfit with a pocket to secrete pencil, notebook and cards – yellow and red. Another is to have two flags, one yellow and the other red and yellow — or was it the other way round? It's fairly clear what the cards, notebook and pencil were for, but less so the flags. These were to offer to lay officials to act as linesmen — now officially known as 'assistant referees', but still called 'linos' amongst other appellations of a less than complimentary nature. If it proved not possible to recruit linesman from amongst the officials or followers of each of the competing teams, then The Referee, in common with many of his colleagues, had to manage without them. This was, in many cases, better than having to put up with the blatant bias and downright ignorance of 'club linos'. "Offside!" yelled one. "Not from a throw-in," whispered The Referee, so as not to embarrass the man concerned. The Referee always gave club linesmen clear instructions, another critical aspect of good refereeing. "Wave your flag when the ball goes out of play," he'd say, "and keep level with the last defender in the opposition's team." The reason for the second of these instructions was a little unclear to most 'linos'. "What about offside, ref?" they'd ask, "and what about foul play? Our boys need protection from this lot you know!" The Referee soon learned that those were issues best left to his own jurisdiction and merely promised to acknowledge any signals the 'linos' made, but not necessarily to act upon them.

Smart kit, equipment, two flags and clear orders and what else? Well, it was important to check the goal nets, firstly making sure that there were some. Not much could be worse than a disputed 'goal' arising from the ball having passed into, and then right through, an improperly secured net! Of even greater importance was to inspect the 'field of play', to use the pompous term in the Laws of the Game book, to ensure that it was appropriately and correctly marked out with white lines, that there were no potentially dangerous objects near the bordering touchlines, that there were no stones or bits of glass lurking on it from the night before and that it was fit for play. Prudent referees always checked that there was an adequate medical box available, not that it would have been of much use in an emergency. Most important of all was the requirement to inspect the boots of the players for worn and dangerous studs and their persons for rings and other adornments that could put opponents at risk of injury. It was wise, also, to give a little speech to each side before they took to the field of play, explaining that people and their families didn't come to the local park to hear a torrent of foul and abusive language and that we were all present to enjoy the game, to play according to the rules, or rather The Laws, and to have a good time. Subject to all these important prerequisites, the good referee could take to the field, provided that he'd not forgotten to bring a reliable and accurate watch!

The Referee was brisk and thorough in all these matters and was careful to exude good manners and confidence to signal to both goalkeepers, and to both linesmen, that the game was about to commence and to make sure that all concerned could hear his whistle, the best being a make called, with stunning appurtenance, a "Thunderer". It should be clear, but often is not, that once the game has commenced, the referee has to be in charge. He, or indeed, she, has, therefore, to reiterate that fact as soon as possible. Thus, The Referee quite deliberately sought an opportunity to blow very hard upon his whistle within a minute or two, or better still, within seconds, of the start to bring the game to a stop, and in no uncertain terms, to lecture a player or players with a frown and a stern word. It didn't really matter who or for what provided that the game stopped dead and everyone saw and heard The Referee establish his authority at an early stage. If all referees followed just this simple precept, then there would be a lot less trouble at football matches. It has been said that teachers ought to be 'firm, fair and fun' and this adage is one that referees would do well to adopt but, perhaps, without the 'fun'.

Referees, including even those officiating in lowly county, local and Sunday leagues, ought to be doing it because they have an abiding love of the game, because they have a desire to contribute to the development of young players, provide opportunities for those participants in the game who are less than gifted, use it as a way to help themselves keep fit or all of these things. They also get paid. Not much mind, but enough to cover their expenses in getting to the matches, usually the equivalent to bus or rail fare or a few pence per gallon if they are obliged or choose to go by private car, and a match fee. These earnings do not ever amount to a princely sum unless, as in recent years, a referee progresses to the highest professional levels and maybe even becomes a full-time pro himself or, of course, herself, although the latter hasn't happened as yet. A lot of referees use their refereeing income to enhance their lives in little ways, such as saving for holidays, purchasing items they wouldn't normally buy, or getting presents for friends and relatives and The Referee was no exception. Each week, after returning home from officiating, The Referee would ritually open what he called "the refereeing tin", a modestly sized and ancient

Russian tea tin that he'd taken a fancy to and acquired from a 'car boot' sale somewhere, and he'd pop his expenses and fee into it. He kept the 'refereeing tin' in a cupboard upstairs, and as the weeks went by, the amount of money in the 'refereeing tin' mounted up. The Referee's daughter was, at that time, a student and whenever she visited him, at some point during her stay, he would say to her, "Fetch the 'refereeing tin'". His daughter, having been introduced to the idea of the 'refereeing tin' and its whereabouts, would dutifully trot off and return with the tin. And no wonder, for when she brought it to him, The Referee would open it up and split the contents equally with her. It was a little bonus for them both and The Referee fondly, but probably incorrectly, believed that it was an inducement for his daughter to visit more often than she might otherwise have done.

The Referee enjoyed refereeing. Apart from anything else, he turned out to be good at it and didn't have to put up with the abuse and vilification that some unfortunates had to endure from players and club officials, who imagined that they were familiar with the laws of the game, but manifestly were not. It was The Referee's view that players and club members ought to be grateful if they even had a referee, especially since the games that did not have one often ended in acrimony and, occasionally, even in violence. The Referee was in the habit of informing players that they, their supporters and any casual spectators were there to enjoy the game and exhorted all concerned to behave appropriately. "This is Division Four of the Amateur League," he might say firmly and with a patient smile to some over-excited young man, "it cannot be that important! Can it?" or "I suggest you stop shouting at everyone else and concentrate on your own game" to another, or perhaps, "You and I both know that you cannot behave like that" as he took the name of a third, or invited a fourth to leave the field for the duration of the remainder of the game for persistent foul and abusive language. So-called 'sending-offs' were rare and happened only a couple of times in The Referee's entire career, although, it has to be said, that the latter was not one of great longevity.

Few people actually realise swearing is a 'sending-off' offence. The Referee didn't much care for swearing, resorting to it himself only when no other vocable would suffice and never on the field of play! Some people, in The Referee's experience, always men, simply cannot stop. One such, playing for a local amateur side of no repute, repeatedly swore. He wasn't being particularly abusive and didn't direct his unattractive words to any particular individual, but he just couldn't stop. Perhaps it was a form of Tourette's syndrome. The Referee appealed to him to moderate his language, and each time that he did so, the player would apologise and promise to do so and each time he would fail. He soon took to turning to The Referee and saying, "Oh, sorry, ref!" every time it occurred. After thirty minutes or so had expired, he did manage to get control of himself and The Referee exploited this success to tell the rest of the players in both teams at half-time, that if this man could manage to play without swearing, then everybody could. A lonely spectator was so impressed by The Referee's achievement, that he walked around the full perimeter of the pitch to tell him so and to thank him for dealing with the swearing so effectively.

Sometimes, people get the wrong idea and, sometimes, it's quite a good thing that they do so. Occasionally, if his game was reasonably close to a railway station, The Referee would cycle to his local station, put his bike on the train and, having arrived at the destination station, would cycle from there to the ground of the club he was to referee. This never amounted to more than a mile or two of cycling, but gave the people associated with the clubs a very different impression. Some of the games were many miles from home, and when asked where he'd set out from, The Referee would always respond accurately, but without mentioning the train and, as a result, he often overheard dressing room exchanges extolling his feats of endurance. "What! He came on a bike! He's going to cycle back!" The Referee acquired a reputation as a 'man of iron' and with it a lot of additional respect. He never let on!

Referees do well to engage with their charges and to share their experiences and expectations provided that it never compromises their position of authority. There are also dilemmas. If the city council worker has failed to turn up, and the changing rooms are not available, should a referee agree to the privation and possible embarrassment of touch-line undressing and dressing? If the weather is inclement, and perhaps worsens, at what point should a referee abandon the game and risk the wrath of the winning side? Or what should a referee do upon arriving at a ground, that he was told by club officers early in the day was fit for play, to find it hard and frosty? And how should a referee respond to a couple of players trailing in his wake as he does his pre-match pitch inspection, who keep repeating, "Its bad ref.

It's bad ref!" Or what about the club secretary, who contacts the referee on a sunny morning to tell him that the ground is not available, or unfit in order, ostensibly, to give the ref time to re-order his day but, in reality, because the club is short of players, or the secretary's wife wants him to go shopping? And how determined should a referee be when contradicting the club linesmen? Absolutely, in the case of the one assisting at a match involving a local side and a team of trustee convicts who shouted, "Our throw ref!" "Not according to your forward," replied The Referee. "He's in for deception!" said the lino wryly. And should referees mix socially with players and officials after games or elsewhere? The answer to that is probably not, or only on a superficial level. The Referee stuck to this wisdom, except for the time he happened upon several young men in a public house of not very high regard on a council estate, quite close to home. The Referee recognised one of the young men as playing for a local football club and nodded politely, whereupon the young man in question returned the greeting effusively, called The Referee over and insisted upon introducing him to his mates and upon buying him a pint. The Referee felt obliged to sit down and made a mental note to say nothing that could compromise himself, the Referees' Association, or the F.A. All went well until one of the company produced an enormous cigarette, lit it, drew gratefully upon it and passed it to the person sitting to his left. The Referee glanced nervously as the large white cylinder went from hand to hand around the group and, of course, from mouth to mouth. Here was a potential calamity. The cigarette finally reached The Referee. He took it, inhaled slowly, paused, exhaled towards the ceiling and calmly

passed it on. "You'll do for me ref," said the young man.
Several others smiled. One even nodded.

Chapter 12

THE TEACHER

The Teacher reached the school gates, walked past and did another circuit of the council estate.

Arriving at the entrance for the fourth time, he hesitated, and then walked slowly across the tarmac toward the doors labelled "Main Entrance". Hostile-looking young men watched his approach with curiosity, rather than malice. A man in his forties emerged from the building and stared with what seemed like unconcealed contempt, before putting a whistle into his mouth and blowing on it with such strength that it screamed sufficiently to startle little groups of boys scattered around the playground away to the left. They hastened to form straggly lines facing the doors, whilst the man with the whistle, with a gorgon-like gaze that must have made the pupils suspect that he hated being there and them even more, waited. He waited until there was sufficient order in the lines, and until a hush had fallen, before indicating with his whistle free hand that it was time to enter the building. When the last boy in the last line had disappeared, the teacher on duty pocketed his whistle — an Acme Thunderer the Teacher learned later — turned and strode into the school without another glance to left or right. As hard as it was to go forward, The Teacher could no longer retreat. He opened the door and went inside.

Teaching, like nursing and other socially desirable occupations, is supposed to be what used to be called a vocation. In those days, for lots of people, that was still so. However, in many cases, perhaps most, people just drifted into teaching because it was then a 'soft option', or it was 'in the family'. The Teacher had an aunt who'd been a teacher and, by all accounts, a very good one. There were rumours that one of his grannies had been a teacher too and his older sister had trained as a teacher and was already working in London. She was good too! Teaching may have been a 'soft option', but doing it in the big cities wasn't. This, The Teacher was about to discover.

It was true that he'd started to train, in the education department of the university from which he'd graduated, but not untypically, at the first sign of difficulty, he took what his father used to describe as "the line of least resistance" and withdrew from the course. He'd considered other options too for that was the time when only a small percentage of the population went on to higher education, so that businesses and manufacturing firms — there were still plenty of those around too — sent their personnel directors out to trawl the universities for clever and thrusting undergraduates, which The Teacher was not. There were loads of opportunities though and it wasn't that The Teacher had to be a teacher, or that he particularly wanted to be a teacher. It just happened. He was lucky too. Teachers were in short supply then, two year training was still extant and it didn't matter if you couldn't communicate very well, or modulate the pitch of your voice, or command respect or demonstrate leadership, or work in a team. You could be socially inept and unable to communicate. You didn't even have to like children very much. If you were a university graduate, you could be a teacher. Large cities and towns, especially in the old industrial north which, especially when approached by train, were still reminiscent of post-war dereliction, recruited pools of young people and dispatched them to schools, often in the most deprived and disadvantaged areas, with the flimsiest interviewing and screening processes and seemingly irrespective of their knowledge of educational theory and philosophy or of their ability to teach. "Where would you like to work? We can take you to have a look at a school now?" The Teacher had been asked by an education officer in a rundown and crumbling town in the north-east. He declined. Instead, he decided upon one of the biggest cities in the north-west, where he found a place to live, a typical bed-sit in a rambling terrace on the cusp of a notorious district best known for drugs, violence and degradation.

The double doors closed noisily behind him, trapping the hem of The Teacher's coat, which tore as he struggled to free it. "Shit!" he thought as he removed the damaged garment, folded it and hung it over his arm in the time honoured way that men did years ago. Inside the building, a kind of medium-level mayhem prevailed for this was what was called a Secondary Modern School. Worse still, it was a Secondary Modern School for Boys.

Most people will be familiar with the eleven plus test, which was introduced in the nineteen-forties as a supposedly objective and fair way of determining what kind of secondary education, from eleven to sixteen or — for those sufficiently fortunate to pass the test — eighteen, children were allocated. It has to be said, that the eleven plus really was intended to be an instrument of social justice that gave ordinary working class children, who were bright enough, the opportunity to go to a Grammar School, where the schooling was to be more academic than that offered by the new Secondary Modern Schools. The Teacher, whose dad was a Gas Fitter and whose mum was, variously, a school cook, a waitress and a housewife, had been one of those working class children. Most people didn't realise and it only became clear as time went on that the eleven plus tests were susceptible to coaching that could mostly only be afforded by better off families, that whether you passed or not depended upon where you lived as the Grammar School places made available in different education authorities varied from ten per cent right up to figures like thirty five per cent, that most places didn't cater for 'late developers', who would have benefited from Grammar School education, but hadn't matured sufficiently to pass the test at age eleven, that there was a marked 'class bias' in the test content favouring middle and upper class children, that because of the existence of single sex schools and the generally more advanced intellectual development of girls at age eleven, the test discriminated against girls when places were allocated in equal numbers in mixed Grammar Schools and where there were more single sex boys schools than single sex girls schools and, finally, that there was a certain amount of downright misallocation. These weaknesses affected the entire lives of thousands of young persons for many years and, astonishingly, most of them, particularly the gender bias favouring boys, are still not widely known or understood. And, at the time, not by The Teacher either!

The Teacher, looking around for the school office, noted that the tumult in the entrance area of the school was of a fairly good-natured kind with pupils of all ages milling around mostly laughing or talking. Several teachers — strictly only those 'on duty' The Teacher learned later — holding mugs of hot tea and, often, cigarettes, neither of which would now be tolerated under 'health and safety' regulations, stood at safe vantage points, bellowing unheard or not understood commands and ignoring the odd sly punch in the ribs or kick to the ankles by one or two amongst the crowd. It didn't take long for The Teacher not to be affronted, much less shocked, by this daily ritual, which faded as fast as it had manifested itself as bodies disappeared down corridors and through doors until the entrance area was deserted, the corridors fell quiet apart from the odd distant bang and shriek and an elderly gentleman in a dark suit, who The Teacher correctly took to be the head teacher, emerged. "Good Morning," he said. "Good Morning," The Teacher replied, and "why didn't you come out of your room and impose some order before now?" he thought. There were no fancy titles like 'bursar' or 'administrator' in those days so, on the way into an inner office, The Teacher was introduced by the man in the suit, Mr Beech, who was indeed the head, but typically, for the times styled himself 'headmaster', to a reasonably good-looking forty year old woman, Mrs Gibson, the school secretary. As he'd already been led to believe at the local education office, The Teacher was expected to teach History, the subject of his degree, some English and, if he wished — which he was pleased to say that he did — some Organised Games, which mostly took the form of football in the winter and cricket in the summer.

The head master, 'acting' as it turned out, showed The Teacher the location of the toilets, the school hall, the changing rooms and the view from his office window down a wooded valley beyond the tarmac playgrounds. "That's 'The Copse,' he announced, "It's quite a popular spot at the weekends". He could have added, "At night, too!" but he didn't. Instead, he announced that 'morning playtime' was approaching and he escorted The Teacher to the staffroom for introductions to the teaching staff. They were all male, all, to a greater or lesser degree, cynics and all members of the National Association of Schoolmasters, an organisation for disaffected male teachers, originally founded upon the premise that men with their familial responsibilities should get higher salaries than mere women and whose leaders made careers out of keeping the teaching force disunited and easy prey for successive governments' bullying and so-called educational reforms. Under pressure to join and at that stage of his career, for this job became one, knowing little of the benefits of trade union membership and even less about trade union solidarity, except that it mollified his new co-workers, The Teacher enlisted. It was only a matter of a few years, however, before he'd learned a few things and he discovered that only one teacher's union endorsed a philosophy that put the emotional, physical and educational well-being of the pupils first, followed by their teachers, their families, equality of opportunity and the organisation of state education — in that order. So, a couple of years later, he left the NAS and joined the National Union of Teachers. Meanwhile, he met his colleagues.

The stylish Mr Beech, the epitome of restraint and good manners, enjoyed what The Teacher's mum would have called 'breeding'. "It's in the breeding, you know," she would say to anyone who'd listen. Meaning that 'breeding' was something that only good quality families displayed and showed itself in the way they behaved in public, like always wearing their best clothes on Sundays, not chewing gum or smoking in the streets, aspiring to a good education and always saying 'please' and 'thank you'. Mr Beech may well have had 'breeding', but another reason for his restraint was that he wasn't far from retirement age, when the best course was to be as nice as pie to everyone and hide in the office all day. He had served the school for a long time, first as a teacher and then as a senior master of some kind, then as deputy head teacher and, finally, as acting head teacher. "This is Mr Rowen...", began the head and there followed a bewildering succession of men between thirty and fifty with worn jackets, patched elbows and corduroy trousers with the wear and tear of teaching in a Secondary Modern school etched upon their faces, along with the usual array of personalities from bright and hopeful, resigned and wistful, sour and indifferent and combinations of these and a myriad of other characteristics. The top man after Beech was Masterson, the senior English teacher. He was sufficiently enlightened to teach the older boys some Shakespeare and even presented a little Elizabethan drama on the annual Parents' Open Evening called, "All for Your

Delight." Not only did The Teacher get no advice about the teaching of English but he hardly had time to get to know 'Masty', as he was affectionately known, before, much to Beech's consternation because it meant more teaching time for him, he – 'Masty' that is – fell and broke a leg playing table tennis during the dinner break shortly after the presentation of the play and never returned! Most of the 'departments', despite some pretentious titles, managed with only one member of staff. English and Mathematics were the exceptions and old Jim Rill not only taught both but, despite tearing around in a mini car — then a 'must have' for trendy young people less than half his age — arrived each morning with barely enough time for a smoke, a cup of tea and, later, to take advantage of The Teacher's nursing experience by having his pulse taken. On one such occasion, Jim suddenly told The Teacher that he made it a rule to wash his hands before going to the toilet in case he'd been in close contact with any of the boys. The Teacher smiled weakly and hoped that this confidence was a joke. It was. Andy was the P.E. teacher, whose unforgettable contribution to the "All for your Delight" event was a bewildering succession of boys in t-shirts and shorts appearing from behind the curtains on one side of the stage in the school hall, vaulting over a gymnasium 'horse' centre stage, before disappearing behind the curtains on the other side to re-appear again shortly afterwards, having nipped behind the safety curtain at the back of the stage. This trick produced the effect of a never-ending troupe of athletic youths when, in fact, there were only about half a dozen boys involved! Andy was something of a misanthrope, who resented young men who came into teaching for what he regarded as "an experiment." The Teacher did his best to demonstrate his greater commitment to education and Andy, ultimately, became a friend and mentor — almost. Sam taught metalwork and spent at least as much time drinking as he did teaching, a habit which, ultimately, was to see him off before his time, whilst Rowen, responsible for woodwork and popular with the boys for his jokes and bonhomie if rather less for his liberal use of corporal punishment, expressed his deep religious beliefs in the contrast between his cheerfulness and his opposition to anything like genuine fun. Rowen's Christianity, it has to said, made crusaders look like the 'Peace Corps'. He was as big a disappointment to the brewers as Sam was a hero, even to the point of objecting to the crate of lager that his colleagues insisted on having on the train back from the annual London outing in the wake of a long dry delay the previous year! The genial Henry taught Science. He was someone to whom The Teacher endeared himself when, almost by chance, he brought into school a handful of foreign postage stamps from his sister's letters and, remembering that Henry's little boy was a junior philatelist, passed them on to Henry for his boy as though he'd thought of little else since being told that, not generally known, fact! The enigmatic Doctor Pratt was something of a mystery for a long time. The mystery included what he taught and why he, who had a PhD, was teaching in such a school. It turned out that he was what used to be called an idealist, a kind of altruistic educational missionary who soon moved on to some other pastoral adventure in the south east. The Geography teacher, known as 'Biggles' because of the knee length white shorts, boots and crisp laundered shirts with turned-up collars that he often wore on field trips and camps, displayed every indication that he was a supreme sceptic with a poorly maintained secret — a kind heart. There were some hints that Biggles was more than just acquainted professionally with Mrs Gibson, but it never came to more than quiet asides at the staff 'night out' and, as The Teacher later discovered, cosy dinners at Biggles' service flat on the other side of the city. Biggles also had a generous disposition and what used to be called a dry sense of humour, which is now known as satire or, at its worst, sarcasm. The art teacher, Cecil, suffered from all the problems that his name and his subject implied. He couldn't keep any semblance of order in his classroom, a situation made worse by the fact that the others, without exception, could! The Teacher felt sorry for 'Ces', particularly when it became apparent that attempting to teach thirty lusty young people history or art after they'd just spent a couple of hours being repressed, bullied or beaten in woodwork classes was fraught with difficulty! And finally, there was the Welshman, The Teacher's immediate boss and mentor in the History Department. It would have been considered an insult to address this man, who was something of a pedant, as 'Dai' or 'Taffy', so he was always called Denis, appropriately enough since that was his name. It was an eclectic mixture from Rowen's cheerful over-use of the tawse, a vicious looking leather strap for the chastisement of wayward pupils, to Cecil's unfailingly unsuccessful struggle to keep order, partly due to the fact that he wasn't allowed access to corporal punishment. These men all had their various foibles and were far from perfect, but it has to be said, that in their different and sometimes idiosyncratic ways, they did care about the boys, about education and about each other. In Doctor Pratt's case, and perhaps others, it was a matter of principle and even sacrifice to work at the sharp edge of what was then called, not entirely without reason, 'the chalk face'.

What they didn't have was ambition. This may have been because of their recognition of their own limitations, the iniquities of the selective system, or simply the process of institutionalisation, which The Nurse had observed in the mental hospital and which was equally obvious in the Secondary Modern School and equally debilitating for the teachers and the taught. It was almost an essential pre-requisite of survival for the staff tasked with instructing, entertaining and inspiring young males, whose backgrounds were fairly humble and whose experiences fairly limited. In the weeks and months that followed, The Teacher learned a lot about what it meant for young people to be labelled as 'failures' at age eleven and about what it means for teachers to work in establishments like boys' Secondary Modern Schools. The fact that the city was moving towards a comprehensive reorganisation of its secondary educational provision only added an element of uncertainty about the future. At his interview for the teaching pool, The Teacher had been asked what his view was of this impending upheaval and he'd done his best to hide the fact that he had no view. The best that he could offer at the time was that he didn't object to it. It didn't seem to matter much and he was briskly dispatched to begin work at The Copse. It was named, with stunning originality, after the rather attractive nearby wooded feature that Mr Beech had pointed out.

Like 'Ces', but not in such a large measure, one of the chief problems that The Teacher encountered in those early days was how to keep order. The pupils had no particular incentive to work hard or please their teachers when their futures were pretty much settled by the eleven plus. Professions or higher education were not for them. The best they could hope for was regular work in a decent job. At least there were plenty of those at the time. Notwithstanding his brief period in the university department of education as a postgraduate, The Teacher didn't really have much idea where to begin, so he approached Denis. Denis escorted him to the history stockroom, indicated where 'sets' of textbooks were available to cover the history syllabus, which began for the eleven and twelve-year-olds with the Romans and progressed chronologically up to the Victorians for those in their final year. 'Sets' meant that there were sufficient copies of a particular book, about thirty-five, to use with a class so that no-one had to share a book. Denis then gave The Teacher a quick seminar on how to teach. "What I do," he said with his voice rising and falling in that peculiar way of the Welsh, "is to talk about it for the first lesson and get the boys to write about it for the second lesson. We have two lessons each week with each class, you see," he added, as though The Teacher wasn't very bright either. "Write about it?" he asked. "Well, copy from the blackboard, really," replied Denis slowly, "but you can use the picture books and get them to trace ..." He tailed off even more slowly and then quickly added, "but whatever you do, don't use the coloured pencils with the 'B' and 'C' classes. They're for the 'A' classes only." There followed another pause, during which both men frowned. Eventually, The Teacher said, "So what do the 'B' and 'C' classes use then?" "These," replied Denis with some emphasis, before reaching above the shelves of history text books for a large cardboard box, in which there was a heap of broken coloured crayons. "Oh," was all that The Teacher could manage to say. It was already clear to The Teacher, that however it was 'dressed up', to tell eleven year olds that they'd failed, that they weren't bright enough for an academic education and had to attend a so-called 'Modern' school and then to allocate them to 'A', 'B' and 'C' groups on the basis of goodness knows what test or questionable primary school records when they got there was likely to have a deleterious effect on those in the lower classes. It led, as The Teacher discovered later, to behaviour that became known as 'the revenge of the 'D' stream' or, in the case of The Copse School, the 'B' and 'C' streams. On top of all that, the lower orders were not allowed to use the colouring pencils! This didn't sound much like good educational practice, even to someone as inexperienced as The Teacher, but as time was short and his schedule of teaching was to begin very shortly, he proceeded at first on the basis that Denis had outlined.

This worked well for about five minutes. The Teacher's workload included trying to impart some knowledge of history to classes in all four year groups, but only one of them was an 'A' class and even that was one of the younger and, therefore, more manageable, classes; 2A. Classes such as 3C, 4B and 4C moving from the rule by tawse and self-laudatory joking of Rowen, the doctor and others to the less authoritarian but still strict regimes, such as those maintained by Biggles, Sam and Denis and thence to Ces and The Teacher were hardly likely to be easy to handle, so small wonder that the latter had problems! With no tawse and no sanctions that he was aware of, what was The Teacher to do when the pupils misbehaved? In practice, they weren't that bad and it was mostly what became known years later in education as 'low-level disruption' like chatting, calling out, inattention, lack of effort and treating The Teacher without respect, as though he was just another encumbrance in their lives and they were just passing the time as best they could in a place they had no wish to be.

One day, The Teacher enquired of Arthur, "What do you do?" Arthur was a young graduate in Classical Chinese, who'd joined the school not long after The Teacher and, unsurprisingly, experienced similar difficulties in the classroom. Only Ces endured worse! "It seems to me," The Teacher continued rather pompously and before Arthur could respond to his real enquiry, "that these lads have no idea of what constitutes reasonable behaviour and decent standards of conduct. Goodness knows what their homes must be like. How can they understand emotions like affection and empathy?" Arthur and The Teacher shared a rare and, in those days, precious thing called a 'free period', which was and is — or maybe used to be now — a time for relaxing in the staff room with a 'fag' and a 'cuppa', preferably in the company of a friendly and respected colleague. The Teacher had come to like Arthur and when the latter ventured to aver, that whilst boys like these may not be able to understand such things, they could, "experience them" and "feel them, just as much as anyone", The Teacher said nothing. He was reluctant to say so, but he knew that Arthur was right. What Arthur didn't have was an answer to the discipline problem.

But Rowen did! "Pick any of 'em," he said, "doesn't matter which one, doesn't matter if he's the worst of 'em. Just grab 'im by the shoulders and throw 'im against the back wall! And make a noise. Shout while you're doing it!" Although The Teacher had to steel himself to do it, he actually tried this strategy! Nowadays, he'd have ended up in court, but to his astonishment, it worked and his class control improved by quite a bit. Soon afterwards, a new, permanent, head teacher was appointed to take over from Beech. He was a more modern and enlightened man, who later became a Labour MP when the Labour Party still represented the interests of the working class and even the poor. The Teacher plucked up the courage to ask if he, The Teacher that is, was sufficiently experienced to use the tawse in circumstances of exceptionally recalcitrant conduct. It was clear that the new head was reluctant to accede to this, but had been unwilling, at this early stage in his headship, to confront the 'old hands' about the rather generous use of corporal punishment and, with some hesitation, conceded. The Teacher swung the tawse only once. It almost made him vomit and he never requested its use again.

Arthur's opinion of the boys wasn't entirely misplaced. The eleven plus was a crude instrument anyway, so that many clever and sensitive children ended up in the wrong educational establishments. Even assuming that some sort of variation in provision at so young an age was a reasonable idea, pupils at schools like The Copse ranged from educationally subnormal to very bright. They were also from a wide variety of homes, most of which were occupied by decent and supportive working class families. It was only as time went on that The Teacher realised that it wasn't only Arthur that had a more positive view of the boys, and in spite of their quirks, their cynicism and their often unpleasant bullying, the staff, on the whole, did their best for their charges.

There was, for example, the annual camp and trips to London every year for the England versus Scotland Schoolboys international match. Apart from the ceaseless and hideous shrieking of 100,000 schoolboy spectators at Wembley Stadium, only surpassed, so The Teacher was told by his sister, by that of the schoolgirls at the annual hockey international, this event was memorable for the occasion when Biggles demonstrated possibly his worst characteristic, his tendency, as The Teacher's mum might have said, to 'carry on regardless'. Some sight-seeing was always included on the agenda and one of the younger boys in his group tugged repeatedly at Biggle's sleeve, pointed at an enormous statue of a long-forgotten mounted hero of the British Empire and whined, "Sir, sir, who's that?" Biggles, without glancing either to the left or the right or breaking stride, continued to look directly ahead in his usual forthright manner, and replied sonorously, "Dick Turpin!" The Teacher, for whom it took many years to get over the onerous sense of responsibility for the young lives in his charge on such occasions, exemplified by constantly scouring the immediate environs and counting the boys in his group, had no idea who the mounted icon might be, but he knew it wasn't Dick Turpin! There were also football teams for every year group and cricket in the summer and annual staff versus boy's fixtures, which the former always won. In his second year, The Teacher was entrusted with the 'under elevens' first year soccer team. They were resplendent in their gold and maroon shirts, but struggled against the much larger city schools in spite of the best efforts at coaching by The Teacher and his wife, who occasionally helped out rather than stand around awaiting the conclusion of what passed for a training session after school. They lost every game except one, which was, ironically, a two-all draw against the biggest of all the other establishments they played! And that would have been a victory, if The Teacher had awarded a third goal to The Copse eleven when the ball went into the opposing goal, but hit an edging stone surrounding the shale pitch and bounced back out again. The Teacher, as always 'bending over backwards' to be even-handed, could not be sure that the football had crossed the line, so his side ended up having to make do with one drawn game and numberless defeats.

One of the innovations introduced at the behest of the new head teacher, aside from adjustments to the curriculum and changes to external testing, neither of which made a shred of difference to the ambience and conduct of the school, was an addition to the extra-curricular calendar in the form of a residential trip by coach to a sometime holiday camp in a decaying seaside town in the south-west. Memorable only for the day Ces fell off his horse, the day that The Teacher and a colleague from another school, Mr Rudge, came across a malfunctioning fruit machine in an arcade, and emptied it, and the night that the coach rocked backwards and forwards quite violently as Rudge and the driver entertained two local females, it was quickly dropped from the diary.

In a lengthy and varied career, one is liable to meet a lot of different people with hugely varying personalities and qualities. A few stand out. One such person was Jack

Rudge. "Mr Rudge will come as soon as he can," said one of the boys in the opposing team, "just as soon as he's sorted the third year team, the gym club and the girl's hockey." This explained why the dozen or so eager eleven-year-olds had arrived unescorted for their match against The Copse's first years and also said much about the commitment of the said Mr Rudge. The game was well under way when Rudge arrived, hastening down the stony slope from the school buildings; tall, slim and athletic in tracksuit and sweatshirt with his long dark hair flowing behind him, an imposing full black beard and forbidding eyes looking for all the world like a commandment striding out of a kerygma! The Teacher was impressed and remained so for many, many years. 'Rudgey', as he was known to his mates, soon afterwards joined the staff at The Copse, where he taught Physical Education and a bit of Maths, even combining the two by teaching classes how to work through quite convoluted calculations drawn from the betting odds at Ascot or York, when it was too inclement for organised games outside and he felt obliged to offer the boys racing on TV as an alternative. He and The Teacher became great friends.

Eventually, The Teacher would have to leave The Copse. The City was reorganising its secondary provision, for one thing, but The Teacher would have good cause to remember many of the boys at The Copse, such as John, a first year. He had informed The Teacher in an essay about his miserable life at the local primary school ending with the plaintive, "And now I am at The Copse and more unhappy than ever before ..." Another was 'Sea Lion Sutcliffe', so-called partly because he was a superb swimmer, but more so because Biggles, with his usual unthinking humour, once told him, "Sutcliffe, I can produce a sea lion that will beat you over four lengths in the pool, but if you can beat that same sea lion by more than ten per cent in the geography exam, you win!" Neither of the 'sea lions' was particularly clever, but nor was Biggles' brand of sarcasm. Buzzer Bundy gained renown for the occasion his granddad sent him to the garage to pump up the tyre on a car wheel and Buzzer inflated it until it exploded and took off half the top of his head. The greater mystery was how Buzzer survived without serious brain injuries — but perhaps not. GCE Winstanley's fame was based entirely upon his parents insistence that their boy was in the academic top flight and should be entered for eight or nine General Certificate of Education papers a year early, when the consensus amongst his teachers was that he'd do well to emulate the famous politician in the probably apocryphal story that told of how he, the politician that is, got through the Harrow public school entrance examination on the strength of scrawling his name, spilling an ink blot, deleting his name and writing it again. In other words, GCE Winstanley could just about manage to write his own name, but little else. Butties Brown acquired eternal celebrity simply by shouting out, "Sir! Can we make butties?" when confronted by fish, chips, peas and bread and butter at the annual camp. Fame sometimes rests upon the flimsiest of foundations! Bull Ball was another, the memory of whom depended upon a simple theme, his habit in cricket of playing forward defensive shots to short balls that struck him with unfailing regularity, and a crack that would make a wrestler wince, on the forehead. The aptly named 'Bull' suffered no apparent ill-effects. On the other hand, there were students who not only shouldn't have been at The

Copse, at least not if the eleven plus test had discerned as it was supposed to, but also, in all likelihood, could have become very successful in later life. Willy Wriggler, for example, never missed an opportunity to show how clever he was, not just by smoking menthol cigarettes behind the canteen, dyeing his hair blue or wearing tight fluorescent trousers, but also by excelling in grandiloquent language and flawless numeracy. Wriggler, doubtless, was sufficiently intelligent and confident to 'make good' in life. So, The Teacher hoped and expected, was Paul, reserved and quiet as 'Willy' was loud, but equally bright and with an athleticism that made him a favourite with most of the staff. Paul brought a note from his mother one day to the effect that she could no longer keep pace with washing his football and sports kit, because there seemed to be something that Paul was involved in every day after school. Such was the dedication of the men of The Copse!

One day, the new head at The Copse, when he was no longer new, took The Teacher to one side and told him about a job in a neighbouring secondary school. "It carries a responsibility allowance,'" the head explained darkly, "it could be just the thing for you." The Teacher took this to mean that the head wanted to get rid of him, so he went to the school in question, where Mr Gates, the head teacher, explained the nature of the job and what was to be expected of the person assuming it. The Teacher wasn't much the wiser after this, but schools like these in big cities were still struggling to find staff in those days, so it wasn't so much a case of applying formally, or being shortlisted and interviewed, as just saying, "Okay, I'll do it. Thanks." Quite how the paper work was completed, The Teacher didn't know and it didn't trouble him at the time, but he started his third year of teaching or, as he, himself sometimes expressed it, "Being in a room with some children" at Moss Newton Secondary Modern Mixed School. Whether The Teacher would have been better off remaining where he was and awaiting the impending reorganisation of secondary schools is a matter for conjecture. It probably wouldn't have mattered much.

Moss Newton was different. Not just because there were girls and women there, but also, because it was organised in a way that wouldn't have been out of place in a pre-war preparatory school. Even The Teacher was surprised, maybe even shocked, to learn that the classes weren't only arranged in age groups, but divided by gender as well! In other words, there was a boys' school and a girls' school together on a single site in one building! There were two staff rooms too, one for female teachers and the other for male teachers. Gates informed The Teacher, however, with a look and semi-smile, that the latter took to indicate some pride, that such were the up-to-date attitudes amongst the staff that this requirement was now ignored. In fact, as The Teacher quickly discovered, both staff rooms were now mixed, the old 'ladies staffroom' being used by the over fifties and the staffroom for 'gentlemen' by the rest; the younger element, so that the enforced division of sex became a voluntary division by age.

History being already covered by one of the male teachers, the genial Jim Coot, The Teacher had agreed with Gates to do some English in the 'boys school' and some games. The Teacher's predecessor at Moss Newton, who had been a favourite of Mr Gates, had taught Geography, but The Teacher was reluctant to commit himself to taking on that subject and the matter had been left unresolved at the interview between Gates and The Teacher. Having been on a course for teachers sponsored by the local education authority towards the end of his time at The Copse, The Teacher offered to throw in some 'Social Education'. This course was some sort of sociological exercise, which purported to deal with the problems of young people at various times and phases of their lives. It was one of those courses where the audience believed that they understood what was being imparted until speakers stopped speaking, at which point, they realised that they didn't. Accordingly, The Teacher followed his habits, learned at school, at university and at The Copse, of taking copious notes and then 'watering them down' for the lesser orders, in this case, the boys of Moss Newton, before regurgitating them as half-baked lessons. The course had been led by an ageing sociologist of some repute and, interestingly, had drawn upon the worldly experience and knowledge of some of the leading lights of the business and entertainment industries, including a popular radio and television presenter and game show host, who, many years later, was tried and imprisoned for sexual offences against young women and girls he'd obtained access to through his professional career. Thus, ultimately, fame became notoriety! Meanwhile, The Teacher wasn't sure that he understood all the complexities of 'Social Education' and Gates certainly didn't. Which was just as well, for trying to impart this half-understood wisdom to teenage boys was not easy! The Teacher did his best and went to enormous trouble to include trips and visits to relevant places of interest and exciting sessions such as canoeing on the boating lake in The Copse, the wooded area below The Copse School. The canoes were stored at The Copse school, so The Teacher was afforded an opportunity to renew acquaintances with his former colleagues, notably 'Rudgey', with whom The Teacher shared much of his social life, which principally consisted of heavy draught beer drinking, playing football and, in 'Rudgey's' case, chasing women. No-one at The Copse seemed to bother with the canoes, so The Teacher had more or less exclusive use of half a dozen of them for his classes of twenty odd lively and uncouth youths. These boys actually enjoyed the thrills, the soakings and the perils of canoeing in those relatively carefree days before 'health and safety' dictated that 'Risk Assessments' made anything the least bit dangerous a bureaucratic nightmare. Years later, The Teacher would blanche at the dangers to which he had exposed young people, himself and his career on field trips, factory visits, hikes and so on. At the city's Town Hall, one of the parties found a large iron bolt on the top floor of the clock tower, picked it up and casually tossed it through the window from where it fell several hundred feet to the crowded pavement below. A shocked passer-by retrieved it and felt obligated to complain to Town Hall staff, who, rightly, blamed The Teacher. "You might have killed somebody," cried The Teacher! The boy concerned just smiled and shrugged, not even nervously.

The Teacher was befriended by Jim Coot and another teacher, not all that much older than himself, Ron Hubbard. Ron was the head of English at the time and a very dedicated and committed pedagogue, who later made the mistake of moving to a mixed race Middle School, where his sincere but clumsy attempts to equalise opportunities in an ethnically diverse community caused such enormous difficulties that he was, regrettably, forced out of the profession before his time. It should be made clear that Ron's first name was not Lafayette and he had no connection with Scientology. Sam's wife, that's Sam from The Copse School, was the Head of the girl's school at Moss Newton and, it has to be said, was far more sensible and far less dependent on alcohol than Sam. She still had what The Teacher felt were somewhat old-fashioned views about how beneficial and life-enhancing it was for the girls' classes to be treated as quite separate entities from those of the boys, but her efforts to raise the expectations and opportunities of the girls weren't helped by the appointment of two young female teachers the same age as The Teacher, but with markedly less control and presence than he had. One of these taught, or rather, tried to teach English and one of the two occasions The Teacher recollected seeing Mr Gates during the school day was when he burst upon the scene to intercept girls from the class of Miss Whatever-her-name-was, following the third time they entered the classroom from the exterior window and, after a period of chaos in the room, egressed through the windows abutting the interior quadrangle. "I'll clip your wings for you lot!" Gates shouted but did little else once the girls had tired of their antics and calm had been restored. The shrieking from the Domestic Science room, where the second of the young women supposedly taught, frequently disturbed the other classes and was so discomposing, that even several of the boys complained to their teachers. The noise could be so disruptive, that The Teacher emerged from his classroom on one occasion and met Jim in the corridor shaking his head, but doing nothing else, except talk about it in the pub later. Sam's wife did her best to counsel her staff, but the only other occasion The Teacher remembered Gates emerging from the confines of his office was to admonish a class lining up on the corridor between lessons. "You're very noisy," he said, "you're very noisy!" The Teacher understood this to be directed at him rather than the class and to mean, "Get this class under control, you useless object!"

One year was probably enough of all this. Secondary school re-organisation finally happened and Moss Newton either closed or was absorbed somehow into the new system. Gates probably retired. What became of Sam's wife and the others isn't known, but The Teacher, following another desultory 'interview' with some long-forgotten men in suits at the Education Offices, moved to one of the large Comprehensive High Schools on the other side of the city. In other words, The Teacher was, in common with all of the educational workforce who hadn't taken the opportunity to retire, move on, or hadn't been 'eased out' somehow, slotted into what was considered to be a suitable post in the new situation of equality of opportunity for all the city's children and young people. Except that, as is now well known, the privileges of the 'well-heeled' minority in society are rather harder to undermine than that and, as hard as a complex reorganisation of secondary education in the interests of equitability had been to achieve, it wasn't equal to the task of outwitting the wiles of the wealthy, whose prerogatives were — and are — entrenched in the private schools, in the few surviving Grammar Schools, in the often misnamed Faith Schools and in the so-called 'comprehensives' situated in the leafy suburbs, where house prices rocketed whenever reorganisation threatened the status quo.

Willington High School, The Teacher's new workplace, was as close as it could be to a truly comprehensive school, where the idea and the ideal of educating all children to the limit of their potential together, regardless of gender, race, ability, social class background, or any other factor, and of providing the buildings, staff and resources to do so then hearteningly existed. And the vast majority of the administrators and teachers were eager to make it work. Willington was born of an amalgamation of two urban secondary schools in a 'catchment area' of modest need being neither, to use the terminology of those times, 'disadvantaged' or 'affluent'. The new school was based, therefore, upon two sites, one of which had housed a Secondary Modern School not unlike The Copse and the other a Technical High School, which was somewhere between a Grammar School and a Modern School and purported to cater for children not of the academic top flight, but not deemed sufficiently 'stupid' for the modern school and, hopefully, with a practical bent. Quite how children had been selected for the Technical High Schools, that only a minority of Local Education Authorities had elected to maintain, was, and still is, a mystery to The Teacher, but it wasn't something that concerned him overly at the time.

It is a fact that the longer you stay somewhere, the less you remember about it, and the older you become the clearer are the memories that are furthest in the past even if they remain the fewest. The Teacher stayed too long at Willington, but that was because he wasn't then able to handle the notion of a career and the system whereby it was realised and he just didn't understand that at the time. In short, he had no ambition as yet, but teaching was, for him, becoming a real job, a profession, maybe even a vocation!

The head teacher at Willington was a one-legged failed parliamentary candidate for the Conservative party. He propelled himself around on a pair of crutches with exemplary vigour and was notable, principally, for his frequent and indubitably genuine way of expressing his gratitude to staff for their hard work, dedication and loyalty. "Thank you very much," he would say at the opening of every meeting and often at various points throughout. So much so, that the staff, not unkindly, would begin to hum or sing the pop song of the same name whenever the head was in the vicinity, which was not all that often. The staff was mostly drawn from the two schools that made up the new mixed comprehensive school. The old Technical school building became the Upper School for the older boys and girls and the old Modern school building became the Lower School and the one in which The Teacher did most of his teaching. The Teacher couldn't help noticing that, and this was a general rule in the comprehensive setting, those teachers who'd previously taught in selective schools, such as the Grammar and Technical schools, were the ones who struggled to make an impact and had the most difficulty in dealing with the less able or more disruptive children. Secretly, The Teacher thought, "Serves 'em right. They've had it easy up to now." He'd been engaged exclusively as a teacher of History and liked to think of himself as a specialist in the field of expertise of the university degree he'd acquired. It wasn't just a third class degree either, even though he wasn't quite sure how this had been achieved alongside his roles as a postman, a factory hand and an ice cream man. It wasn't long, however, before the Head of Lower School, whose self-important attitude made The Teacher, rather unfairly, think that he'd have made a decent Gauleiter in Germany during the war, approached the latter and asked him if he'd mind assisting the school in fulfilling its obligations to the children by teaching a bit of English to some of the younger children. "Certainly not! I'm a History specialist! I couldn't possibly do that!" was what The Teacher wanted to say, but following a brief pause, he heard himself say, "Oh, okay ..." He wanted to add something about helping out in whatever way he could, but the Head of Lower School, having obtained the response he wanted and expected, was already disappearing rapidly down the corridor. Eventually, The Teacher wanted to approach his Head of Department, an affable lady, who owed her promotion, like so many in those days, to what was called "being in the right place at the right time", and ask her if, or rather, when, he could get some Sixth Form teaching, then seen as some of the best and most useful teaching experience and an avenue to wider opportunities, promotion and more pay. He never did approach her, much less ask her, and he had to remain content with teaching up to the General Certificate of Education (GCE) and the less academic version of external exams for fifteen and sixteen-year-olds the Certificate of Secondary Education. He never taught the Sixth Form.

The Teacher did do some games though. And he ran the under fifteens football team at the weekends and, along with a colleague, ran several basketball teams after school. The under fifteens was one of his most productive ventures. It was rather like managing a proper football team, except that it took up much of his spare time and nearly every Saturday morning in the season, so that, with the addition of playing football for the grandly named City Education Committee Association Football Club (CEC) on Saturday afternoons with 'Rudgey' and a collection of like-minded young men, and a few pints at the Teachers' Centre afterwards, winter weekends were something of a 'write-off' for his wife and fairly young daughter. This situation was exacerbated by The Teacher's insistence on embarking upon a succession of coaching qualifications in the coaching of football, basketball, cricket and swimming. Whilst all this caused some friction, The Teacher tried hard, and largely succeeded, in not letting it trouble him too much for quite a number of years. His handling of the under - fifteens, meanwhile, culminated in their reaching the final of a regional trophy, which, had The Teacher been a little more creatively bold and modified his strict defensive 'sweeper system' to suit the conditions and the opposition, might well have been won and the national finals come into sight. It was not to be, The Teacher didn't have sufficient flair to take off the 'sweeper' and bring on another 'striker' and the chance for glory was lost.

That is not to say that The Teacher wasn't a success. His pedagogy was developing nicely and exposure to a wider range of teaching methods and styles was proving very beneficial. He learned quickly and his class control improved immensely too. On one occasion, The Teacher was taking a history class in a science laboratory, normally the domain of Miss Black, an elderly old

Xanthippe who had some sort of senior pastoral role. Goodness knows why the class had to be moved to such an inappropriate venue, but about halfway through the session, the door opened to admit a teenage boy of troubled mind, who peremptorily strode to the front of the room, opened a drawer in the teacher's bench and extracted what appeared to be a small box of pills! Ignoring everyone in the room, the boy turned and began to make his way back to the door, where he paused and turned again as if to challenge anyone to demand an explanation. The perplexed class looked from the boy to The Teacher, who wisely cocked his head very slightly, pursed his lips and raised his eyebrows just sufficiently to keep control of the situation. Several seconds elapsed before the boy opted to offer an elucidation. "It's okay, sir," he announced, "Miss Black allows me to go into her drawers!" Several of the more precocious girls in the class interpreted this as a lewd inference and began to chuckle, until a frown from The Teacher, followed quickly by widened eyes, silenced them. The Teacher then allowed himself a smile, dismissed the boy and shared quietly in the humour of the moment by turning to his class and shrugging his shoulders. The class responded by smiling and returning to their tasks. It was a measure of The Teacher's increasing stature and presence that he was able to stay in control merely with gestures and facial expressions! Miss Black's laboratory was the one The Teacher borrowed for his lunch-time film shows, entertaining packages of Woody Woodpecker cartoons and abridged Tom Mix westerns hired for nothing from the local authority and raising much-needed funds for the History department. The Teacher kept good order in a lab full of appreciative and gay, in the traditional sense of that word, youngsters, even on the occasion that the sound stopped and The Teacher announced a guarantee of a full refund of the few pence they'd paid for admission if he couldn't get it back on before the chase at the end of the western. He did. By this time, some of his English classes were doing so well that the Head of English commended him to the senior leadership and his History teaching was imaginative and could be quite stimulating. So much so, that one of the younger boys raised his hand in the time honoured fashion to indicate a wish to speak and said, "This History is really good isn't it sir?" "What makes you say that, Phillip?" said The Teacher. "Well," said Phillip, "you never know when you're going to run into an Anglo-Saxon do you?" On top of that, The Teacher managed to persuade the recalcitrant 'Bully Bailey', sixteen years of age, feared by even the most experienced staff and the scourge of the upper school, to wear his school uniform blazer. The crumpled and badly frayed object was kept in a locker on the corridor and Bailey would bring it out and don it only to please The Teacher, for whom he had a mysterious respect and he wore it only for The Teacher's lessons after which it would disappear into the locker until the following week. This kind of response from the more difficult pupils did give rise to increased confidence and a desire for change. It came in an unexpected form.

It is hard to credit nowadays, but in those days, Education Authorities offered each year something called 'secondment', an opportunity to have a term, or even a full academic year, of paid leave of absence to work or to study somewhere else. These 'secondments' were available in very limited numbers to only a small number of teachers that had given a certain minimum in terms of length of service and provided that the staff concerned could find a place on a suitable course of study or work that the senior officers in the education authority deemed to be appropriate for enhancing the skills and knowledge of the applicant in a way that would be considered to be of some subsequent benefit to the authority. The Teacher looked around for something to do for a year and found it at a local university, only a couple of lengthy bus journeys from where he lived. He was surprised to find something appropriate to apply for, but even more surprised when his application was accepted! The course was a Diploma in Compensatory Education. The Teacher didn't have a clear idea what 'compensatory education' might be and his surmise was that not many other people did and that, because of this, applications were few and that is why he was able to secure a place. Self-deprecating though this inference was, The Teacher never regretted his first secondment — to his surprise, he was to get a second some years later — and he learned a lot.

It was a matter of conjecture, and still is, whether it is possible to 'compensate' disadvantaged youngsters from deprived and poverty-stricken environments, but The Teacher soon came to believe that it was important to try. As one learned commentator put it, "Education cannot compensate for society." It can't, but The Teacher understood that it can go a long way to improving the prospects and the lives of the poor and the downtrodden, so that, following many hours of listening to enlightened educationalists, sociologists and community workers, many more visiting inner-city schools and institutions, whole days in the magnificent city library, with its façade of Portland stone, writing papers, researching for months and producing a dissertation on sociometric friendship patterns in mixed race primary schools and after several searching examinations, The Teacher was, to his astonishment, awarded a distinction in the discipline and had undergone something of a 'Damascene' revelation. Notwithstanding the movement for comprehensive education, he recognised the continuing gross inequities in society and in schools. At the end of that academic year, The Teacher joined the Labour Party.

Then, The Teacher made a mistake. He returned to Willington. He made three more mistakes that year, perhaps more. Most people learn when they are very young what they're not good at, but momentarily forgetting that his own teacher had told him in no uncertain terms, when he was ten years old, that he could not sing, he tried to join the staff choir and he compounded this error by trying to get into the teachers' band as, of all things, a trumpet player! What he did not do, and most certainly should have, was try to get out of Willington long before he did, two years later, when a team mate in the CECAFC, called Derek, casually mentioned that he was leaving his 'junior' school for a deputy headship in another town. "Why don't you do it?" the team mate suggested, as though the post was his to allocate to whomever he chose. In practice, it was because the head teacher of the primary school, which was quite close to Willington, had asked Derek if he knew any suitable colleagues and to make some enquiries amongst his friends in the football team and in another organisation called The City Teachers Physical Education Association. The City Teachers PE Association, with an exclusively male membership, had less to do with physical exercise than beer drinking on Friday nights and was renowned for being a market place for promotion posts in the city's primary schools, in which the domination of males in senior positions was then as great a scandal as anywhere in the country. The Teacher's interest in primary schools and the education of five to ten year-olds had been stimulated by his course in Compensatory Education but, with his standard hesitancy when confronted with anything new or unfamiliar, he only agreed to "think about it" and had it not been for Derek's persistence and the concerns of Derek's head teacher that he might end up with a raw recruit from the city 'teaching pool', or worse, a woman, then nothing would have happened. As things turned out, Derek persuaded The Teacher to visit the school where the head had a chat with him and, there being no other candidates, the job was his. Up to this point in his career, The Teacher still hadn't really undergone anything approaching a proper interview!

Primary education was still reasonably sensibly structured in those days and the children were organised into three years of five, six and seven-year old classes called 'infants' and four years of eight to eleven-year old classes called 'juniors'. It was during their final year at the 'junior' stage, that children had been required to take the grossly unfair 'eleven-plus' exam. Most often, these 'infant' and 'junior' classes were called 'departments' in a Primary School, but less frequently, they were separate Infant and Junior Schools, each with their own head teachers and staffs. Edward Road Junior School was housed on the second floor of one of those gaunt, old Victorian school buildings which, if it had been a big department store on the High Street, would have been called the first floor, because it was immediately over the ground floor. The Teacher always supposed that the 'infants' occupied the ground floor for reasons of convenience and safety, but that, also, may have been just another English idiosyncrasy. The building was fronted by a large tarmac play area, the 'junior' playground, and at the rear of the building was a smaller, but similarly paved, 'infant playground'; the whole area being enclosed by a stone wall topped by spiked iron railings, that had survived being removed and disposed of for the 'war effort'. Between the perimeter and the 'junior' playground, there were some rose beds, which the head teacher of the Junior School spent many hours planting and pruning when, in the opinion of The Teacher, he should really have been managing the school. "Which was more surprising," The Teacher mused years later, "that the head emerged from his office to tend to them, that the roses bloomed profusely, or that they were never vandalised?" It was an ordinary working class locality in the days, when residents had some respect for their surroundings.

Edward Road was a big school and, therefore, had eight classes, two in each year group with the usual heterogeneous collection of teachers. The deputy head, Arnold, was old-fashioned and unhealthy, but a very likeable and helpful source of advice for The Teacher, especially about how much influence could be exercised umpiring inter-schools cricket matches. "You can only control one end," he would say sagaciously, tapping an index finger on one side of his nose, "you have to trust the other chap at the other end." This was precisely the problem The Teacher encountered again and again in school sports competitions. Some colleagues were so keen for their charges to succeed, that they resorted, sometimes totally unwittingly, to tactics that could only be described as bordering upon downright cheating! Sometimes, it actually was downright cheating too, like giving goals that clearly had not crossed the goal line, calling 'not out' with the batsman plumb in front of the 'stumps', or declaring a batsman 'in' when he was well short of the crease! The Teacher liked Arnold; not only was he supportive but his political position in the staffroom, where he often rambled on about the injustices of society, was close to what The Teacher now believed in. Arnold was also close to retirement and he died almost immediately, thereafter. Arnold, as was customary for deputy heads then, taught one of the oldest classes, the 'junior fours'. The other belonged to the formidable Mrs Green, a gruff but kindly woman in the twilight of her career, who insisted upon ancient protocols, such as always occupying the same armchair in the staff-room, one of the most comfortable, and woe betide any who sat in it. Mrs Green collected for the Teachers Benevolent and Orphans Fund and expected regular contributions from all. Those who failed to do so, together with anyone who, even inadvertently, occupied her chair, would feel what used to be called the 'rough edge of her tongue'. There was no doubt that the fund, founded originally by the biggest of the teachers' trade unions over a century previously for the promotion of "self-help and thrift against times of sickness and distress", benefitted from Mrs Green's fierce countenance and sharp invocations. It was a worthy enterprise. It helped many teachers through difficult periods with advice and loans and grants and was one in which The Teacher became involved as an elected member of its board of governors much, much later when it was simply the TBF. The classes in the next youngest year group, the 'junior threes', were taught by The Teacher and by Ruby, a similar chimera, who would sit with Mrs Green during play and dinner breaks and rail against the inferior prospects and position of women teachers like a kind of quasi-feminist. One of the 'junior twos' was in charge of Elaine, memorable for being the wife of the Teacher's understudy in the CECAFC, the reserve team goalkeeper, and for displaying an outward facing sign in the window of her classroom during a spell of hot summer weather, emblazoned with the words "NO WASPS ALLOWED" in big letters. She said that it seemed to do the trick and convinced some of the children that wasps were quite good readers. The other 'junior two' class was taken by a pretty young female teacher, who played the piano during the school's assemblies, whilst the children and their teachers sang lustily and The Teacher, notwithstanding the fact of being a husband and father by this time, nearly fainted with suppressed desire! That leaves the 'junior one' classes, the first of which was Carole's, a plain young woman, about whom The Teacher, somewhat inappropriately, was forever humming 'Oh Carole' and declining offers of yoghurt, and the second of which was taught by a recently qualified female, whose abrasive and inelastic-faced right-wing attitudes 'rubbed' Arnold 'up the wrong way' and fairly shocked The Teacher.

In the motile environs of a 'junior' school, The Teacher was, at first, in constant fear of treading on the children and, when crossing the 'infant' playground, regularly ambushed and embarrassed by microscopic toddlers wanting to hold his hand. He wouldn't have bothered unless he needed to get to and from the shops and, later, to get to the nearby library on Fridays, where he sought out 'The Teacher' newspaper to peruse the 'vacancies' section. That isn't to say that The Teacher was unhappy at Edward Street, it was just that, after a relatively short period of time, he began to believe that if people like Derek and some of the other primary school specialists he encountered in the CEC football team and elsewhere could be deputy head teachers, then anybody could! In fact, it hadn't taken The Teacher all that long to adjust from pretending to be a specialist teacher of history in a comprehensive school of over one thousand students to making a reasonably realistic attempt to inculcate a mixed-ability group of ten year olds with some knowledge and skills of mathematics, English, geography and even a little science, physical education and art, or was that just daubing paint? The Teacher moved rapidly from the head's instructions to put the 'A' group on the 'Alpha' maths book, the 'B' group on the 'Beta' maths book, hear every child read — he didn't say what — every week, plough through the history and geography syllabus and, by implication, to somehow take care of the "dunderheads", a term The Teacher had first heard his teacher auntie use some years previously, to a rather more integrated and balanced approach, that took into account, at least to an extent that The Teacher was able to cope with, the aptitudes and interests of all the children. This was personal development of a very high order. When asked to provide something for the mixed-age 'clubs' afternoon, The Teacher offered to set up a 'woodwork club'. This wasn't the unmitigated disaster expected, but it was most certainly a risky adventure in which strict rules had to be laid down for the use of tools such as saws, chisels, screwdrivers and hammers and the progress of which took several years off the Teacher's life, or so he later claimed. The Teacher also became good at organising sports for 'junior' aged boys and was so committed and successful, that Arnold told him that the head had noticed, goodness knows how, and he was rewarded with a new football kit in gold and blue for the school football team.

It has to be borne in mind that, at that time, the leadership of primary education was largely male and the rank and file largely female, so that, after a couple of years serving his time as a kind of apprentice primary school teacher at Edward Street, The Teacher felt able to begin applying for a deputy headship! Thus, ambition began to blossom in the wake of sound but unexceptional development and, ultimately, after a string of unsuccessful applications, The Teacher obtained an interview at a primary school in the same education authority on the other side of the city. 'Rudgey', having taken a similar route as The Teacher from secondary to primary education, but being rather better, or more suitably, trained and qualified, was already a deputy head by this juncture and, over ale in the public bar of a city centre hostelry one night, nonchalantly informed The Teacher that he, The Teacher, was the "favourite for the job." 'Rudgey' may have just been encouraging his pal, but he, 'Rudgey', had served at the school in question and may have had access to privileged information. The Teacher, having imbibed heavily as he often did, was outraged that 'Rudgey' should have access to such information, if he did, but The Teacher didn't challenge his friend and he never found out the truth of it and, in the end, it didn't matter.

The Teacher could only ever recall two of the questions he was asked at the interview. The first was posited by the head teacher, who wanted to know how The Teacher felt about the children sitting the entrance examination for Direct Grant – semi-public which, of course, really meant semi-private – Grammar Schools. The Teacher replied that he had no objection to this procedure and, in the light of his secondary experience; he didn't envisage any academic or practical problem with it. In other words, he lied. The second was a question from an inspector, who fancied himself, wrongly, as something of an avant-garde progressive, but was, in fact, a popinjay, who said to The Teacher slowly and carefully whilst smirking and looking around at his fellow interviewers for approbation, "What makes you laugh?" "Tom and Jerry," replied The Teacher. On such flimsy evidence as this, The Teacher became a Deputy Head Teacher.

Chapter 13

THE DEPUTY

Mr John, 'Old John' to everyone else, pursed his lips and looked at The Deputy grimly, "I've been here for twenty one years," he boasted, and, slapping a pile of slim, buff-coloured A4 sized books, embossed with the city crest on to the large wooden table at the front of the room, he added, "and I've got twenty identical record books!"

The Deputy looked puzzled. "What happened to the other one?" he asked. "Ah," said Old John, beaming as though he'd caught The Deputy breaking into the infant department's 'dressing up' box. "I was acting head for a year," he pronounced triumphantly. Indeed he had been, and the head had informed The Deputy that he was of the view that Old John had merited "further promotion" to a permanent headship and that this would surely have been attained, had it not been for the 'new-fangled' notions emanating from the city's education officers and inspectors. "You might find these useful," said Old John, pushing the pile of record books across the table towards The Deputy, who, even more certain that he would not find them useful than he was that it was right that his predecessor had never become a head teacher, said, "Thank you." Old John went on to explain how he arranged his classroom. "I have the brightest boy here, in front of my table," he explained, "the next cleverest at the front of the next row and so on, in order, until you get over there" he added, pointing to a desk in the far left-hand corner of the room at the back of the row furthest away from his table. "Who sits there?" The Deputy ventured to enquire. "Well," said Old John, "the dullest boy sits there. I don't care what anyone else thinks, I don't have any fancy groups or special cases, I just get on with it. They're all treated the same and they all have to 'sink or swim'. It's the best way and I get good results!" The Deputy, whilst being tempted to ask Old John what he did with the girls, elected not to respond to this archaic approach to organisation and teaching. Instead, and in order to divert Old John away from anything directly educational, he enquired about who looked after all the tightly packed pot plants that he'd noticed lining every window of every classroom, the corridors, the school hall and even some of the toilets! "You do," replied Old John and went on to expound at great length about the educative benefits of the plants and how much they inspired everyone and raised moral and what to do with them all at holiday times. At this point, The Deputy fell into a deep reverie and only roused himself in time to hear Old John telling him how important it was to strip off and get into the water with the children. The Deputy later learned that this piece of advice was in connection with the teaching of swimming, the risk of being accused of something dreadful being much less then. Within a month of starting at the school, The Deputy had managed, through a combination of neglect and over-watering by his squad of 'pot plant monitors', to reduce the pot plants by half, before persuading the head to let him hand the task over to a recently appointed and inexperienced colleague.

Escaping from the one-sided exchange in what had been Old John's classroom and was imminently to become his, The Deputy proceeded to the school office to fulfil an appointment with 'Big H', the head teacher of Leafold, that being the name of his new school. Big H introduced him to Mrs Wildon, the school secretary, who turned out to be as saturnine as she looked, and then ushered The Deputy through a door labelled "Headmaster's Office" into a room that was larger than his auntie's 'front room'. A connecting door at the back of the room led into an equally impressive toilet, cloak and washroom. "This is the headmaster's suite," Big H told him, "I think we'll keep it that way for now." This didn't bother The Deputy overmuch, particularly when it transpired that there were sufficient toilets for each of the remaining males on the teaching staff to identify their own personal toilet, whilst the myriad female staff members shared a block of three between them! The Deputy's was situated at one side of the school hall where he could 'perform' in peace. "I don't even need to close the door," he thought to himself. He was disturbed only upon one occasion when, standing to urinate, a glance over his left shoulder revealed several members of the infant staff on the Hall stage preparing to rehearse something or other. The situation called for a calm response and The Deputy reached backwards with his right leg, whilst balancing upon the other to adroitly push the door shut with his foot. Thereafter, he secured all toilet doors before beginning upon anything...

The head owed the epithet 'Big H' to the caretaker, who also had a penchant for quite witty, if rather facetious aphorisms. So did the self-styled 'King', a young male teacher appointed at the same time as The Deputy and completing what Big H thought of as a master stroke of recruitment in obtaining two young men, firstly to deploy The King to replace Rudgey, secondly to dispose The Deputy to take over from Old John, and thirdly, to utilise both of them to go some way to balancing the preponderance of females surrounding him. It might be added that it also made it easier for him to hide in the office, or to don his blazer and tie and slip away to join other elderly men to do the things that he felt were important, like organising schools football in the city.

The caretaker, The King and even The Deputy, bestowed upon the 'regiment of women' soubriquets to suit their appearance or personality and to facilitate reference to them in 'heart-to-hearts' and corridor gossip without, should it be overheard, identifying who was the subject of the conversation. The head of infants, for example, who resembled the fat Habsburg bailiff in the William Tell fable, became known as 'Gessler' a name, it has to be said, that her actions and attitudes fully merited. Other nicknames were less complimentary, such as 'Dogface', a close ally of Gessler, and 'Doom' another hatchet-faced old woman who took the 'backwards' classes in the juniors. When they weren't poring over jigsaw puzzles in the staffroom, this trio were forming a phalanx of traditionalists to plot against the progressive educational notions of The King. Of the several remaining women in the juniors, one was of

Eastern European ancestry and had been inveigled by Big H, who was blissfully unaware of the racist connotations, to agree to 'change' her name from Svikovsky to Smith on the grounds that it would be easier for the children to manage. The King was outraged and, although he and The Deputy were willing to challenge Big H on this issue, the teacher in question was equivocal and nothing was done. Miss 'Smith' and the others were reluctant to involve themselves in The King's ambitious designs and neither was 'Silverback', the man who had taken over the pot plants, most of which would have made better teachers than he ever would, and was in the second year infant class, or the plump woman in the reception class, who was remarkable more for her size than her presence in the classroom; or perhaps both! The King always sought the endorsement of The Deputy for his proposals and The Deputy, to his shame, was ambivalent. However, in attempting to mediate between the resistance and antediluvian approaches of Gessler's group, The King's avowed frustration and advanced aspirations and Big H's expectations and desire for continuity and a quiet life, he learned a great deal about the role of the deputy head teacher.

If Big H was not strong on diversity, he was even less so on gender equality and would have insisted upon the women all wearing what he called "appropriate dress", meaning frocks, at all times if he could have got away with it. But even one or two of the younger women at Leafold were sufficiently progressive, and sufficiently bold, to insist upon their right to wear trousers if they so wished. Now, The Deputy had learned how to operate a film projector, probably from some course or other on modern technological teaching aids, and took to showing educational films in the school hall now and again to improve the general knowledge, and sometimes to entertain, all the classes in the school hall. One such film was an enthralling, but entirely unsuitable, short about careers in the gas industry, entitled "A Fitting Future". This film actually had the Deputy's father in a supporting role, that being, in truth, the reason he'd ordered it. The sight of his dad, resplendent, riding his gas fitter's bicycle with its front carrier full of tools down a rural street, whilst waving and smiling like some working class monarch was truly a sight to behold! Big H, whilst not fully in tune with their educational purpose was aware of The Deputy's film shows and recognised, for instance, that other staff could get a break whilst they were being shown. In the course of one of these presentations, Big H slipped into the hall and sidled up to The Deputy to beseech him, that under no circumstances, should the women be permitted access to the film projector on the grounds that women were simply not able to handle such intricate machines. Co-incidentally, one of the younger female teachers had already approached The Deputy on this subject and asked to be allowed to use the projector, arguing that it would save him the trouble of setting it up and operating it on her behalf. Following several weeks of cajolery and earnest debate about the mental capacity and frailties of women, The Deputy was able to persuade Big H, using the very same arguments that had been presented by the young female teacher, to allow him to train any of the women who wished to be trained in the use of the film projector. Big H continued to express grave reservations, but eventually conceded, and several of the women subsequently attended an after-school seminar set up by

177

The Deputy. Not long afterwards, The Deputy was passing the hall when the same young female teacher, who'd led the projector insurrection, was showing a film to her class. Glancing through a window in one of the hall doors, The Deputy saw the young teacher standing just in front of the projector, behind the seated children, blissfully unaware of the smoke pouring from the machine. The Deputy dashed in, stopped the projector and extricated the film. No harm was done and neither he nor the young woman had any idea what it was that had caused this malfunction, but both swore quietly not to reveal it.

All teachers keep records. Records are an essential part of planning what to teach and evaluating what has been taught. If you ask pupils what makes a good teacher, they nearly always include variations of 'firm', 'fair' and 'fun' to which should be added 'well-founded', 'well-informed' and 'well-flexible'; That is to say, well-prepared and ready to change direction according to how the class or the group or the individual child responds. That is why, although he did have a look at one of them out of curiosity, The Deputy quickly consigned Old John's twenty identical record books to the dust bin along with, on one famous occasion, his class register, thereby perpetrating one of the great unsolved mysteries of education for, as one 'old hand' once conspiratorially informed him, "You can smoke in the stockroom, you can streak from here to the town centre, you can even bugger the chairman of the governors but, whatever you do, do not mess up your register!" There is always at least a grain of truth in such apocryphal anecdotes, which probably derives from the stress upon attendance and numbers on roll, which became of even greater importance than it was in Victorian times as, from the late twentieth century, government legislation began the transformation of head teachers from educators to executives, schools into faux corporations and children into commodities with a price on their heads to be traded and 'delivered' things like 'subjects'. Notwithstanding this regression to, and growth of, bureaucracy, planning and evaluation remained important. From his earliest days at The Copse, The Deputy had kept copious records, often spending entire Friday evenings working, and on into the small hours, in order to be ready for Monday morning and the week ahead. As time went on, he refined his technique and his practice to reflect his developing skills as a teacher, changes in curriculum and teaching methods, and the needs of the children he taught, as determined by their ages, aptitudes and abilities.

Although The King could be a source of some difficulty, even anguish, he, although not in the same class as Rudgey, was, as the song says, also a smoker, a joker, a midnight toper - and a footballer. Thus, The King, Rudgey and The Deputy occasionally turned out for the same side of one or other of the several CEC elevens, though more often, the latter two featured in the first eleven, particularly after The Deputy had become the goalkeeper following a crisis in that position and had discovered that it was something that he could do quite well to the point where, on one occasion, he was selected for the League representative team and famously appeared on the back page of the Daily Telegraph, albeit in a font so tiny that few people ever knew! It was customary for CEC players to gather in the city Teacher's Centre following games and imbibe large quantities of beer, consume innumerable meat pies, if they hadn't been left in the boot of the club captain's car for days on end, smoke, and then, in the days when it was possible to do so, drive to their respective places of residence. Logically, this interest in sport translated into vicarious activities in school and The Deputy and The King between them ran a number of teams, including two football teams, a nine-a-side rugby team, a cricket team, boys and girl's athletic squads, swimming teams, girl's netball and even a mixed chess team! They organised the city wide competitions in football, 'B' team football, rugby and athletics. During the course of one of the latter, Rudgey, having been pressed into service as a race-starting official and being pestered continually, mostly by irritating little boys, aimed his starting pistol at one of them and fired off several blanks, before being restrained by a concerned colleague, who, unlike 'The King', The Deputy and others, had failed to see what used to be called 'the funny side of it'. Notwithstanding Arnold's maxim at Edward Street, The King and The Deputy became somewhat obsessed with winning and Leafold actually triumphed regularly in a number of disciplines and competitions. Big H shared this preoccupation with sport, and although his role in the city with his 'blazer and tie' buddies was devoted almost entirely to the selection of the secondary age city football teams, he did take it upon himself to arrange the annual trip to Wembley for the Schoolboy International. On these occasions, he would regulate the boys with regimental authoritarianism, directing them when and where to buy their 'favours', as he called rosettes, and souvenirs, when to use the toilets and where to sit and when to stand, notably when the band struck up the national anthem, though not that of the opposition. On a memorably hot London day, The King and The Deputy had barely settled into their seats behind Big H, holding foaming pots of beer, when he ordered the assembly to its feet and the embarrassed pair had to do their best to stand erect and mouth the words of the dreary English anthem, whilst taking care not to spill the beer on Big H's brylcreem laden head immediately below them.

The King had another talent. He was a gifted musician and had performed with a 'pop' group. The group was singularly unsuccessful, but The King's school-based operettas were received with acclaim by colleagues, parents and friends. The most outstanding of The King's' works was 'Captain Jack', an authentic tale of a nineteenth century North American Indian chief, whose real name was Kintpuash. The story tells of the misfortunes of the Modoc Indians and the brutality of the United States cavalry ending with the execution of Kintpuash and the destruction of the Modocs. A truly lavish and moving adventure and not in the same genre as 'Rock Bottington', The King's parody of 'Dick Whittington'. The role of The Deputy in all this was as prompt, costume organiser and stage hand, but it was a privilege and, as a kindly inspector said to him following a performance of 'Captain Jack', "Children forget lots of things, but they always remember being involved in things that give them opportunities, value their contribution and esteem their worth." The Deputy didn't need to be told that, but he politely concurred. "That's true," he said.

Now, the ambition that had begun to flower in The Deputy didn't extend to wanting to aspire to the role of head teacher, until two things occurred. The first of these was meeting more and more of the dilettantes, who were already performing in it. Accordingly, The Deputy, encouraged by the perdurable example of The King, began to take professional development seriously and do everything he feasibly could to equip himself for promotion. He often promulgated this with The King and together, they attended lectures, courses and seminars deemed appropriate for those aspiring to educational leadership. It has to be admitted, that some of these had more to do with being able to include the title of the lecture or course and the name of the provider on curriculum vitae and application forms than with the value of their content. In these circumstances, The King might suggest that they pretend to have a fight or walk into the auditorium and begin the lecture as though it were they who were giving it with the idea that when the genuine tutor arrived, they would feign shock and outrage. These divagations, never realised, were supposed to make their lives a little more interesting. The city education authority offered its own programme of courses for its teaching force, some of them residential. These afforded opportunities to get close to local authority 'inspectors', later rebranded as 'advisers' and later still 'consultants', to impress them. This, The Deputy found very difficult, but he and The King did manage to build up quite an impressive chronology of information to list in the section headed 'courses of further study'. The second thing was when Rudgey became a head teacher.

The Deputy, inexplicably and needlessly, decided to add a second degree to his qualifications and enrolled on a Master of Education degree at the university, the real one, not the polytechnic that later became a 'B' list university as higher education was expanded to further politicians' careers and cheapen and degrade the entire system. Following three years of part time study, including lectures and examinations in such esoteric subjects as sociology, educational psychology, social psychology and goodness knows what else, The Deputy was able to add the letters MED to his signature and at the end of his name on letter-heads but, of course, he never did. Highlights included the day a dour lecturer in sociology collected his papers into a sheaf, tapped them on the lectern and closed the session with, "Well, I seem to have read my notes in the wrong order, but no-one appears to have noticed" and strode from the classroom, the briskest thing he ever did, before his bemused audience could say anything. Attendance was mandatory, along with passing the exams and writing a research dissertation. A few minutes prior to the opening lecture in social psychology, an eccentric-looking man with joined eyebrows and wearing a red and black sweater leaned over to The Deputy and whispered, "Look here, old chap, I'm Litnovski. Just write your signature on this piece of paper and I'll write mine for you. If you can't make it to one of these lectures, I'll sign you in if you'll do the same for me." The Deputy, eager to be complaisant, replied, "Okay, fair enough." He never heard from Litnovski again, except for a note about six months later, mysteriously delivered by another student and saying, "I live in the hope that you are still signing me into the social psychology lectures – Litnovski." The Deputy was.

In order to acquire the skills necessary to analyse the data in his chosen research dissertation, it was essential that The Deputy attended lectures on basic statistical analysis. It was also important that he didn't miss playing for The Immaculate Conception Pirates Basketball club. The fixtures clashed with the basic statistics course, so instead, he decided to risk the advanced statistical analysis course. This course proved to be a salutary lesson in humility and how it must feel to be in a remedial class or in any class if you're particularly thick! For the first twenty minutes of each session, The Deputy would lean forward, wide-eyed, and concentrate hard on trying to keep up with what was going on, before slumping back into his seat exhausted, 'switching off', avoiding eye-contact with the speaker, who droned relentlessly on, and escaping at the close with as much dignity as he could manage. "Small wonder the 'D streamers' are vandals," he thought, as he hurried off to the gymnasium to get his own back on the basketball and on the opposition. The Deputy, somehow, acquired enough understanding of, or how to use without understanding, analysis of variance, 'lines of best fit', and regression analysis and so on, so that he was able to investigate "The Effects of Gender, Intelligence and Personality on a block Design Intelligence Test." The Deputy had a young daughter by then and he and she spent many relatively contented and peaceful hours in the city library, she with her crayons and colouring books and he summarising previous research and producing a tome of over one hundred and eighty pages. The qualification was duly awarded. It proved to be of little use, unless it impressed prospective employers or usefully contributed to the sum of knowledge on intelligence testing, neither of which The Deputy had any way of knowing. He did have the satisfaction, if that's what it was, of replying, "Just the two," when a young colleague enquired as to whether he had a degree, those being the days when not every teacher had one. He promised himself that, one day, he would return to the university with his child, go and have lunch in the 'Boffin Bar' again and visit the university library to ascertain how many times his work had been taken from its shelves. Of course, he never did.

What he did do, however, was to start applying for head teacher posts. It is astonishing how quickly the art of form filling and writing the covering 'letter of application' can be mastered, so that most reasonably intelligent candidates are able to use the language and expound their peculiar philosophy of education in such a way that impresses the quidnuncs and the 'princes of darkness' that inhabit the alleys of educational opportunity. The Deputy began to get interviews for approximately every fourth job he applied for and, ultimately, was successful in getting a headship in a neighbouring town, which flabbergasted his mother-in-law, delighted his wife, pleased most of his friends and was, a friendly inspector asseverated, "Probably a good thing; a fresh start in a different education authority."

Chapter 14

THE HEAD TEACHER (Part 1)

"Don't change a thing for the first year!" Newly appointed head teachers often receive this kind of advice. They always ignore it.

The nomenclature Edgemount was entirely suitable for the Head Teacher's new school, standing, as it did, on the rim of a hill overlooking a hamlet-like suburb of the town with an expanse of fields to the rear. The situation was an odd one, in that, although the setting was primarily an urban one, the school field did get invaded from time to time by animals such as sheep and other livestock. On one notable occasion, the Head Teacher, accompanied by two boys, set out to drive away two sizeable horses which had strayed on to the field through a broken fence section. "You two circle round behind them," said the Head Teacher, "and they'll move down the field towards me. Don't make too much noise, we don't want to frighten them." The two boys, delighting in the drover role but also a fraction wary, kept close to the boundary of the field as they moved cautiously into position. Once behind the horses, which were grazing contentedly, and at what they considered to be a safe distance, the boys began to clap their hands, jump up and down and whoop and shout loudly with the result that the startled horses set off at a gallop towards the Head Teacher who, petrified but unwilling to show it, froze as the two creatures raced towards him. The horses divided as they neared him and passed at pace, one on each side, the closest of them brushing the Head Teacher's shoulder as it careered towards the gap in the fence and across the adjacent field. It wasn't so much the proximity of the beasts that frightened the Head Teacher, he barely noticed the touch and the warmth of their breath, it was the bared teeth and the cavernous nostrils that alarmed him! "Well done, boys," the Head Teacher called, "you can go back to class now. Thanks!" Thinking that he'd have been better to have asked a couple of girls, he followed the boys into the building, made for his and the secretary's shared office — fortunately, she wasn't there at the time — threw himself into the large swivel chair behind his desk, lit a cigarette and inhaled gratefully. He would also have gone into his secret store of whisky carefully hidden in one of the cupboards but he hadn't yet installed it.

The deputy at Edgemount, Max, was another quite gifted man. He had applied for the headship, but hadn't been shortlisted, his adviser having told him that he wasn't quite ready for promotion. He bore the Head Teacher no ill-will, quite the reverse, in fact, and was entirely helpful and supportive throughout the Head Teacher's time there. Max wasn't in the same league as The King but he too had been in a pop group of sorts and he also specialised in writing and producing musical plays, utilising all the oldest children and exploiting any talent amongst the teachers and other staff that was available. A succession of these events included 'Mohr and the Mouse', a re-working of the story of how the carol 'Silent Night' came to be written and performed in the early nineteenth century, when Joseph Mohr, a German priest, took his lyrics to the local schoolmaster and organist who produced the tune. In Max's slightly apocryphal version, Mohr was the local priest who wrote the words and the music, which was arranged for the guitar because a mouse had chewed through the church organ pipes. Another was more accurately based upon Dickens's classic tale of redemption, featuring Ebenezer Scrooge singing 'I Don't Like Christmas' to the tune of the Boomtown Rats hit, 'I Don't Like Mondays', whilst a third, equally stunning and called "Carrots" after the red-haired waif who tragically died because the orphanage was full to capacity, romanticised the story of Doctor Thomas John Barnardo and the origin of "No Destitute Child Ever Refused Admission". Max, when approached by a scruffy twentieth century 'waif' about costumes, replied with laudable restraint and a gentle smile, "Just come as you are". And, finally, 'The Little Match Girl' with its melancholic theme and heart-breaking finale. As on previous occasions for both Max's and 'The King's' extravaganzas, The Head Teacher had a supporting role in costumes, props or lighting and the parents were as overwhelmed as they always are. Max could make films too! He had a camera and a projector and he made a brilliant film called 'The Phantom Litter Dropper Snatcher' with lots of tricks, such as the phantom disappearing and re-appearing on the school roof to spot and swoop down to snatch recalcitrant litter droppers from the playground. Where *was* 'health and safety' then? Max was also good at something called 'display'. He was clever with glue, nails and screws and could erect hardboard display boards on any kind of surface and on any kind of wall. He might, from time to time, accidentally nail the odd book to the wall, but with a few bits of sugar paper and children's pictures, he could transform a school hall into a nineteenth century arcade, a 'cowboy' backdrop for the parent Teacher Association hoe down or a Christmas themed exhibition, including a nativity scene to bring tears to your eyes and three wise men arriving, as if from nowhere, with the fourth, Artaban, heading in the opposite direction for added interest!

Edgemount's teachers were nothing if not traditional. All the more reason for not following the standard recommendation concerning the first year of headship, the converse of which was, and probably still is, 'strike now, or at least before the iron freezes!' Winnie, with sizeable irony, taught what she called the 'babies' classes in a manner more appropriate to a 'prep school'. Her notion of the teaching of phonics, for example, began with 'A' and progressed to 'Z'. No wonder the teacher in the next class up, age wise, promptly resigned when asked to work with Winnie in two 'vertically grouped' year one and year two infant classes for the following academic year! Little need be said about Doris, in 'top infants' whilst the young teacher in 'junior one', having surprised the Head Teacher by expressing support for private health care, something he considered to be 'beyond the Pale', surprised him again by struggling to implement a 'modern maths' scheme he'd arbitrarily introduced. A 'moveable feast', as she expressed it, of 'concrete operations' that enshrined the idea that the understanding of processes in mathematics was an essential precursor to genuine learning, if 'learning' was to be defined as 'a more or less permanent change in behaviour' as many experts averred. An unwise neologism, as it turned out, in view of the major area of discontinuity represented by the teacher in the next class up, whose opinions on practically everything would not have disappointed Genghis Khan! "She looks a bit like him too," The Head Teacher pondered as she adumbrated her opposition to anything with the slightest hint of progressive education about it during staff-room interludes. Jen, in the third year junior class, was okay if a trifle weird. She unsettled the Head Teacher with her 'bohemian' attire and her habit of sitting cross-legged on the floor surrounded by children. Max, who eventually and deservedly, became the head teacher of a small school not far from Edgemount, took the oldest class of ten to eleven-year-olds and was broadly supportive of the Head Teacher's innovations, which included a new reading scheme and the mathematics that was being trialled in the junior one class in direct contrast to the 'trick and tick' teaching supported by the rote learning beloved of 'traditionalists'. In return, the Head Teacher endorsed Max's dedication to 'special needs' children and helped him with his applications for promotion. This usually took the form of a 'mock interview', which they refined into as formal a procedure as possible. Max, in role as candidate, sat on an upright school chair a yard or two from the Head Teacher's desk facing the desk, or coffee table if the simulation was being enacted at Max's or The Head Teacher's house, behind which were placed a row of three or four chairs, all slightly higher than Max's, enabling The Head teacher to occupy a central position dominating proceedings, whilst flanked by an enormous five feet tall toy rabbit that his mother had made for a seaside carnival procession some years previously and, if no real person was available, such as either or both of their respective spouses, a large cardboard cut-out of an ageing female with facial hair posing as an education officer. Generally, the head teacher would introduce the 'Reverend Rabbit', the chair of governors of the imaginary primary school and Mrs Huntingdon-Browne from County Hall, to 'set the scene' and relax the candidate before proceeding to demand that Mr Max "tell the governors" all about his position on the primary curriculum, 'special needs' children, 'parental involvement' or whatever the latest initiatives were in the days when primary education still benefitted from Lady Plowden's 1966 report extolling the virtues of a 'broad and balanced curriculum' that subsequently enriched the lives of generations of pupils and teachers. Max would respond as best he could and The Head Teacher would evaluate Max's responses unless, as often happened when the women were present, one or other of the participants began to chuckle and the whole charade descended into farce, another bottle was opened and they'd all watch a black and white porn film on Max's sixteen millimetre projector and collapse laughing at that instead, whilst secretly marvelling at the staying power of some of the 'actors'! Whilst Max's later promotion may have owed something to these sessions, as The Head Teacher always claimed, it remains a matter of debate whether they were a critical factor. Interestingly, acting upon the advice of another 'significant other' in his educational life, The Head Teacher later abandoned sitting behind a large desk in a threatening position, in favour of shoving the desk against a wall and turning to encompass whomsoever was in the room in a more democratic and agreeable manner.

One of the head's duties in the days before online banking, was to take any monies collected to the bank if the caretaker couldn't, or wouldn't, do so. This included such things as dinner money, school funds, petty cash and collections for the Christmas Panto, theatre visits, and summer camps and so on. Some teachers, like The King at Leafold had their own idiosyncratic collection and banking system, which generally resulted in them living off the 'Alice in Wonderland' money for half a term until the time came to pay for the tickets, at which point, their personal bank account would take what The Head Teacher's dad used to call "a nasty knock". Not that The Head Teacher's dad ever had something as avant-garde as a bank account, but he did know what banks were for, because his nephew, The Head Teacher's cousin, was a bank manager in the days when banks were honest institutions working for the public good, instead of a bunch of brigands working for their own enrichment, as is the case at present. As you'd expect, school bank accounts were subject then to strict rules and still are, so that only two or three designated signatories, in the case of Edgemount the school secretary Mrs Leftwrinckle and Max, are permitted. Almost every week, The Head Teacher would forget to ask one or other of these two to sign the 'paying in book', or the cheques, and would arrive at the bank and be standing in one of the inevitable lengthy queues, something for which banks and other public places are still deservedly criticised, and realise that he would again have to forge Max's signature or go back to school and get it. He opted for the former course so often that, on the infrequent occasions that Max deputised on 'bank duty' he, Max, had to carefully copy the Head Teacher's version of his, Max's, signature! On one of these nefarious missions, The Head Teacher was interrupted in this activity by a man in a suit he took to be a bank employee. Fearing he'd been 'caught in the act', The Head Teacher's confusion turned to relief when the man turned out to be some sort of representative, who with the connivance of the bank, was selling an early genus of tax evasion that is now very common amongst the more generously remunerated classes. "Do you think you should be paying less tax?" was the man in the suit's opening gambit. This would have normally outraged The Head Teacher but, relieved that he hadn't been exposed as a forger, he replied, "No, I believe that we should all pay our fair share of taxes for the common good. Otherwise, how would schools and hospitals be funded? And…" He got no further, for the 'suit', typically avoiding eye contact, had glanced down at the Fabian Society tie The Head Teacher had routinely taken to wearing and its woven precept, "The inevitability of Socialism" and promptly lost interest.

Most primary schools have, for many years, tried hard to become involved in their communities even if that involvement extends only as far as encouraging the parents of their scholars to support the school, to help out at functions such as Sports Day, concerts and fund-raising ventures, to offer whatever skills they may have to help in classrooms, with football teams, to accompany school cultural, educational and recreational trips and even to make minor improvements to the fabric of the school. Thus, nearly all schools have a 'Parent's Association', or better still, a 'Parent-Teachers

Association', or best of all, a 'Parent, Teachers and Friends Association' thereby drawing upon all and sundry in their neighbourhoods. Edgemount was no exception. Now, it is a fact that most of the active participants in these 'associations' are women. It is also true that they become active in the 'Parent-Teacher Association' or PTA for short, for one or more of several possible reasons placing them in several distinct categories. Firstly, they join in because they want to secure advantages for their own children, secondly, because they want to ensure that their children don't 'miss out' on any opportunities or extra-curricular activities, thirdly, because they are financially reasonably well-off and have little to do to occupy their time and fourthly, because they are lonely and need some company. There may even be some who genuinely wish to offer their talents for the general well-being of all the children but these are very rare and it was the fourth category that was significant at Edgemount.

One day, late in the Autumn Term, The Head Teacher was conversing at the school doors with a particularly spirited PTA member called Mrs Storm, when a close friend of The Head Teacher arrived unexpectedly, strode up the short slope from the main gate, ignored Mrs Storm, looked at The Head Teacher with lips like a corpse and eyes as hard as marbles, thrust a package at The Head Teacher and said, "Here's your birthday present!" She then spun around and strode away as rapidly as she'd appeared, leaving The Head Teacher staring after her in stunned silence. Eventually, The Head Teacher turned to look at Mrs Storm. Her eyes had narrowed very slightly and there was an almost imperceptible smirk on her face, as though she'd just drawn certain conclusions concerning The Head Teacher's private life that would be worth sharing with those friends that she could trust — if any!

Within days, Mrs Storm called upon The Head Teacher again, taking care, as it transpired later, to choose a day and a time when Mrs Leftwrinkle, a woman most inappropriately named in light of her girth, her right-wing affiliations and her habit of sticking old pennies to her dog's ears with sellotape in order to make them droop sufficiently appealingly to make entering the animal for 'county set' dog shows a viable proposition, was off duty. Mrs Storm's pretext had something to do with costumes for the school play, and in no time at all, she had accepted the invitation of The Head Teacher to visit the stockroom where such things were stored. There, she turned to The Head Teacher, smiled engagingly and said, "I've been trying to get you into bed for months!" The Head Teacher did his utmost to conceal the fact that this was, for him, an entirely unexpected turn of events and, there being no bed available in the stock room and in even less time than it took to get there, the relationship was cemented comfortably, if rather irreverently, amongst the heaps of shepherd's costumes, upon the flowing robes of Joseph, Artaban and the magi.

Few men become members of PTAs because they have a genuine and altruistic interest, but more often, because their egos are bigger than their brains and because they want to show off. Normally, there aren't many such men but, together with the rather more numerous dissatisfied women, there are often sufficient to ensure that the PTA meets fairly regularly, often retires to a local hostelry and, equally often, organises events with opportunities for all sorts of social intercourse. Edgemount PTA was typical and once Sadie Storm's "year for teachers", as she candidly expressed it, had expired, The Head Teacher moved on to enjoy the favours of Georgia, who was on the point of leaving her husband, but later returned to him so that The Head Teacher, although he was earnest in his affection for her, could play the part of the abandoned lover for all he was worth. And then there was Laura, whose husband 'worked away', so that there were ample chances to exploit the realisation that, as she put it, she and The Head Teacher "wanted each other". The Head Teacher's trysts in darkened stockrooms, the staffroom, Max's house and elsewhere began to acquire almost as much notoriety as the County Councillor Chair of Edgemount's governing body, whose reputation suffered grievously following the sighting of a naked man in full flight across the moor beyond her isolated cottage.

This isn't to say that The Head Teacher had entirely lost his moral compass! Along with Max, Jen and occasionally others, he spent an enormous amount of time furthering the interests of Edgemount children, pursuing runaways across the wet grass on the council estate, attending to the injuries and hospitalisation of certain boys and making a religion of always being present if an Edgemount child was involved in something from a swimming competition to a singing event and lots more besides. Indeed, it was at Edgemount that The Head Teacher first became involved with Local Authority Social Services. It is the duty of Social Workers to look after those children and their families that are considered to be what used to be described as 'at risk', to support those families and to intervene appropriately when things went wrong and especially when children were in any danger of harm. The Head Teacher discovered that Social Workers, with the exception of those that suffer from cognitive distortion and the resultant verbal diarrhoea, are decent, dedicated and hard-working professionals, who get no praise when things go well and loads of blame when things go wrong. The Head Teacher had also become intimate, in the sense of friendly and close, with a group of nuns living on the council estate and serving its inhabitants. Nuns have also, in recent years, earned some unwelcome notoriety, but whilst these were pragmatic, they were also practical and pious. Their role was to help and support poor and needy families and their children, rather than exploit, persecute and abuse them. At least that is what Max and The Head Teacher assumed, having no evidence that it was otherwise. Both The Head Teacher and Max worked closely with the nuns, mostly on utilitarian tasks such as replacing broken windows, painting, redecorating homes and supervising young offenders doing community service as an alternative to a fine or imprisonment. In return, the nuns would visit Edgemount, bringing cakes and biscuits they'd made, which Max and The Head Teacher shared with their colleagues in the staffroom.

Thus, the reputation of The Head Teacher was what might be termed 'mixed' and, having made some quite successful innovations at Edgemount and been asked to speak on local authority professional development courses for teachers, his educational achievements were reasonable. The combination of lothario and leader was, however, becoming untenable and The Head Teacher, correctly sensing that he should move not just to a new school, but to a new town, began to seek a fresh challenge and a bigger school in many and varied places.

Consistent with his previous experience, The Head Teacher was successful in obtaining interviews for approximately one in four of the posts for which he applied, the big difference now was that the interviews were far more rigorous and demanding. One of the first of these was significant, in that it provided a lesson that The Head Teacher would never forget. The several candidates gathered at the school, a large urban primary, at the beginning of the school day which, fortunately, happened to be the day of the monthly 'Pet's Assembly'! Immediately upon reaching the sanctuary of the staffroom to await their turn for interview, having run a gauntlet of barking dogs, screeching parrots, hissing cats, snakes and other beasts, fowl and fish, the candidates flung themselves into armchairs and vowed — almost in unison — that the demise of "Pet's Assembly" was to be the first change they'd introduce if offered the post! The general rule about introducing animals into schools is, "Don't!" The Head Teacher remembered only too well how the metalwork teacher at The Copse had tried to help an errant boy come into school more often and stay for rather longer by getting Henry, the Science teacher, to put the lad in charge of feeding the laboratory mice, an appointment that ended with all the mice dead in the gutter and the boy in the hands of the police! He could recall, also, the ceremonial cremation of the school hamster at Edgemount. The lifeless creature's cadaver, having just been shuffled from the blade of the caretaker's coal shovel into the school central heating boiler, began to curl and twist in the heat occasioning one of the two children privileged to witness this solemn event, believing the animal to be still alive, to burst into tears and the other into giggles! These memories had already made The Head Teacher an implacable opponent of animals in schools. Although it was modified later by a certain colleague, whom he allowed to bring a rabbit named Farabundo into his school, closely followed by a guinea pig called Rosa, his opinion remained that it was better to take the children to the animals than the animals to the children.

In the event, The Head Teacher didn't get the opportunity of ending the 'Pet's Assembly', wherever it was! However, head teacher appointments were not yet two-day bonanzas of panels, presentations, pageants and power points, so that his edification and knowledge rendered him able to go before panels of governors and local education authority (LEA) advisers with some confidence and his search was enhanced by the increasing numbers of ageing head teachers seeking to take early retirement. Sometimes, a retirement was conditional upon the existing head teacher's replacement accruing no additional cost to the LEA and the fact that, as a relatively youthful candidate, The Head Teacher was comparatively inexpensive added to his potential and he was offered a headship at a very large primary school in a modestly sized and historic town, close to the seaside, about sixty miles further to the North. Whilst this dismayed The Head Teacher's parents, particularly his mother, both of whom had been born and bred on the South coast and thought that anything north of Yeovil must be inhabited by Hottentots, and compounded their despair arising from their son's previous marriage to someone from the North-West, where the natives were reputed to be miserly and speak like imbeciles, it did represent quite a good career move for The Head Teacher. He accepted the post.

Chapter 15

THE HEADTEACHER (Part 2)

Modestly sized historic towns are not always what they seem to be and this one had considerable pockets of atrophy, including run-down council estates and crumbling terraces. As for the populace, in some important respects, the prejudices of The Head Teacher's parents were not misplaced!

The school, inappositely called Wheatfield's, had been constructed in 1939 and, whilst it did have quite a big grassed area sloping away from the rear, was as remote from the wheat and the fields, which may once have graced its environs as the surrounding social housing was from the weed-strewn flower beds and lawns and the decaying grandeur of the nineteenth century mansion in the local park; also called Wheatfield's. The Head Teacher was only the third head of the school, the first two having served for the first forty-four years of its existence between them, almost equally, and had established a very good reputation, such that it was oversubscribed. The oversubscription led the parents of unsuccessful applicants to exploit the 'appeals' system, which was weighted in favour of moving the problem of a shortage of primary school places away from the desks of LEA education officers and on to the desks of the local head teachers — as a sympathetic but helpless LEA adviser said to The Head Teacher, "Bums on seats comes before the quality of educational provision." The single admission criterion at the time of The Head Teacher's arrival was simply 'first-come first served', which had the advantage, from the perspective of the first two heads and most of the governors, that the school filled up in the first instance with the children of those parents who realised what the situation was and acted early enough to ensure that their offspring got places and those who 'left it late', the "dross" as one of The Head Teacher's predecessors described them, were passed on to the next school down the road; the equally inappropriately named Riverside. There was plenty of "dross" to go round however and quite a lot ended up at Wheatfield's too.

Quite a lot became a majority of over seventy-five per cent as The Head Teacher persuaded his governing body to amend the admissions criteria to reflect residential proximity to the school and to include measures of deprivation and disadvantage. In fact, The Head Teacher and the head of Riverside quickly adopted a joint policy that resulted in much fairer access to both schools, but tended to penalise Wheatfield's in terms of both the academic potential, or rather the lack of it, and the demanding nature of incoming pupils. This was exacerbated by the increased numbers following appeals, but would have mattered less had the dreadful Eleven Plus not still been operating in the town owing to the powerful lobby of the governors and parents of the single sex girls grammar school and the even more exclusive semi-private boys grammar school, the alma mater of a Conservative government minister, who was just as famous for the bedding of his secretary as for the magic associated with his 'old school tie'! The Head Teacher was, of course, totally opposed to selection, but had been assured at interview that the LEA planned to introduce a scheme of reorganisation into comprehensive secondary schools. It never happened and now, it never will.

Organisation at Wheatfield's reflected the omnipresent inequities of the eleven-plus examination. All the 'junior' classes, those that would, in the ever-changing language of today, be termed years three to six, were divided into 'A' streams' and 'B streams'. There being sixty to seventy children in each age group, they were split into two groups of thirty-two or thirty-three according to whether they were, again in the stilted language of The Headteacher's predecessor, 'quicker' or 'slower'. The dividing line between these two groups was entirely based upon having roughly equal numbers in each class, rather than upon any meaningful definition of their ability or potential and this kind of arbitrary distinction, of course, happened in thousands of primary schools all over the country and in some still does. At the same time as he had expressed his opposition to the eleven plus, The Head Teacher had unequivocally undertaken to end streaming and, urged on by, among others, the head at Riverside who shared his progressive educational philosophy and soon became a friend as well as a colleague, determined to do so quickly. That meant ignoring the usual caveats about not frightening the existing staff by moving too rapidly and, instead, following the aforementioned apophthegm to 'strike while the iron is hot, or at least before it freezes'!

As it happened, had The Head Teacher not acted swiftly, he might have been thwarted by the incipient opposition in the staff-room expressed regularly by the senior staff, most notably, the deputy, Colin, and the 'head of infants' as the women in charge of the reception and year one and two classes were then described. Long before all this, an old friend of The Head Teacher's had joined the army, an act which quickly ended the friendship, but not before the former had described the military distinction between non-commissioned and commissioned officers and the concomitant traits of 'NCO tendencies' and 'officer qualities'. The educational setting might not be very much like that of the military, but Colin, although he could display the latter, was much stronger on the former, so that The Head Teacher was ultimately constrained to request that Colin behave less like a sergeant major and more like a lieutenant. As time went on, whenever The Head Teacher wanted to introduce something new or to support a member-of-staff in a fresh venture, or to resolve an issue affecting curriculum or organisation, the first and most crucial introspection was always, "How can I get this past Colin?" Colin told The Head Teacher that he had applied for the headship at Wheatfield's, he hadn't been shortlisted and he declared himself "willing to learn." He wasn't, or possibly couldn't, and neither could most of the other teachers, three of whom The Head Teacher came upon in a huddle in the infant corridor one day. "Is this a rehearsal for 'Macbeth'?" he asked, but got only silence and quizzical gazes in reply.

Being a head teacher can be a lonely occupation and on this occasion, like others until he became less sensitive to and more immured from criticism, the fear of criticism and the fear of failure filled him with dread. Schools, of course, are just institutions, the same as banks, offices, factories, shops and other workplaces with the usual range of individuals. Teachers, however, are distinctive in that they tend to be very ordinary or very special. One of the former, an eminently forgettable and commonplace practitioner, persuaded the 'Head of Infants' to seek an audience with the new head to ask for a ruling upon whether the desks in each classroom should be arranged in rows, as they then were, or re-organised into groups, as the staff suspected that the new head would prefer. The Head Teacher refused to give a direction at first but, in the end, was prevailed upon to rule, because of the absence of a firm line from the top concerning the issue was causing distress and uncertainty. So, as expected, The Head Teacher pronounced in favour of groups. It made no difference to the archaic teaching styles, but at least it looked more up-to-date.

Hugh had worked in a bank and, therefore, fell into the ordinary category, but he had also been the manager of a supermarket, when he'd detained an elderly shoplifter only to discover, whilst awaiting the arrival of the police, that the felon had offloaded the stolen goods! With inestimable resourcefulness, Hugh diverted the attention of the criminal and the shop's security person and planted a large tin of white gloss paint in the unsuspecting detainee's rucksack! It didn't occur to the police to wonder what the unfortunate old tramp wanted with a ten litre can of paint and justice took its inevitable course. Hugh was a decent enough person though and he had the good grace to tell The Head Teacher that he regretted the incident now that he was older and wiser. Unfortunately, Hugh was to become one of the first casualties of the policies of the Conservative and New Labour governments of the late twentieth and early twenty-first centuries, which applied 'market forces' to education and turned schools into mini corporations in competition with each other for pupils and were financed according to how many 'customers' they could attract. What did it for Hugh, who had been a strong and popular, if rather old-fashioned teacher, and, as time went on, lots of other perfectly capable pedagogues, was the relentless pressure of targets and school league tables based upon tests, by any scientific standard utterly invalid and unreliable and the never-ending revision of the curriculum — it was said that the only constant in teachers lives was change — and the ever-present threat of a visit from the new 'educational Stasi' called Ofsted; the so-called Office for Standards in Education. Ofsted was a Tory government invention made up of 'educational prostitutes', many of whom would not have lasted half an hour in the classes of the people they were inspecting. Hugh ended up in a grocery shop, whilst Ofsted flourished under successive Conservative and New Labour governments. Whatever makes governments and ministers of education believe that arrogance, bullying and threats were the way to incentivise a workforce remains a mystery, unless, as usual, their principal objective was short-term, if fallacious, demonstrable educational gains as revealed by the specious unscientific quasi-test scores that would be sufficient to ensure the advancement of their personal careers and their return at the next General Election.

Those who recall George Bernard Shaw's rather unjust adage, "He who can, does. He who cannot, teaches" and the perceptive additions by later scholars, "He who cannot teach, teaches teachers" and "He who cannot teach teachers, does educational research" will not be surprised to learn that an additional, final, line was appended, "He who can do none of these things, becomes an Ofsted inspector."

Other members of the teaching staff at Wheatfield's were more resilient. Jenny had come late into teaching and she was a fairly resolute character, who coped with the successive waves of government enterprise and their impact upon her professional security. She managed to withstand most of it but, in spite of her obvious steadfastness, she decided to resume smoking. The Head Teacher, passing Jenny's classroom one evening after school, stopped for a chat. He became fixated by the lettering and words in large, careful cursive script on her blackboard immediately behind her as they conversed. 'ph', 'f' and 'gh' appeared at the top with some examples of words such as 'photograph', 'fish' and 'cough'. What fascinated The Head Teacher was written at the foot of it all in a rather less mature hand — 'ghuck ophph'!

Tom, a genial fellow, who, like Jenny, had qualified late after a career in the merchant navy was used to bending before rather than resisting ill-winds. Tom was a stalwart of the NAS, the aforesaid organisation for those teachers with few principles beyond self-protection and defence of pay and conditions, and he was one of the first to recognise that The Head Teacher, a member and activist of the only teachers union that did have policies to protect children and their teachers and policies for the better development of education and policies for professional teacher unity that might have saved it from the relentless government onslaught, would be fair. Support was also forthcoming from Belinda, about thirty years old, pert, blonde and loquacious, rather like an educational Cindy Doll. Once the new head had become a familiar figure, in the sense of routine and cordial, it didn't take long for Belinda to approach him after school one day on a rather sensitive and private matter. "I've only ever had my Robby," she told him coyly, "if I was to have someone else, it would have to be someone I respected." This encouraged The Head Teacher to identify a meeting to which he could accompany Belinda. She was the coordinator for mathematics, so a gathering at County Hall of primary school maths specialists served the purpose, after which they drove in his car to a secluded local beauty spot ostensibly to chat, but both knew the reality. "What happens?" She asked. It having been many years since The Head Teacher had been in such a position, he wasn't all that sure, but he responded with, "Well, most of the action takes place in the passenger seat. It may be over quite quickly the first time." It was.

Some of the others, like Miss Monaghan or 'Moaning Minnie' as The Head Teacher privately dubbed her were broadly supportive of The Head Teacher's aims and values. 'Minnie' was a good teacher and a committed trade unionist, but just about as miserable as it was possible to be. She'd been appointed in the term immediately before The Head Teacher took over along with an ambitious young man, who would have been head teacher material if he'd been a bit brighter and, because of that, was malleable and cooperative. It was a source of considerable irritation to The Head Teacher that these posts had not been filled on a temporary basis, so that he could have started at Wheatfield's by making a couple of key permanent appointments himself. It would have been useful experience too for he'd only had the opportunity to do so once previously, at Edgemount, when over one hundred and fifty applications had to be sifted and short-listed and his abiding memory was of a young and beguiling newly qualified candidate with an enchanting smile. The post went to a more experienced woman but, as he watched the youngster skip away down the school drive, The Head Teacher yearned to open the office window, lean out, call to her and say, "Wait! We've reconsidered. We want you. The job is yours!" He didn't.

Fortunately, notwithstanding "Moaning Minnie" and the young man, he didn't have to wait long for similar opportunities at Wheatfield's, as further teaching vacancies arose and the first of these had lasting implications. The school needed an infant teacher. Politely spurning what was to become Colin's recurrent suggestion that they advertise locally, shortlist and appoint some experienced old crone of his acquaintance, The Head Teacher insisted upon advertising all vacancies nationally to draw upon the widest possible pool of talent and to attract the most gifted candidates. He also obtained the agreement of the Chairman of the governing Body of the school, a solid and traditional Labour and Co-operative devotee, that for every post, at least one newly qualified person should be short-listed. It has to be said that The Head Teacher, although at first he tended to do most of it himself, was always scrupulously honest, going to enormous pains to be fair and rigorous in the advertising, long–listing, which involved reducing the applicants to manageable numbers for more consideration, as well as short-listing, interviewing and selection processes. And he took care to get the panel of governors to include several 'reserves', in order of preference, so that, in the event of any of their selections dropping out, the short list could be readily augmented. On this first occasion, five people were short-listed, all women but, when one dropped out, The Head Teacher requested the permission of his 'Chair' to call upon the first of the two or three 'reserves', who was, as it happened, newly qualified. As is customary, all the candidates were invited to make appointments to see the school before interview and the 'reserve' turned out to be a stunning, raven-haired young woman, who clearly knew more about the school and The Head Teacher's philosophy than the rest. She was a clever girl and was astute enough to recognise palpable left wing tendencies, besides being by far the best at interview and was offered, and accepted, the post. The Head Teacher didn't realise the full significance of all this until much, much later.

Shortly afterwards, completely by chance, The Head Teacher visited his local for a dinner time pint of bitter. He was alone in the public bar and began chatting to the bar maid, a delectable and affable young woman with an accent that made The Head Teacher suspect that she'd break into "Blaydon Races" at any second and that revealed her origins more clearly than the labels on food products hide theirs! They discussed the nuances of television soap operas and he thought to himself, "This kid is pretty smart, what's she doing working behind the bar on this estate?" It transpired that the barmaid was a student working part-time, would shortly qualify as a teacher and was busy applying for a full-time job in teaching. The Head Teacher mentioned a vacancy that was coming up at Wheatfield's. The young barmaid applied and joined him there the following autumn. Two more young female teachers soon followed and salacious rumours began to circulate about the advantages of wearing red knickers for interviews at Wheatfields. These were nothing but egregious whispers, however, for The Head Teacher, whilst he didn't always know quite how to conduct himself, he did know how to conduct the selection of teachers in a manner that was fair and objective; 'proper order'! The Head Teacher joked that he was their mentor and these were his "creatures", that he had taken "lumps of clay" to mould into preceptors of exceptional practice and each year, usually during the 'staff night out' and after imbibing more than he should, he would announce the annual "I owe it all to The Head Teacher" awards. Some of his acolytes, especially those who had worked in other schools and did not feel entirely indebted to The Head Teacher for the fact that they were able to keep up their mortgage payments, resisted the "creature" nomenclature, but in The Head Teacher's version of life, they all came around in the end to conceding that they owed everything to him. This is not to say, by any means, that The Head Teacher was intimate with all his "creatures", just two; and one who, with admirable forbearance, he managed to resist because, at the time, he was committed to joining one of the others in another bedroom. He didn't feel able to cope with two women and a residential course for teachers on how to deal with young people and bereavement led by a simpering sciolist, who began each session by placing his hands together in an attitude of prayer and muttering, "Has anyone got anything they wish to unpack?" As much as this irritated all those present, it wasn't as bad as seeing the same ground-breaker turn into a raging antagonist on the Monopoly board after a couple of drinks in the evening. At one sitting, participants were asked to describe what animal they might imagine themselves to be and following a succession of kittens, puppy dogs and teddy bears, The Head Teacher suggested a camel. When asked to explain why later, warmed by alcohol, he simply stated that a camel is never without hump! The Head Teacher may have been a married man and a parent for some years at this stage, but it is axiomatic that prior to entering into such a union, you should try to ensure that your wife has something between the ears as well as something between the legs.

The grief and bereavement course was one of many for The Head Teacher's thirst for CPD, continuing professional development — or it may have been 'personal development' — exhibited during his time with The King endured into both his headships. Furthermore, he was generous in encouraging staff, both teaching and non-teaching, to do the same. He was also magnanimous and fair in dealing with all the demands emanating from governments successively vying to outdo one another in their hard-line and often vindictive educational policies. For example, Tom, a loyal NAS member, was quick to concede that The Head Teacher had been more than benevolent in determining the distribution of tasks and meetings allocated under the one thousand, two hundred and sixty-five hours annually that some civil servant in the Department for Education had advised the government minister of the day was the most that it could expect to 'screw' out of teachers without risking a serious backlash. "He doesn't have to do that," was how Tom put it at the time.

Meanwhile, the process of de-streaming had been prepared for by allocating equal numbers of boys and girls of all abilities to each of the two classes in every year group and this was enacted at the start of the school year following The Head Teacher's appointment; the first opportunity. Sometime later, when the teachers were getting used to coping with 'mixed ability' groups and when the iron had cooled quite considerably, The Head Teacher ventured to introduce a couple of other changes, one of them of little import and the other cataclysmic. An education authority adviser once said to The Head Teacher, "If you see two people crossing a school playground, you can always tell which one is the head teacher." "How?" asked The Head Teacher. "The head will be the one picking up the litter," replied the adviser. Fed up with the litter, The Head Teacher, after minimal consultation with staff, decided to canvass the support of parents for a complete ban on crisps and sweets and chocolate. He not only cited the litter problem, but also the benefits to the children of a healthy diet and introduced more bins, including a large fibreglass animal called Bonzo with an enormous mouth that growled, "Thank you very much" whenever it was fed with scraps of litter. Bonzo was removed again within a week when the pupils started tearing up each other's exercise books and whatever else they could find to feed it! On the plus side, The Head Teacher was able to report that a large two-thirds majority of parents favoured the prohibition of crisps and sweets and he introduced the ban. He did not reveal that the number of parents that had responded to his canvass was three; two in favour and one against! The other and more far reaching change was to turn the entire school around by moving the youngest reception and infant classes to the 'open-plan' suite at the opposite end of the school and to reverse the entire 'infant' and 'junior' departments, or 'key stage one' and key stage two' in modern, and ever-changing, parlance. This was a monumental and complex undertaking and involved moving, every chair, desk and table, every item of equipment and every book, pen and piece of paper from one end of the school to the other. It also provided an ideal opportunity for The Head Teacher, his 'muse' and those supporting the move to hire rubbish skips and throw out a load of out-dated materials and old-fashioned books and for Tom and others less enamoured of it to burrow into the skips and retrieve as much as they could. With careful planning, done nightly in local public houses by The Head Teacher and his coterie, the job was completed in a fortnight, with only a small amount of disruption. The Head Teacher's report to governors was favourably received and it just goes to show that there are things that must be done at once, others later and still more at any old time!

If you ask young children to rank order the most important people in their school, the Caretaker is always at the top of the list. This is because he and it always is a 'he', is the most ubiquitous member of staff and the one the pupils see most often. Frequently, he is the one with the most authority too, or so the children believe. Incidentally, the children would probably put their class teacher second, the head of department third and, perhaps then, remember the head teacher, especially if he or she led the 'whole school' assemblies often enough. On the other hand, they might not and if asked "What about Mr So and so," they are quite likely to say, "Oh him! What does he do?" Which is rather like the reaction Tom got when he'd just received his pay slip from The Head Teacher's precursor; a monthly occurrence and the latter's excuse for spying on his teaching staff. "Look, children," said Tom, holding up the small buff-coloured envelope. "My wages, not much is it?" A child frowned, raised his hand and asked with genuine curiosity, "Where do you work?"

Of course the caretaker, or 'site supervisor' as they were later re-christened during one of the periodic government drives for changing titles in order to exact a greater variety of jobs and more work from them, is and has always been a vital cog in the educational wheel. And caretakers have always been fully aware of the indispensable importance of their role. That's why 'Shanghai Sid' at Willington was forever striding around the school with a broom or a screwdriver, telling anyone who'd listen how enormous his workload was and how useless his assistant in the lower school was. And that's why Edgemount's partially sighted caretaker spent so much of his time wheeling barrow loads of ash and clinker from the boiler room to his own back garden, taking care to pause and address as many people as possible in both directions. If only he'd been as enthusiastic about the cleaning and his role as cleaner leader but, as the vast majority of the women who work as poorly paid school cleaners will attest, caretakers are much better at telling them how to clean than doing it themselves. That's not to say that caretakers aren't good workers too, they do plenty of other jobs, they just don't much care for the cleaning! As Edgemount's man said one evening, when he unexpectedly entered the school office just as The Head Teacher was employing a guillotine to cut off the bottom six inches of a blue and orange striped football shirt, "Now I've seen everything!" Caretakers frequently have their own personal eccentricities like the one at Edward Street, who was never without his brown three-quarter length coat, looking for the entire world like a 1950s high street grocer. He was obsessed with the arrangements for the distribution of the children's break-time milk which Mrs Thatcher 'stole' and which was then replaced by many local education authorities and he carefully painted 'CUP'S', with the apostrophe, in big letters on the waste bins. Or, like the caretaker at Leafold who, like most of his contemporaries, had his secret hideaway. His habit of retreating to his lair in the cellar for a snooze was cruelly exposed, when Big H caught him there during working hours, a minor disgrace, which all the teachers got to know about and considerably worsened his already jaundiced attitude towards the teaching profession. Referring to Gessler, Doom or one of others, he'd say with a grimace, "You can break coal on 'er face!" Or, "She's so tight she can plait sawdust!" Or, and this was his best, "A glance from her can boil cheese!" And finally, with reference to all teachers, "They ought to cut their money by half and give it to the miners!" This was, of course, in the days when there were miners to give it to.

Caretaking reached a pinnacle of excellence with Barry, at Wheatfield's. Barry had a reputation for strength, hard work and loyalty. It was said that he could carry a school piano under each arm and a third in his teeth, that he could buff the floor of the school hall at the same time as shovelling several tons of coal in the boiler room and that, where women were concerned, his maxim was, "No fence too high!" What Barry couldn't do himself, he could admonish and assist with or offer advice. At about five o'clock one evening, when builders were proposing to erect a 'test wall' to see how well the bricks they were to use for a classroom extension matched the existing brickwork, Barry told them, "If you build that tonight, it will be gone in the morning." They built it and it was! Another incident occurred when electricians were re-wiring a section of the school and, needing to pass an electric cable from one end of a long corridor to the other, were on the point of taking up the wooden parquet flooring to do so.

"Wait," said Barry, before disappearing in the direction of his house at the end of the front drive. He returned a few minutes later carrying a ferret to the leg of which he tied a piece of string. "Take up a couple of blocks at each end of the corridor," he said, "attach the cable to this string, I'll put the ferret in, you replace the blocks at this end and he'll seek the light at the far end." The electricians looked very doubtful but, after The Head Teacher agreed to the strategy, they acceded and, sure enough, the ferret dragged the cable below the floor the length of the corridor before emerging at the far end with the cable behind it. "There! I told you so," cried Barry in triumph, and quite right too, for he'd just saved the authority a lot of time and money and protected the parquet corridor floor from unnecessary disruption and possible damage.

Apart from the essential scaling of fences, Barry and The Head Teacher shared another, rather curious and sordid but eminently attainable, ambition. It began when The Head Teacher, busy with some task or other in a relatively remote part of the school halfway between the entrance area and the far end of the building, nipped into one of the infant washrooms to relieve himself, just at the moment when Barry was checking that he hadn't missed anyone working late before locking up for the night. Far from being surprised, much less shocked, Barry conjectured about who might have used the same wash basin during the day and the conversation between the two went on to speculate which of the young and decorous females might have used the very same bowl for washing their hands. It barely becomes a working man to behave in such a contemptible manner, much less a professional with two university degrees, one of them a Master's in Education, and an advanced diploma in Compensatory Education. The pair decided that it would be a jolly wheeze to pee in every sink in the school, just to imagine the delicate hands being cleansed therein the following day, regardless that they, the sinks that is, would have been thoroughly scrubbed and rinsed overnight. They never embarked upon this depraved scheme, or The Head Teacher didn't rather, not so much because of any moral considerations, but rather, because there were so many sinks.

The Head Teacher discovered Barry's 'hideaway' by chance, when he saw the caretaker emerge from a door into the playground during a Parents' Evening when the children's mums and dads, guardians, aunties, uncles, younger siblings and dogs come into school, some by invitation, to berate the teachers for the children's failings and to give the head a hard time. Not many heads and teachers, even in quite innocuous schools in pleasant settings, go for very long without being threatened and, in many cases attacked, by irate parents. In fairness to the parents, many do come in to learn about their offspring's progress and to support the staff in helping them to reach their potential. Parents' Evening can be a busy time for heads too for, in between fending off the more persistent of the parents, they have to make periodic patrols to protect the staff, make tea for everyone at regular intervals and chase errant miscreants and myrmidons away from the premises. It was this trepidatious duty that The Head Teacher was engaged upon when he saw Barry. He watched Barry make off towards his house and thought, "I've not noticed that door before, and it must lead into a stockroom or something." He was surprised a second or two later, when the door opened again and Mrs Burlyman came out! "Gosh, what's Mrs Burlyman doing in there?" he thought. Inside the building, The Head Teacher walked from his office, down the infant corridor, across the hall and into the junior corridor to roughly where he guessed the inside of the mysterious door might be. Locating what he thought must be the door at the far end of one of the washrooms, he went over and tried the handle only to find that it was locked. The following day, he tackled Barry about the strange door and was told that the door he'd tried wasn't the one that led into the playground but another that led, as The Head Teacher had surmised, into a stockroom that, in turn, led to the exterior door. "Problem solved," said The Head Teacher, "show me this stockroom please, Barry," he added. Barry dutifully escorted his boss to the stockroom, opened the door and they both entered a capacious T-shaped vestibule. "I keep the toilet rolls and paper towels here," said Barry and, indeed, there were lots of cardboard boxes piled up in the two arms of the T attesting to that and, at the top of the T, was the door leading to the outside. "There's still plenty of room in here," said The Head Teacher, "have you got a spare key, Barry?" "Of course," said Barry grinning broadly and tapping the side of his nose with his right forefinger, "I'll get one for you." "I'll wait here," said The Head Teacher. Barry left and The Head Teacher was able to examine the room closely, before concluding that the main stem of the T was almost like a wide passageway between the washroom and the outside door leading into the playground. Glancing down, The Head Teacher was intrigued to notice that the floor was covered by two gymnasium mats! "That explains why Tom was short of two gym mats," he mused. Tom was nominally in charge of physical education and had been pestering The Head Teacher about PE equipment including a shortage of mats for gymnastics. Later, having taken early retirement, Tom briefly became the Head of PE in a private school. Briefly, because he wasn't used to and couldn't cope with children who all did exactly as they were told, got changed, lined up, followed instructions and remained silent, thus making the lessons so long that Tom, accustomed to the lengthy preparations, exhaustive searches for PE kit, watching those without and keeping order with those that did, that were all a feature in physical activities at Wheatfield's, had to resign, defeated by good behaviour! Meanwhile, The Head Teacher, picturing once again the stealthy emergence of Mrs Burlyman, had realised what the mats were in the passage for. "I get it", he said to himself darkly just as Barry returned and handed him the spare key. "We'll keep quiet about this," he said to the caretaker, "No need for anyone to know about this place is there? Just between me and you? Our secret, okay?"

Barry shrugged, smiled, widened his eyes slightly and nodded, "Our 'secret passage' eh?" he said.

The Head Teacher had already decided to share his knowledge of the 'secret passage' with Belinda. He had become her habitual 'gentleman caller' and visited her almost every Friday evening after basketball matches. This was an exercise in closet furtiveness, for his habit was to telephone to make sure that Belinda's husband had gone to the Ex-Servicemen's Club, or wherever it was he spent his time, and then to drive or cycle to a nearby street or pub car park from where he'd steal along the poorly lit streets and alleys for his assignation. Every teacher had some free time at school, particularly those with additional responsibilities and Belinda's fell upon Mondays, so that The Head Teacher, having introduced her to the secret passage, was able to entertain her there on a regular basis. For a long time, it was Monday morning, Friday night, school trips and the odd weekend away. The trouble with having an affair with Belinda was having to listen to her in between times for Belinda could, to use an old-fashioned expression, 'talk the hind leg off a donkey' about anything to anyone. This prolixity proved to be very effective when used in interviews with colleagues, parents, prospective employers, inspectors and on the telephone, but wasn't really appropriate in the dimly-lit intimacy of a suburban B&B. Paradise not so much by the 'dash board light' as the bedside lamp and, in fact, The Head Teacher found it close to unendurable, which accounted for his taciturnity in her presence. However, he may well have been, in the words of the song, 'praying for the end of time ...' but endure it he did and this happy liaison was sustained a lot longer than it deserved to be. That is until the day that his periodic, and totally unprofessional, habit of opening the classroom door of the black-haired beauty who'd captivated him at interview and saying, "When are you going to run away with me?" got a response other than titters from the children and what he thought was a serene, forbidding smile from its target. Only after the smile transmogrified into companionable, even coquettish, did he consider a move from flirting to philandering might be 'on the cards'! It took quite a long time, but the first of his 'creatures' was to become much more than that, but far too respected to be asked to take a turn in the caretaker's 'secret passage'.

The school secretary will also figure quite highly on young children's lists of important people in school, if only because they are almost as omnipresent as caretakers and do so many different jobs. Frequently re-named 'bursars', for the same reasons as caretakers became site supervisors, school secretaries answer telephones, collect money for all sorts of things, do all manner of bureaucratic tasks and protect the head from unwarranted interference. Some secretaries regard that as their most important role the second most important, although they'd probably not admit to it, being to pass on in its entirety all the local gossip, spreading it as far as possible whilst maximising its importance and warning of the dire consequences likely to emanate therefrom. Mrs Wildon at Leafold was almost equally strong in both her principal duties. She could jealously guard Big H as protector supreme, whilst smearing all and sundry and helping with the staffroom jigsaw puzzle all at the same time. Regrettably, she died unexpectedly, which occasioned the episode when The Deputy and The King inadvertently embarrassed Big H by arriving wearing black ties. Caught on the corridor in his shirt sleeves and tieless, Big H scuttled into his suite to adjust his dress. Commensurately strong in the idle talk field was Mrs Leftwrinkle, who enjoyed heaping calumny upon The Head Teacher's rivals in the locality, such that The Head Teacher took great care to keep anything the slightest bit confidential well out of her earshot. Mrs Smith, the elderly incumbent at Wheatfield's, was an exception to the general rule and it was said of her, that if you got on well with your mum, she was "just like Mrs Smith" and if you didn't, you wished that she was! Unfortunately, Mrs Smith 'went on' very soon after The Head Teacher's arrival at Wheatfield's to be replaced by Dorothy, of whom it was said that whatever you imparted to her would appear in print on the sugar bags at ASDA by the following morning! Dorothy had some very fixed ideas about right and wrong and anything that she didn't agree with was wrong. Seeking advice from The Head Teacher about the behaviour of one of her errant daughters, in itself a bit like asking for directions from a blind man, Dorothy concluded wearily, "They just won't obey the rules." The Head Teacher, desperate to do something other than listen, turned slightly, glanced across the room at her and replied, "You'd better change the rules, Dorothy." Afterwards, he lost count of the number of times he overheard her say, "And do you know what he said then ...?"

Everyone remembers 'dinner ladies' but it isn't often you come across a 'dinner man'! Wheatfield's had one and the children ran rings around him. Not only were they impertinent and called him rude names but they raced around him in circles whilst doing so. This gentleman was also a lollipop person and he could be seen each morning before school trying, and failing, to persuade his charges to cross the road safely. The Head Teacher was often tempted to stop and assist but he'd been warned about taking on the responsibilities of a Local Authority School Crossing Patrol Officer when, sometime previously, for the sake of the well-being of the children, he'd taken up the 'yellow jacket' and pole of a sick lollipop lady only to be told by someone in charge of road safety that, should anything go wrong, he'd 'be liable.' The age of litigation having been imported from the United States, The Head Teacher was mindful of the day a curtain rail on a classroom wall collapsed on to the head of a ten year old boy, whose parents assured The Head Teacher their lad had suffered no injury, but came into school a few days later to talk about 'trauma' and 'delayed shock' and 'potential brain damage'. The Head Teacher, from his knowledge of the child concerned was certain that the parent's original diagnosis was spot on. Nonetheless, he took the precaution of referring the matter to the appropriate local authority official and the boy's parents, in due course, got the money they were after. So, The Head Teacher gave up his brief spell with the 'lollipop' and immediately had to fend off a succession of complaints from other parents that he didn't care about their children's welfare!

There are, of course, two kinds of 'dinner ladies'. Those who serve and, in the days when the food was edible and nutritious, cooked it and those whose job it is to look after the children during the 'dinner break'. Strictly speaking, those in the first category are kitchen staff or cooks and those in the second are 'welfare staff' but to the children they're all 'dinner ladies'. The Head

Teacher's mum had worked in school kitchens and worked her way up to 'veg cook' or something like that but she never reached the dizzy heights of a 'kitchen supervisor' at the top of the school catering tree. None of them could be described as 'chefs', of course, because none of them are men and they get paid a pittance as do their colleagues doing the 'welfare' work and the only perk of the job is, or was, nicking left-over food which, at the time The Head Teacher's mum was doing it could result in what she dramatically described as 'instant dismissal'! Of the two kinds of 'dinner lady', neither attracts much respect from the pupils or, indeed, the teachers but it is the 'welfare staff' that has the more arduous role. They vary a great deal in their ability to look after, control, or even relate to children, but most of them believe firmly in the sergeant major approach to discipline relying upon much regimentation and stentorian instruction. This kind of control only works when used sparingly and when it is backed up by authority, reason and effective sanctions none of which the average 'dinner lady' can command. Thus, dinner ladies struggle to keep control and the situation was exacerbated when teachers, with some justification, withdrew their voluntary and unpaid 'dinner duty' role.

Some families cannot afford the price of school dinners, so arrangements are made for their children to have 'free school meals'. The days of special 'free' tickets or separate queues to humiliate such children were long gone by The Head Teacher's time and the local authority could be very helpful concerning children whose parents couldn't afford school trips, bus fares or even school meals. And sometimes it could be very difficult! "You'll have to speak to them about Peacock, he already owes £42.50," said his secretary one day, handing The Head Teacher his own telephone with the one in the outer office still on her desk, so that she could listen in to his conversation. "Peacock doesn't owe anything," responded The Head Teacher dourly as he put the receiver to his ear and heard the local authority school meals section clerk intone into it, "All dinners MUST be paid for in advance!" "Yes," replied The Head Teacher, "I understand that, but what if a child has no dinner money on collection day?" "All dinners MUST be paid for in advance." "Yes, yes, I know. So, are you saying that I let the child go hungry?" "All dinners MUST be paid for in advance." "Peacock isn't the only one, it's a problem here, and we can't refuse children food … can we?" "All dinners MUST be paid for in advance." In the end, albeit that some parents took advantage, Peacock got fed and the school meals section got its money.

Several solutions offered themselves over the years to the problem of dinner breaks, once the meals had been eaten and the children dispersed into playgrounds. The first of these was the provision of bats, balls and skipping ropes for the children to play with, the second was the zoning of play areas into quiet areas, games and football sectors, the third was the introduction of the 'naughty book' in which the names of miscreants would be entered, and the fourth was training for 'dinner ladies'. All these innovations made The Head Teacher feel good for a while, but none of them worked for any length of time. The 'dinner ladies' were unable to stop more unruly children from using the bats to beat each other about the head and the ropes to attempt mock executions. Children in the quiet zones were constantly being run down by the over exuberant footballers and the 'naughty book' was filled, within days, with the names of the wayward and those courting notoriety, sadly, it ran to several volumes within the first week! As for the 'training', if anyone can get a 'dinner lady' to distinguish between mildly errant behaviour that can safely be ignored, effervescence that needs a gentle reprimand and dangerously ferocious conduct that has to be stopped at all costs, then that person, apart from being a psychiatrist, psychologist and seer of the very highest order, will also make a fortune. In the end, the only strategy that worked was for The Head Teacher to spend the entire dinner break patrolling every play area and every corner of the school grounds, intermittently nipping indoors to turf out any capricious youngsters who'd sneaked inside, and grabbing a cup of tea and a smoke if the atmosphere outside appeared to promise an incident-free lunchtime. If he ate at all, it was when all the pupils had returned to class for the afternoon. There was always a risk that something awful might happen and now and again it did, if a fight or an assault of some kind occurred. The Head Teacher came to the conclusion that it was less trouble to patrol all the time, than chance a disturbance that resulted in an injury and the consequent investigation and involvement of parents. What saved the day, in the end, was the introduction of the 'Senior Midday Supervisor', a slightly better-paid post which, if you could get a well-respected teacher to do it, took an enormous amount of pressure off the head. At Wheatfield's, Hugh had a go and took it in turns with the young PE teacher both of whom were good enough to bring some joy and some relief into the life of The Head Teacher!

It was small wonder that the likelihood of incidents during the dinner break was quite high given that three quarters of the school's intake came off the estates, where the large majority of decent working class families were forever having their reputations and lives tarnished by a minority of hooligans, rascals and drug takers. There was a fair amount of real poverty too, so that the governors, staff and PTA had to do whatever they could to even up the opportunities for all the children. In these circumstances, it is no surprise that some very difficult and badly behaved children, 'challenging' is now the word used to describe them, were regularly admitted to the school. Similarly, that educational psychologists and social workers were amongst the most regular visitors to and supporters of the school. The latter, when they weren't, in the words of one outspoken colleague of The Head Teacher, "too far up their own backsides" and not into a surfeit of what the 'black-haired girl' called "cognitive diarrhoea", or something like that, could be very valuable in supporting schools with problems, whilst the former, the Educational psychologists, whilst being an odd lot had, in those days, access to certain levels of support that weren't normally available. Hence, the game was to exaggerate the symptoms displayed by the disturbed, deprived and disaffected child, keep copious records of their behaviour, involve their parents in discussions and refer them to the 'Ed Psyc'. The first Ed Psyc The Head Teacher ever encountered came dashing into the entrance area at Edgemount and begged for immediate access to the gent's toilet which, together with the fact that he was an active union member, endeared him forever to The Head Teacher. The second, at Wheatfield's, was a chain smoking, hard-drinking eccentric, who was generous with the local authority's resources when, as was usually the case, he was giving them to the children of underprivileged families in disadvantaged schools. Regrettably, his life span was cut short by his lifestyle. His successor, and the third memorable member of his profession, was an earnest young man, who managed to cut off several fingers in an accident with a lawn mower, took up running marathons and had a vehement exchange with a visiting workman over a parking space in the school car park. At first, the Ed Psyc flatly refused to accede to the man's rather strongly worded requests to move his vehicle so that his van could get in. The situation began to escalate and The Head Teacher intervened and suggested that the Ed Psyc move his car and then discuss the matter further, which he did. The workman turned to The Head Teacher with undisguised irritation to ask, "Who is that bloke?" "He's an educational psychologist," replied The Head Teacher, "he's a very intelligent man," he added, as though to offer a palliative. The workman frowned with increasing incredulity, curled a lip with contempt and said, "Well, God help the kids!" By the time the Ed Psyc had moved his car and returned, still fuming about the workman, the latter had gone about his business in the school kitchen and The Head Teacher wisely declined to tell the 'Ed Psyc' where he'd gone. By far the best, and most productive, of all the Ed Psycs was an elderly chap called out of retirement to help cope with the growing demand for provision, who believed implicitly all that he was told by schools, had a healthy disregard for circuitous procedures and processed more cases in one day than two or three of his colleagues could manage in a week. Eccentric they may have been, a bit weird even, but all these men provided invaluable help for

Wheatfield's children. Besides, having your head 'shrunk' by an educational psychologist was quite fun and, when the routine of the obligatory battery of psychometric tests had been completed, the parents baffled into consent, the farrago of forms filled in and dispatched and following a lengthy wait, all kinds of support might ensue such as a teaching assistant, extra resources for a variety of ailments, equipment for all manner of afflictions and, best of all, a spell at the 'Tutorial Centre' which provided more direct tuition for the pupil and a respite from disruption for the school — for the other children as well as the teachers and staff.

When you become a teacher, you quickly discover that some children are more memorable than others and it is usually those with names like the aforementioned Peacock or names such as Chantelle and Wayne that you recollect most often. No-one found out who demolished the 'test wall' for the extension, or who broke into the school, one of many such incursions, and stole the 'state of the art' calculators, but The Head Teacher knew enough to send a message via those 'in the know' on the estate to Tayvon asking for 'first refusal' should he be looking for someone discreet to 'sell them on' to. The calculators, precursors of more modern technology, disappeared with the newly up-dated English Policy, which the English Co-ordinator, a posh title for the teacher in charge of that subject, had left hanging from her chair in a plastic supermarket bag. An incidental theft as likely to be as inadvertent as the policy was unlikely to be recovered. Tayvon had what is still called 'form' in certain quarters and so did Cale. Cale was one of several notorious brothers who took exception to the fact that The Head Teacher had confiscated his axe, on the grounds that it wasn't a suitable prop for war games in the playground. The Head Teacher suspected that it was Cale who returned to school late one evening for a stroll along the roof, not an uncommon pastime for the locals, but unusual in that, whoever it was this time, kicked in eight hundred pounds worth of glass domes in the ceilings. At Wheatfield's, 'breaking glass' wasn't associated with the name of a pop song, but it was a fairly frequent occurrence costing, at its peak, several hundred pounds a month! The sight of ten year old Daron retreating slowly up the arterial road into the estate, eyes narrowed and tossing his open-bladed Stanley knife from hand to hand as Colin, equally slowly, followed Daron, asking him to surrender the weapon and return to school for his dinner remained seared in The Head Teacher's memory for a very long time. It was one of those times that Colin excelled himself. Daron's Stanley knife ended up in The Head Teacher's desk drawer-full of confiscated items along with Cale's axe and Kyrone's ring the size of a knuckleduster and equally dangerous. Every time one of the boys came to implore him for the return of some such object, The Head Teacher would solemnly tell them that they should ask one of their parents or guardians to call in for it, when he would be happy to return it and have a chat and a cup of tea with them. The implication wasn't lost on the boys and not a single axe, knife or ring was ever disturbed again.

One of the guns was though! A young child burst in to The Head Teacher's office one morning, just before school, in a state of considerable agitation. "It's Blake Anderson!" he shouted, "He's up the tree again!" The Head Teacher didn't admonish the child for his unseemly intrusion, accepting that Blake was a well-known transgressor and it could easily be something of an emergency. The climbing of the trees in the school grounds was not allowed, although plenty of it went on in the evenings and at weekends, for even in those days there was some regard for health and safety. Instead of upbraiding the intruder, The Head Teacher went to his desk and opened the drawer of confiscated articles and withdrew a quite realistic black plastic hand gun. He crossed to the window facing onto the playground, opened it and, holding up the gun as if in readiness for firing it, said, with mock urgency, "Where? Where is he?" Far from pleading for mercy on Blake's behalf, the youngster hurried across to the window and frantically gesticulated towards one of the largest of the trees where, sure enough, Blake Anderson was clambering amongst the branches. Even as The Head Teacher took aim, the young boy continued to fixate upon Blake expectantly, before repeatedly looking from Blake to The Head Teacher and back again, as though awaiting the next development with an element of eagerness. The Head Teacher lowered the gun and said, "Go and tell Blake to come and see me please." Clearly crestfallen, the informant nodded and hurried away.

Not long afterwards, The Head Teacher was conducting a meeting with Hugh, when the office door burst open again to admit another excited pupil. This time, it was about Kyrone and the hot news, literally, was to the effect that Kyrone had set fire to one of the junior cloakrooms. "Alright, calm down," The Head Teacher said, "we'll see to it. You get off back to your class." Hugh smiled at the preposterous idea that Kyrone, odd though he was, disturbed even, would set alight part of the fabric of his own school. "Ought we to take a look?" he suggested. "I suppose so," replied The Head Teacher wearily and they exited the office, paused at the secretary's office to let Dorothy know where they were going and strolled along the infant corridor, past the cloakrooms and across the hall. Leaving the hall by the double doors leading onto the junior corridor, they were confronted by a pall of smoke bowling along from the direction of a cloakroom. "Good grief!" exclaimed Hugh, "he damn well has; the little blighter!" A very efficient evacuation followed, during which no one was seriously hurt, but several children were slightly injured from bumping into fire extinguishers propping open the fire doors on the junior corridor. The relief of The Head Teacher was tempered by thinking about what he might do to Kyrone and the complaints from staff concerning blocked exits. He was reminded of the time at Edgemount, when Max had returned from a course on Health and Safety in schools to report that national statistics informed that not a single child had ever been burned, scorched or even singed by an outbreak of fire, but that several thousand had suffered injuries from blocked fire doors, locked fire doors and misplaced fire extinguishers!

Some children are less dangerous, but more disruptive. Terry arrived on roller blades when no one else would have dreamed of it and when Terry decided that a lesson wouldn't happen, it didn't. He knew the score too. "You can't touch me," he would say, "go on, try it and see what happens!" Nobody wanted to touch Terry, but if he was in a bad mood, then the only way to be sure of not penalising all the other children in his class was to evacuate them to another room such as the library or the school hall. The knock on effect of that was that the library would be out of use for a while and nobody could do P.E. Cody wasn't disruptive, but he was somewhat clumsy. The Schools Museum Service, an excellent resource for primary education, could be booked to bring in units on certain themes, such as the Stone Age, Victoriana, and transport and so on. These would include artefacts, costumes and relics to illustrate history, geography and so on which the children would be able to see and to handle. Cody wasn't attempting to use the stone-age weapon aggressively, but he was posturing with it and pretending to hurl it across the room; or so he said when he released it. The Head Teacher was summoned and arrived just in time to hear Cody's teacher saying, "Two thousand years of history and you manage to break it into pieces in two seconds!" It was a replica, of course, but neither the teacher nor Cody seemed to know that.

Not all of the children's problems were behavioural. The Head Teacher was in the habit of taking a little Vietnamese refugee child to a language class once a week; teachers do things like that. On the way there and back, he tried to engage the child with vocabulary like "house" and "man" and "dog" before moving on to "legs" and "roof" and "hat". Quite a refined stage had been reached, when the Head Teacher spotted a dog and asked the girl, "How many legs?" "Four," she replied with obvious delight, just as a three-legged dog ran across the road! Some children are disabled, or ill. Like Raymond who was what was then termed 'partially sighted'. The rest of the children, as is usually the case in such circumstances, went to enormous lengths to help and protect Raymond, whilst The Head Teacher took full advantage of Raymond's disability to obtain counselling for him, equipment for him, such as a special desk, large print books and an early form of computer, education for the other children about sight loss and its consequences and — best of all — new sun blinds in every room down the length of one side of the building as Raymond progressed through the school. Towards the end of this process and late in the school year, The Head Teacher was explaining to a local authority buildings officer that he was in the ultimate room when Raymond, being a clever boy, interceded to say, "But I won't be in this r..." "Oh, yes, you will be, Raymond," interjected The Head Teacher rapidly, "Oh, yes, you will." Help was available for children then and it got better and better. A fellow basketball player of The Head Teacher's acquaintance, who'd started his career as a teacher of Geography before deciding that, to get anywhere, he'd have to specialise in something, even tried to put it around that special loud versions of children's classics were available from County Hall for deaf children! Even Tom, the acknowledged expert in the full exploitation of the County film library, whose 'hits' included the seasonal series "Children in Summer", Children in Winter" and so on. "Charcoal Burner" — the most boring film for schools ever made — and, best of all, "A Fitting Future" which The Head Teacher had shown at Leafold and had his dad in a cameo role on his Gas Company bicycle. Even Tom didn't believe the tale about the loud books! Neither did the Head Teacher and he found it hard to believe in the gadget the school's service for deaf children provided for a hearing impaired boy at Wheatfield's at about the same time as Raymond was securing the new window blinds. This little 'gizmo' was attached to the boy's hearing aids with a corresponding device hanging around the teacher's neck, acting to amplify whatever she said and enable the child to take part in normal class lessons. The only drawback to this wonderful device was getting the teacher to remember to switch it off at play time. Small wonder that the deaf boy attracted a group of older admirers at one end of the playground, tuning into the staffroom news, gossip, trivialities and petty squabbles!

Caretakers and cleaners can get very cross when children abuse resources such as paper towels and toilet rolls. The solution for the damage done to boxes of paper towels and the utilisation of paper towels for uses other than hand drying was relatively simple. By the time The Head Teacher had decided to ask Barry why the paper towels were no longer stored in the secret passage with the toilet rolls — "There's enough room to hold dances in here," he confided to Belinda — the Education Authority had installed a new health and safety measure in all the washrooms; automatic hand dryers! "Piss misers!" Colin christened them in light of the strict instructions, largely ignored, given to all the boys to wash and dry their hands after using the urinals. Of course, the end result was that most of the children came into the hall for their dinner with wet hands, but at least the paper towel problem was solved and the electricity expended on the hand dryers was less than the savings made on the hugely reduced supplies of paper towels! The toilet roll difficulty was a little more intractable in that certain children liked to put them in the toilet bowls. "These people need our help, children," The Head Teacher announced pompously, during one of his morning assemblies, "Your help I mean. There must be something wrong with them!" There was, but they weren't in need of being exposed by their peers for psychiatric help, they just thought it was great fun to block the toilets with the toilet rolls. After sufficient toilet rolls had been wasted and several drains had been blocked, The Head Teacher came up with the answer. Each teacher was to have two toilet rolls in their classroom and, whenever a child wished to visit the toilet other than to wash paintbrushes, wash their hands or urinate, he or she would be issued with one of the class toilet rolls and return it to their teacher afterwards. A brilliant scheme, as long as the child and the teacher remembered to take or send the toilet roll! The point at which six year old Shanelle realised that she'd forgotten to take the toilet roll was immediately after she'd finished 'pooing', as she termed it. What was she to do? She came out of the cubicle into the cloakroom, took the nearest coat off its peg and used it to clean herself before replacing it. Naturally, Lavonne, the child who found her coat in such a condition at 'home time', was a trifle upset, but not nearly as much as her mum was! Shanelle was quite frank about what had happened, so that her mum was as embarrassed as the victim's mum was vexed. In the end, the whole thing was resolved amicably between the parents, Lavonne's mum got Shanelle's coat cleaned, the two girls remained friends and the two mums became friends. Barry wasn't very happy, but the only person who suffered was The Head Teacher, who was firmly rebuked by both mothers, and several staff and promptly abandoned the disastrous toilet roll policy. It was impossible to tell how many other children had found themselves in a similar predicament, but details of the incident quickly spread and, not surprisingly, with the toilet rolls back in the toilets, the children concerned tired of the game of throwing them into the toilet bowls and, eventually, it subsided.

Most of the children at Wheatfield's were perfectly well behaved and came from what governments now like to call 'hard-working families', an all-embracing euphemism for decent, respectable, law-abiding and supine. The children went on to the secondary schools, the tendency being for the schools to choose them rather than the other way around. The available 'choices' included selective schools, faith schools, so-called 'comprehensive' schools and 'modern' schools, which The Head Teacher liked to describe as "discrimination and inequality erected into a system of education", and then on to jobs, careers or, in some cases, higher education. A sizeable number went on to unemployment too or other forms of occupation. When asked about the successes of the school's ex-pupils, The Head Teacher often chose to identify the school's alumni in terms of what he described as three typical examples. The first was convicted for drug running and 'sent down' for a lengthy term, the second was a well-known newsreader on television and the third was a successful stand-up comedian.

Nurture has a far greater effect upon our children than nature, so they tend to reflect the life-styles and behaviour of their parents. That is why parents are so central to the lives and chances of their offspring and that is why schools do their utmost to encourage parents to involve themselves in the education and training of their children in a partnership. During the sessions allocated for parents to consult their children's teachers, normally Parent's Evenings, it is customary for teachers to sit at desks in a communal area, such as the school hall or a science laboratory or to remain in their classrooms. Either way, arrangements are made for parents, and possibly others acting in their stead, to queue to see whatever teachers they feel they need to see or have been specifically requested to see. Seats are usually provided for them. Most schools have improved upon this by allocating specific times and getting the parents to make appointments. There is still a certain amount of waiting, because some parents will always overstay their allotted time, especially if their child is naughty or not doing too well academically. The Head Teacher had never forgotten one of his first, at Moss Newton, when a man and a woman sat down in front of him and began to talk at length about their child. From their use of the pronoun 'she', The Head Teacher, still a lowly teacher at the time, quickly concluded that the child was a girl, but each time he attempted to elicit the child's identity, one or other of her parents began to speak again. There was a clear assumption on the part of the couple that he knew their child intimately and, eventually, they stopped and looked at him expectantly. A short silence followed before the man spoke again. "We're not so much bothered about the History," he said, "but English is important isn't it?" The woman then broke in to add, "And how she gets on with the others, that's very important isn't it?" This one-sided discussion had gone on for so long that it seemed rude to risk asking, "Who is she?" for fear that the parents would be offended. The remainder of the meeting was, therefore, couched in terms so general that they could have applied to any child anywhere until the indomitable pair rose to leave, looking more than a little perplexed.

Whilst he was able, by a process of eliminating all the boys and girls whose parents attended that Parents Evening, to narrow it down a bit, The Head Teacher never did find out who that girl was, but in no time at all he learned a thing or two about impressing mums, dads, guardians, grandparents and anyone else who came wanting to know things, to take up his time and to threaten his peace of mind. One ploy, for example, was to greet any remotely reasonably presented woman attending a Parents Evening alone with something like, "Oh, I was hoping her mother would be able to come!"

By the time he got to Wheatfield's, The Head Teacher had learned that the role of the head during parent's evenings was threefold. Firstly, the head must support the teachers. He or she has to protect them from unwelcome threats and abuse and make them cups of tea, the latter providing excellent cover for looking out for and thwarting incidents of the former. Secondly, the head must accept his or her share of dealing directly with parents, especially those with grievances. At such times, The Head Teacher always called to mind, and freely gave to others, the advice he'd had from an old hand at The Copse in his early days, "Never sit down! If you sit down they'll trap you behind the desk and you'll be there forever!" Whilst it isn't easy to conduct an interview standing up, this was sound advice and good counsel to which The Head Teacher later added, "Keep on the move!" Thirdly, and finally, the head should have somewhere to hide other than his or her office.

Concomitant with Parents Evening is the writing of reports on all the children and it is one of the most dull, detested and debilitating tasks of the teaching profession. In his early days at The Copse, The Teacher tended to write blunt comments such as, "Takes no interest and does no work!" or sardonic and sarcastic remarks criticising the boys for lack of attention, laziness or bad behaviour. This went on, until he realised that prosaic statements like these were not only unlikely to get any positive response from the boys and their mums and dads, were not even criticisms of the pupils, but of the teacher — himself. This was first, very gently but precisely pointed out by Mr Beech at The Copse and, thereafter, he progressed to writing informed and helpful comments in reports, at such length that colleagues began to protest that he was too long-winded, even pedantic! Ultimately, the Teacher and, subsequently, The Deputy, learned how to strike a balance between pithy, appropriate and supportive observations and provocative, but apposite, interjections that would be useful to the student concerned and helpful for parents and other teachers.

Parents, as you'd expect, don't only appear on Parent's Evening. Sometimes, they telephone and, even though there are always arrangements in place for the secretary, bursar, personal assistant, or whatever the fancy title is nowadays, to shield the boss from unwelcome intrusions, a wise head will sometimes accept calls. Of course, it's usually parents described as 'pushy' that are bold enough to call the head. Parents like Mrs Gurlingham St John, who called one morning to complain about the number of stray dogs in the area at the weekends and the possibility that faeces deposited on the school field might present a serious health risk to the children at play times and during the dinner break. The

Head Teacher glanced out of the window as Mrs Gurlingham St John was speaking, just in time to see one of the Riverside youngsters, drop his trousers, squat and deposit right in the middle of the field! "It's not even playtime, that lad must be playing truant," thought The Head Teacher, before saying aloud, "Mrs Gurlingham St John, it may be worse than you think …"

Sometimes, parents call personally and often, when they arrive at the school door, they do so without appointments, so that heads face the dilemma of either turning them away, or getting the office staff to do so, thus risking seeming to be unwelcoming, or agreeing to see the parent, thus risking the possibility of exposure to an outraged or infuriated individual. Statistics from union surveys suggest that heads and teachers are often vulnerable to abuse and even violence! Not from Mr Gerston though, or 'Fred' as he preferred to be called by all and sundry. Fred lived just around the corner from the school and had, recently and belatedly, discovered that there was a second child at home approaching the school starting age. His first born being already a pupil at Wheatfield's, Fred had decided to approach The Head Teacher concerning the sibling, a boy. "What's the boy's name, Fred?" said The Head Teacher. "Stephen," replied Fred. The Head Teacher sat down at his desk and took a pen and a notepad from a drawer. "Sit down, Fred," he said and then asked, "And how do you spell that?" "I'm not at all sure about that," replied Fred, "I'm not right good at spelling, you'll have to ask his mum." "Okay," said The Head Teacher, "what is Stephen's birth date?" "Oh, I'm not at all sure about that," said Fred again, "I'm not right good with numbers, you'll have to ask his mum." "Okay," said the Head Teacher, "why do you want Stephen to come here?" "I came here," said Fred emphatically, "this is a very good school!" The irony of this escaped Fred and The Head Teacher, now accustomed to late enrolments and lack of clarity about names, ages and even numbers of children, chose to ignore it, but did allow himself a wry smile and an imperceptible sigh. The Head Teacher suspired again when Doris's mum came in to complain about the red hand mark on her daughter's thigh caused, she claimed, by a teacher's overzealous methods of correction. It took tact and diplomacy of a very high order to deal with situations such as this and, later, to upbraid the teacher concerned. In the end Doris's mum, a happy-go-lucky woman from the estate, went away happy, especially after The Head Teacher promised to get her an alarm clock to cope with her children's — there were several — congenital lateness for school. It worked for a while until a loss of patience arising from a late night and not much sleep resulted in the alarm clock being tossed through a window, resulting in an expense for the local council and the children losing even more time of the morning sessions at school.

In contrast to Fred and Doris's mum, some parents were far more volatile. One such was Mr Honeywell, whose daughter approached one of the male members of staff to complain that she was being bullied by another girl. Bullying is an issue that schools would be wise to take very seriously and to protect themselves with a policy to deal with the power relationships between the persecutors who often turn out to be, in their turn, the bullied, and the persecuted. Tom, or it may have been Hugh, did his best to deal with the problem and thought, indeed, that he had. Not to the girl's satisfaction, however! She absented herself from the premises and went home to tell her mother, who telephoned her father, who was working some considerable distance away in some metropolis or other. The Father, Mr Honeywell, hopped into his car straightaway and drove to the school, parked it directly outside the main entrance, entered the building, and, ignoring the pleas of the secretarial staff, burst through the office door to confront The Head Teacher and Tom – or it might have been Hugh – and announce that he'd just driven sixty miles to sort it out! The Head Teacher attempted to explain that the teacher had dealt with the matter, that his, Mr Honeywell's, daughter shouldn't have put herself into danger by leaving the school and going home during school hours and it hadn't been at all necessary to make such a journey on such a trivial errand. This succeeded only in enraging Mr Honeywell, who shouted incoherently, frothed at the mouth, waved his clenched fists up and down before the cowering Tom, or perhaps, Hugh, before retreating as far as the open door, turning and shrieking, "If I come back, dig a hole!" A day or two later, The Head Teacher went to Tom, no, it was definitely Hugh, and said, "I've written to Mr Honeywell., Hugh. I've said, 'Dear Mr Honeywell, we have now dug our holes and would be very grateful if you would come into school to discuss ...'" The Head Teacher managed to maintain a serious countenance for only as long as Hugh did not!

Sometimes teachers are absent from school. Head teachers used to hate this, because it often meant that they would have to take the class for the day, but it did give the head an opportunity to get to know the children. Wise head teachers bought copies, or small libraries, of books with titles such as, "A Miscellany of Unexpected Lessons" or "Shut up and Crayon!" Another, and rather better, way a head could familiarise herself or himself with the pupils was to do some individual work, or small group work, with all the reception children during their first term. In this way, their peculiarities and personalities could be assimilated and their names learned forever along with those of the nice and the naughty! Once enough names had been absorbed in these ways, it was easy for The Head Teacher to impress visitors to the school by greeting children by name, as they perambulated around the corridors and classrooms of the building. "You seem to know all the children," astonished callers would intone admiringly. "Yes," The Head Teacher would smile and say, inclining his head slightly in a suitably reverend manner, whilst thinking, "that's what you're supposed to believe." And The Head Teacher discovered another way to impress. When forced to be on his own with them, he secretly trained some classes to chorus a response whenever he came in to their classroom and greeted them. After saying something inconsequential by way of introduction to the teacher, he would turn to the children and say, "Good morning, children." The class responded in unison, "Good morning Oh Great One!" whilst the accompanying guest became wide-eyed. The children thought it was great fun, but it was necessary to take care which tactic was employed to dumbfound each visitor, for some were not taken with the "Oh Great One" ceremony, whilst others were not taken in by The Head Teacher's wily selection of which to children to greet by name.

However, a certain route to adulation is the extent to which ordinary persons are affected by most teachers' facility to calm a large gathering of young people simply by standing in front of them in silence. The secret lies in the curiosity of children and the *'presence'* of the teacher. "Watch this," The Head Teacher whispered to a local dignitary as both approached the school hall, where the entire body of children had been mustered for what is still called 'morning assembly' and the noise emanating therefrom would have been sufficient to close a canning factory on health and safety grounds. "I'll just go to the front," The Head Teacher continued, "and they'll all go quiet." The Head Teacher strode to the front of the hall. The teachers aligned along each side took to a little gentle hissing and tutting, intended to convey to the masses between them that something approaching order was required; it didn't. The Head Teacher stood in front of the assembled ranks. He said nothing, but his eyes were flickering from side to side, barely perceptibly and not sufficient to betray the fear raging inside him that they, the children, were not going to fall silent. But, little by little, they surely did and The Head Teacher was able to stand erect and allow himself a glance at the visitor and a tiny smile of triumph. Silence fell. It had worked again!

Leading the school 'morning assembly' is, of course, one of the regular tasks of all head teachers and the books available to help with this would fill half a local library and are a very useful tool for busy heads. Often, cunning head teachers, using the guise of 'professional development' as a reason or rather, excuse, to persuade other colleagues, especially deputy head teachers, to accept a share of this onerous duty. This is no surprise, for even having been given an 'assembly' book as a leaving present from his or her previous school and received another for several birthdays and Christmases, many of which offer boring and irrelevant material anyway, the average head would still struggle to present a fascinating assembly *every* morning! The Head Teacher was better than most. Following an invective from one of a series of nasty, self-seeking and incompetent Ministers of State for Education to the effect that heads were not taking sufficiently seriously the 'mainly Christian' flavour of the school assembly and, having spent twenty minutes haranguing the children about their bad behaviour, The Head Teacher walked tight-lipped to the hall door, opened it, paused, turned and added, "By the way, Jesus agrees with everything I've just said!" It is necessary to add that it was a somewhat rare occurrence for the Head Teacher to move from the ethical teachings inherent in his usual sermonising to anything clearly identifiable as Christian. One such shift happened when he'd returned from a trade union delegation — or perhaps a volunteer work brigade — in Central America with a tiny box of colourful woven 'worry dolls' he'd acquired in Nicaragua. There were six dolls and The Head Teacher, having introduced the carton of dolls to the children, explained that at the end of each day beginning with Monday, you could tell your troubles and worries to one of the little dolls before going to sleep and in the morning all would be well! The children were fascinated by this concept and The Head Teacher didn't have to wait long before one of them raised an arm to enquire, "What about the seventh day, there's seven days in a week?" This being precisely the question expected, The Head Teacher was able to respond in appropriately reverent tones, "The seventh day is Sunday and you can share your problems with Jesus."

In the course of his teaching career, The Head Teacher had seen thousands of assemblies performed by others and most of these had varied from dull exhortations to behave in a rather more selfless manner to tedious narratives that were supposed to reflect the beneficial outcomes of the same and outright sermons based upon dubious religious texts. He'd witnessed the new head at The Copse hectoring the boys without having much effect upon their attitudes or conduct, he'd dozed off looking fixedly and embarrassingly at one of the fifteen year old girls at Willington and he'd admired the young female teacher at the piano at Edward Street. As a deputy, he'd even had to take over when Big H wasn't available, most famously for an end-of-year awards stint, when the latter was off sick. The most memorable part on this occasion was when he rewarded the talents of an erstwhile athlete by describing him as "able to jump further than any other boy of his age in the entire city," before adding, "which, sometimes, is just as well." At Edgemount, as a newly promoted leader, the taking of assembly became a regular occurrence but few stood out. One that did, followed the death of John Lennon, which The Head Teacher heard about in his rather uncertain car on its even more uncertain radio on the way to school. The Head Teacher tuned in the hall radio upon his arrival at school that day and the children filed into the hall to the melancholy strains of 'Imagine there's no heaven ...' followed by a lengthy peroration by The Head Teacher about the life of what he described as "One of the greatest folk heroes of our times." Something of an overstatement, perhaps, but not worthy of the disdain, made obvious by her clicking and clucking, whilst waiting vainly at the piano for the usual hymn, of the only member of staff still present. It should be made clear that kindly heads often allowed teachers the assembly time to prepare their lessons in those days. The grateful staff hurried down to the staff-room for a gossip and a cup of tea, leaving the available musicians to take turns at the piano. There being only one such at Edgemount, privately known to The Head Teacher and Max as "The Poisoned Dwarf" as much for her appearance as for her personality, and it was she who sat grimacing on the day John Lennon died. It was The Poisoned Dwarf who opposed any belligerence on the part of teachers over pay and conditions and who opposed most of the out-of-hours activities promoted by Max and all of the innovations introduced by The Head Teacher. Of course, there is always one, or more, who feel that they have to frustrate change and, to his regret, The Head Teacher allowed "The Poisoned Dwarf" to put him off sufficiently on this occasion to call a halt before he'd really wanted to; something he never allowed to happen again. It was also at Edgemount that the local mayor made an annual tour of the all the schools. The first time this occurred, The Head Teacher prepared the assembled children with a few questions intended to elicit what they knew about the role of a mayor which, being as it didn't amount to much, he felt it incumbent upon himself to supplement with a little information, including the cocked hat and red robes, that they were to look out for when the mayor arrived. Some of the older children seemed surprised that their mayor was a woman and that she was adorned in a flowing blue robe! The Head Teacher made a mental note to remember to say something about both these contingencies when the mayor had left. The basis of most of what the mayor had to say revolved around how wonderful it was to worship the baby Jesus and how wonderful it was that another baby had been born recently, a baby prince into the illustrious House of Saxe-Coburg-Gotha or words to that effect. When she'd finished, The Head Teacher explained to the children that each one of them and all their baby brothers and sisters at home were just as precious as the rich and privileged baby prince whilst the mayor looked on aghast!

At Wheatfield's, The Head Teacher's assemblies fell into several categories. They were either run-of-the-mill, out-of-the-book homilies on morality, rambling descriptions of events in his or the children's lives, stern lectures on how to behave, plaintive appeals for them to rescue the world, or by far the best, robust yarns that entailed a bit of fun and excitement. "Hands up all those who kick dogs? Asked The Head Teacher one morning. Not a single hand went up. "I see," he said, "well, hands up all those who strangle cats!" Again, not a single hand went up. "Well, hands up all those who throw stones at budgies then!" evinced the same response. The Head Teacher allowed a long pause to build the tension, before finally asking, "Then why do you do all that to each other?" One day, The Head Teacher produced a genie's lamp that he'd picked up from a junk shop and looked just like a prop for a pantomime. "Look at this, children," he said, "what do you think it is?" Having drawn, from the more widely read and older amongst his audience, following some carefully worked questioning, that it was rather like Aladdin's lamp, The Head Teacher carried on with, "Well, what do you think I should do with it?" After a suitably drawn out exchange in which the children repeatedly implored him to rub it, and The Head Teacher repeatedly protested that something dangerous might happen, he allowed himself to be persuaded and he slowly and carefully rubbed the lamp, whilst saying aloud, "Okay, I'm rubbing the lamp now!" "What is your wish, Master?" boomed the preposterously deep voice of the caretaker, planted behind curtains at the back of the hall. When the hubbub had died away, The Head Teacher said, "My wish is for all the children of Wheatfield's Primary School to be kind and helpful." "Impossible, Master," came the response. Not many of the children really believed that the lamp had produced a genie, but if only one of them became a bit more considerate for a while, then it was worth it as far as The Head Teacher was concerned. Besides, it was fun. So was standing at the front knitting with enormous needles and red and white wool, whilst the children came into the hall. "I'm making a scarf for my cat, children," he said with sepulchral solemnity, "can you hang on while I finish this row please?" The Head Teacher completed the row with painstaking care amidst funereal silence. "The secret of good knitting is in the tension children," he explained unsmilingly, but with ever so slightly widened eyes. Quite what the point of all this is long forgotten, but there must have been one. As there was with the tin of Irish stew, relabelled with a wrapper from a similar-sized tin of dog food. "Look at these, children," said The Head Teacher and, proceeding to read from the list of contents on the label, then added, "It sounds good enough for me to eat, never mind the dog!" None of the children considered it odd when he produced a tin opener conveniently from his coat pocket, proceeded to open the tin and sniff its content, before extolling it again and suggesting that he might taste it. At this point, some of the children seemed shocked and others protested. The Head Teacher went on to sample the content of the tin, in reality cold, but quite nice, Irish Stew of course, before going on to explain the moral involved about not judging tins by their labels, books by their covers or people by their appearances. A point also well made in the story involving a birthday gift of a book, which its recipient passed on as uninteresting and unopened to someone else for their birthday. It was then that The Head Teacher, posing as the second recipient, opened with a flourish the children's story book he had bought for the purpose and pretended not to notice a ten pound note fall out and flutter to the floor. The ten pound note fell amongst the youngest children, those most unlikely to try and steal it and, when it had had been retrieved and passed back to The Head Teacher, he said, "Ah! You see children, books have hidden treasures." So do hats when you have a collection of about twenty and you can persuade a line-up of young people to try them on, whilst you explain where they all come from. "This straw Stetson is from Cuba," began The Head Teacher, "and this is called a 'boater' children, rich people wear them; this is a floppy hat that Miss Weaver gave me for my birthday — and goes rather well alongside her tawdry looking 'Cinderella' outfits," he could well have added — "and this is a Sandinista army hat from Nicaragua, and this one is a flat cap that working class men wear, and this one is a bowler hat for the upper classes — as worn by wealthy crooks in the city of London," he might have continued. It is not difficult to see how assemblies can become political, if heads allow them to, like the head of Riverside Primary School's friend in Scotland who described Che Guevara's dilemma as having to choose between the stethoscope and the Kalashnikov! Or The Head Teacher's own anti-war session as he fashioned a white crane from a piece of paper, whilst celebrating, if that is the right word, the anniversary of Hiroshima, Dresden or Guernica. However, it was, and perhaps still is, safe to raise issues such as apartheid, sexism and racism; carefully, but less so to dwell upon those of homophobia, peace and social class!

Teachers used to love their jobs and enjoy their lives, which is why The Head Teacher encouraged anyone who'd listen, including his own daughter, to become teachers and cajoled and impelled his 'creatures' to seek promotion. All of them became heads or 'leaders', the latest fashionable locution, of one kind or another. Teaching is hard work and teachers need and deserve professional integrity, lengthy holidays and a hearty breakfast. The first two of these have been under threat for a long time and the third is often skipped. The long and continuing attack upon teachers and their conditions of service having culminated in a substantial reduction of pay, an impending increase in length of service to the point where it would not be impossible to be taught by your great grandma, and pressures resulting in a significant proportion of teachers failing to get beyond five years of service alongside appreciable early demises through debility, dismissals and death; small wonder that schools have difficulty recruiting head teachers and finding someone to organise the staffroom tea fund! As time went on, The Head Teacher felt constrained to write to the leading national educational journal to apologise to everyone he'd ever exhorted to become a teacher.

In practice, staffroom tea funds, like the 'teachers' night out' collections, never balance, and as much as The Head Teacher tried to persuade young people into pedagogy, he, equally, discouraged them from becoming impromptu treasurers for their colleagues refreshment, rest and recuperation. Staffrooms in many schools used to be fairly grotty places and the greater the pressures upon staff, the grottier they became. The piles of unwashed cups in the sinks and on the draining boards, the dirty plates on the tables and the half-read newspapers strewn upon the chairs testified to this and the smoker's corners reeked of dirty ashtrays and unfinished cigarette ends. At The Copse, 'Biggles' used to smoke half a tipped cigarette during morning playtime and then stand it on end, so that it went out and he could pick it up again at dinner time, re-light it and finish it off. At one time, of course, nearly everyone smoked and, possibly in common with others, one of the teachers at Wheatfield's got so fed up that she took up smoking again, having previously given up for a number of years! At Wheatfield's, the smokers took over a washroom and toilet that became known as 'The Swamp' and The Head Teacher's 'creatures' took to gathering in his office on winter mornings before school to warm themselves and to make toast before the bars of the electric fire. All this changed when smoking became less popular and was finally banned, at which point, the inveterate addicts took to fouling the areas immediately outside the front entrance, thereby creating another eyesore requiring remediation and rules about 'dog ends', matches and acceptable standards.

The ritual of the 'teacher's night out', the TNO, carried on, and in spite of the problems besetting the profession, it remains a minor institution in schools. The all-male 'booze-ups' of The Copse contrasted with the slightly more sedate mixed occasions of the Moss Newton staff, though, in both cases, it tended to be the younger elements that were always present. On one of the first of these, The Teacher, as he then was, wore, as most men did in those days, his new best suit. It was charcoal grey, as they nearly all were then, with hand-stitched edges and he liked it. It was the custom to ease trousers at the knee by pulling them up a little when sitting, an action which forthwith tore a hole across the right leg and caused The Teacher to spend the remainder of the evening with his hand on his knee. The TNOs at big schools such as Willington tended to fragment into factions according to subjects taught, age or interests, and at some schools, like Edward Street and Edgemount, especially in situations in which staff were drawn from a widely scattered area, the TNO assumed a less important place in the school calendar and were, consequently, less well-attended. At Leafold and Wheatfield's, however, the TNO was a fixture of some moment and everybody who didn't want to become the subject of conversation there was certain to be present. Big H took charge and ordered the wine. "Four bottles of Blue Nun and two of Mateus Rose," he said, without even glancing at the wine waiter. "Hang on," interposed The King, "what if someone wants something different or some red wine? Shall I ask?" Big H said nothing and glanced around the room, while The King asked each colleague in turn what they wanted to drink and jotted it down on a beer mat, before looking across the table at Big H with obvious satisfaction. Big H then looked up at the wine waiter and said briskly, "Right. That's four bottles of Blue Nun and two of Mateus Rose." The King's lips parted, but he didn't speak. He looked at The Deputy, who didn't speak, and everyone's head dropped as they fell to scrutinising their copy of the menu. This procedure varied little and it was only when Big H was sick and failed to join the throng that red wine, beer and soft drinks were included in the initial drinks order. And that was the only time anyone had much fun and that was principally because Rudgey and his inevitable fund of bawdy songs and raunchy jests had been permitted by acclaim to re-join his ex-colleagues for the evening. TNOs at Wheatfield's started life as 'professionals only', which meant 'teachers only', a situation which the egalitarian principles of The Head Teacher soon changed, by manipulating the vote by cunning and persuasive lobbying before staff meetings, to include non-teaching staff. Another unwritten rule, or rather, custom, was that spouses remained excluded with the exception of Tom's wife, who knew the rule, but chose to ignore it, the woman concerned being what might nowadays be termed a 'cougar' and was then more likely to be called a 'harridan' or maybe a 'harpy', no-one bothered to challenge her, least of all her husband. The money required for TNOs, whether collected beforehand or solicited on the night was, and most likely still is, never enough to cover the bill. This wouldn't matter if the head, or the chair of governors if present, or both together with whoever is sufficiently generous to 'chip in' to avoid embarrassing scenes, manages to amass the shortfall, before half-drunk people begin accusing other half-drunk people of not 'shelling out' their full share. Or worse, as once happened in the Chinese restaurant chosen for a Wheatfield's TNO, a member of the party starts to dispute details of the bill and question the integrity of the restaurateur. Just at the point at which the proprietor appeared to be losing patience and the more timid diners swore that they heard, amidst raised voices, the sound of machetes being sharpened from the direction of the kitchen, The Head Teacher produced enough cash to make up the shortfall and several of his supporters, including, he was pleased to note, the black-haired girl, threw enough on the table to make up an acceptable tip. The group left hurriedly. Only slightly less embarrassing was the occasion on the final morning of a summer term, when the black-haired girl, perhaps to celebrate her promotion to a deputy headship in another school, organised a breakfast meeting for any or all of the teaching staff at the outlet of a restaurant chain close to the school. The Head Teacher's wife was informed of this arrangement by someone other than him and, suspecting that something was amiss, she turned up at the same time as the fried eggs, realised that she was in error — this time, at least — and said, bizarrely, "I've found your underpants in the washing machine," before leaving.

Schools, at least state schools run by LEAs, have always been rooted in their communities. The fact that most of them still are is in spite of, rather than because of, government education policies which now appear to be heading for a 'fire sale' of all schools via 'academisation'. This community involvement goes much deeper than, but always includes, parental involvement. Both of these were once non-existent, then became fashionable and, finally, became fundamental to the activities and well-being of schools, their personnel and their families. This might sound a bit pompous, but it's true, and teachers, who give up an astonishing amount of their own time, deserve the gratitude of their charges, the families and people in the neighbourhood of their schools. Those who have ever seen the looks on the faces of the elderly when a school choir performs in an old folk's home, or witnessed the tears flowing amongst the audience during a performance of 'Joseph and His Amazing Technicolour Dreamcoat', or observed mums and dads watching an infant nativity scene, or accompanied children distributing parcels at The Homeless Action Shelter will know about the contribution that schools and teachers have made. Mind you, it didn't always work and the 'Parents' room at Wheatfield's, which became more like an opium den than a 'drop-in centre' for meetings and informal exchanges, had to be quietly closed following a violent altercation between two of those it was intended to serve. But, overall, the enormous and positive contribution made by teachers over many years has been put at risk by the actions of governments and ministers of state, who wouldn't know the difference between a state school and a bag of bananas and have no conception of what life is like outside their own sheltered milieu.

One of the Head Teacher's weaknesses was to allow his enthusiasm for something that he felt was worthy to preclude the deployment of common sense and to exclude the sound advice of other rational counsellors. He had, somewhat late in life, become an adherent of the Co-operative movement and its political wing and, thereby, the Woodcraft Folk, which was, and is, like the cubs and scouts but without the sexism, militarism, religion and flag-wagging devotion to the royal family – a kind of 'scouting for socialists!' Assisted in this venture by Belinda and her husband Robby and several mums, there being a heavy demand for good wholesome after-school provision, two mixed groups of 'pioneers' were recruited and met weekly in the school hall, where the customary activities included working for the award of a variety of 'badges', singing and co-operative games. The latter was something The Head Teacher introduced later as an alternative to the competitive running and jumping normally included in the primary school annual sports day and, during one of the first of these, following a lull when The Head Teacher was awaiting his next mixed-age group for some diverting activity that he was supervising, one of the more forward of the mums spectating that afternoon called out to him. "I saw you on Sunday, who was that young woman with the dark hair?" A number of other mother's heads turned expectedly towards him as The Head Teacher replied with consummate aplomb, "That was my auntie." This was greeted by a tittering of merriment from the spectators and a grunt of disbelief from the questioner, just as The Head Teacher's next group of children arrived to rescue him from any further embarrassment and Sports Day resumed! Meanwhile, the Woodcraft Folk group's helpers were keen to expand the interests to include the tradition of camping and this was most easily accomplished by making use of LEA facilities with tents erected by the resident outdoor pursuits centre employees, hiring 'camping barns' or, as a last resort, hiring tents and erecting them on private campsites. This was all good fun and, ultimately, the Woodcraft Folk being a democratic organisation, the residential Woodcraft Folk Annual Conference was included with The Head Teacher attending as leader, accompanied by one or other of the female helpers providing a tasty alternative to the garrulous Belinda.

However, inspired by, amongst others, the black-haired girl of whom he'd become increasingly enamoured, The Head Teacher's most remarkable community initiative was the planting of four hundred and fifty saplings across the top of the school field at Wheatfield's, between the edge of the field and the dilapidated fence beyond which the estate lowered. Each child in every class planted a tree labelled with their own name on a little tag, assisted by a small army of staff, volunteers and parents and supported by the advice and encouragement of a local environmental group and some money from the LEA. Once the project was complete, vandals swept onto the field in the evenings to tear up the little plants and scatter them across the field and beyond and every Sunday morning a small team led by The Head Teacher and the black-haired girl collected as many of the uprooted trees as they could locate and replanted them. This process endured until the vandals wearied of the game and the restoration party could go on no longer. Not many of the trees survived, however, and the last time The Head Teacher strolled across the terrain, he counted twenty-one!

The lesson from this experience was not that you shouldn't try to involve the community in enhancing the environment, nor that you should give up in the face of adversity, but that you should persist and do your best for as long as you are able. That is what The Head Teacher told his governors, his colleagues, the PTA, the children and anyone else who'd listen. And that was why he persevered with his politics, only giving up on the Labour Party when it became clear from its behaviour, rather than from its manifesto, that it was no longer the party of the poor and would no longer champion the interests of their children. On the contrary, it began, and continued, to espouse what can only be described as right wing or downright Tory policies! Accordingly, The Head Teacher, having switched from the NAS early in his career and, to the bafflement of certain of his fellow heads, having spurned the advances of the nakedly self-interested National Association of Head teachers, became active in the NUT. As a deputy, he'd taken part in the action to relieve teachers of the compulsion to do dinner duties, when the union advice was to leave the premises at lunch times to avoid confrontations with the head, resulting in schoolteachers crammed on to local park benches blowing on their freezing fingers and eating their sandwiches, or cupping their hands around a match to light one another's cigarettes, or hunched in cars in side streets near their schools with the engine running to keep warm. And he'd survived the defection of several NUT members at Edgemount, when the 'poisoned dwarf' enticed them away over some trivial dispute, leaving only himself and Max as representatives of the NUT. And he'd loyally struck over pay and conditions and gone to the rallies and, grateful for Colin's loyalty, which made it possible, he'd persuaded the governors at Wheatfield's to close the school on strike days. And, within months of them both joining the staff at Wheatfield's, The Head Teacher and his initial appointment there, the young black-haired woman, carried the banner of the local NUT Association outside the local hospital at a demonstration against government cuts to the National Health Service. As a delegate to the NUT national conference, The Head Teacher was enabled to enjoy the allure of a number of British seaside resorts and the charms of several inland towns and cities, to discover the exquisite beauty of 'double entry book-keeping' as treasurer of the local association and to unravel the intricacies of tax returns as assistant treasurer to the NUT county division. All of these afforded opportunities to develop his relationship with the black-haired object of his admiration.

The Head Teacher never really understood why he was offered what was, for him, a second secondment, unless it was the outcome of him repeatedly making contributions and boldly attacking successive governments during meetings with the LEA advisers, officers and head teachers. At one such meeting, whilst making a criticism of what become known as 'local financial management of schools', a Tory strategy posing as giving schools greater freedom and independence but, in reality, one for making schools compete with one another in a 'market' for clients and one step away from a start on the privatisation of provision, The Head Teacher declared, that if he'd wanted to be a store manager, he'd have joined Tesco! At another, The Head Teacher remonstrated that the obsession with targets and testing — cherished by both Conservative and New Labour ministers of education as a 'quick fix' to exalt themselves and increase the likelihood of re-election — was distorting the broad and balanced curriculum that had so often been demonstrated to be the optimum route to enrichment, love of learning and improved standards and was risking the place of such things as art, music, history and multi-cultural education in schools' educational programmes. A few days later, The Head Teacher's telephone rang and the senior adviser for primary education informed him that the LEA was looking for a serving head teacher to make a training video on anti-racist and multi-cultural education and asked him if he'd consider a twelve week secondment to lead the project. An office and telephone close to the LEA multi-cultural education centre would be available as a base, cameras and equipment would be provided along with the services of the adviser for 'traveller education' and the whole thing would be supervised by the senior adviser for 'multi-cultural services'. Colin agreed to be 'acting head' at Wheatfield's for the term and The Head Teacher, whilst being unsure where to start, agreed to be the titular 'researcher' which, in practice, meant writing an outline script and 'story board', and to do all the preparatory work and co-operate with Eddie, the 'traveller education' specialist, who would be responsible for filming, editing and technical assistance – whatever that was! From being uncertain at the outset of what he was supposed to be doing, The Head Teacher progressed to a fairly intimate knowledge of what was happening in the authority's schools and a few telephone calls revealed a wealth of activity and learning about comparative religion, art, literature, festivals, customs, music, food and language in the multi-ethnic LEA and an enormous amount of hard work and goodwill by dedicated teachers and parents for the benefit of the children, schools and their communities. Eddie was an obese toper and joker who, whenever The Head Teacher booked lunch at a participating school, reacted with feigned shock and said, "What, is there no pub?" He turned out to be very intelligent and a first-class cameraman and technician though, and, thanks to the co-operation of all the schools, hours and hours of film were produced that had to be cut down to about forty minutes of pithy action and commentary. Eddie had a clever idea about the latter and found a man with a voice like an Eton educated cricket commentator, who, when he finally appeared on camera, turned out to be as black as coal! Another nice touch, amongst many, was to do a 'close-up' of an elderly white English female teacher talking to a mixed class of white and Asian teenagers and then pan from her to the youngsters sitting, or lounging, in various postures of inattention and have the teacher, a dual linguist, suddenly switch to speaking Urdu. The astonished reaction of the class was captured on the film. Close to completion, Eddie rang his senior colleague at the 'multi-cultural education' centre and said, "Nearly done Dave, we're just adding the credits. Your name will appear at the start of course, are there two Bs in 'Gobshite' or one?" Reflecting later, when a conceited, resentful and grudging specialist criticised the finalised film as 'patronising' and 'inaccurate', The Head Teacher thought, "Just look at the pictures of young children sharing, learning and working together without a trace of animosity, competition or fear" and he concluded that it was okay.

In his time at Wheatfield's, The Head Teacher, thanks largely to a change of political control at County Hall, enjoyed a board of governors that was sympathetic with his ideals and supportive of his attempts to defend education against the government thrust to pretend to enhance parental choice, whilst, in reality, imposing a myriad of selective admission processes like aptitude testing, faith criteria and appeals against rejection if the school of choice was full. All of this boiled down, in the end, to selection by social class, to persist in school 'league tables' based upon fallacious tests and to make substantial cuts in resources. Many of the governors, including parent governors, joined in the battle for the future of education through the rallies and demonstrations organised by 'Fight against Cuts in Education'. FACE may now be long gone, but the battle goes on. In fact, during the fourteen years The Head Teacher was at Wheatfield's, there were only two chairs of the governing body. The first was active in the Co-operative movement and the local Labour Party and the second was the local Church of England vicar. The former was so supportive of The Head teacher, that he frequently requested that he, The Head Teacher, mark the list of candidates for jobs to save him, the chair of governors, and the trouble of having to read their applications. "You know these things," he'd say with a wink, whilst the latter won the Head Teacher's heart forever by staunchly supporting the activities of FACE and the NUT testing boycott and by being so overcome with emotion that he was unable to address the assembled parents following the final night of "Joseph...!" Both were committed, hard-working and reliable.

Ofsted called upon The Head Teacher only once and that was sufficient to make him determine that it would never be twice. He freely conceded that it was his opinion that, had the punitive and bullying inspection regimes set up by the Tories and endorsed by New Labour been in place earlier, he would surely have fallen victim to them. The large buff enveloped arrived one November, in the days when ministers of education at least had the decency to give schools some advance warning and The Head Teacher opted not to ruin Christmas for the staff by sharing it with them, but waited until January to do so. It transpired that the lead inspector had some recent relevant experience of education, which is not always the case now, and was perceptive enough to observe that there were no "fat children", as he expressed it, in the school. Providentially, he was in the hall when a bull mastiff dog that had slipped its collar on the school, field bounded in through an open door amidst shrieking children and panicking welfare staff. No-one was hurt and The Head Teacher managed to seize the dog by the head and return it without mishap to its apologetic owner, who should not, of course, have been exercising it on the school field. The lead inspector told The Head Teacher that he stayed in a caravan to save on money and retain more of his allowances, which The Head Teacher considered to be a bit mean but, of course, didn't say so. He came in unexpectedly one afternoon, after school, and discovered The Head Teacher on his hands and knees in the hall, assisting some teachers with some preparations, which impressed the former and gratified the latter. The lead inspector was quite friendly, unlike some of his companions and, fortunately, The Head Teacher managed to find them accommodation for the duration of their stay in Barry's house which had been recently vacated, when Barry and his wife moved to another property, not council-owned, in order to prepare for future retirement. This had the advantage of keeping the inspection team at a distance in modest temperatures and enabling the teachers to share experiences and ideas for last-minute strategies for defending themselves. If it sounds like a battle, that is exactly how teachers see it and that is how schools prepare for it often with help from the LEA advisory service. The latter is not always as useful as it might be and the visit of Wheatfield's adviser was memorable for his dire warnings about the severity of Ofsted and the certainty of tears and recriminations. The Head Teacher was at pains to forestall the worst of his imprecations and had prepared a ditty, based upon the bear Balou's song from 'The Jungle Book', lampooning the adviser and Ofsted in the hope of lightening the mood of the staff. Heads do go to a great deal of trouble, again with the connivance of the LEA, to find easy options for weak teachers, to 'export' them temporarily through exchange or feigned sickness or 'hide' them during inspections. It has become a game and heads that can play the game are more likely to survive intact. Wheatfields, in spite of poor or non-existent, test results — the school, with the backing of the governors and parents, had boycotted the government's national tests — was pronounced 'satisfactory', a category which in 'government speak' now means 'unsatisfactory', but was then deemed enough to escape punishment. The Head Teacher made all the inspectors accept a Wheatfield's school calendar, replete with pictures and produced by the children and teachers they'd so recently been persecuting, which embarrassed some of them into a donation. A celebration followed without them!

Now and again, you make tangible decisions in life and not long afterwards, The Head Teacher decided that it was time to go. He had co-operated with the LEA in the past by accepting what were called 'knock-on' redundancies, where a teacher from an overstaffed establishment would move to another with vacancies, or to facilitate additional 'voluntary redundancies' in the second school involved. He had succeeded, with the assistance and support of the vicar, in securing several 'early retirements' with enhancement of pension years, which means a slight increase in pension, for several staff. Others, like the 'black-haired' girl, had gone to promotions. Nowadays, forty per cent of newly qualified teachers no longer get beyond five years of service and those that do rapidly begin to anticipate the day that they can finish and it is increasingly difficult to recruit head teachers. Both of these phenomena come courtesy of the government. By contrast, The Head Teacher never tired of relating the story of his aunt, who'd been a teacher for forty years and volunteered not for redundancy or retirement, but to continue working for an additional year, not to add to her pension pot, but simply because she loved teaching. Those days ended ages ago and The Head Teacher now approached the authority on his own behalf, to say that he was prepared to go as well.

The first entry The Head Teacher ever made in the Wheatfield's school log book included a quotation from a medieval philosopher called Peter Abelard, who'd had the great misfortune to fall in love with a nun called Heloise, with calamitous consequences. Abelard described his feelings before a disquisition as "all unprepared and trusting to my genius". The last entry suggested that there'd been more turmoil in education in the last fourteen years, than in the previous forty-four year history of the school. It concluded, "It is unwise to look back but the same oscillation between fear and hope, anxiety and expectation occurs."

Chapter 16

THE LECTURER

If you ask children today what they want to do when they grow up, they'll tell you that they want to be pop singers or footballers. They don't want to be lawyers or teachers and certainly not train drivers or air hostesses! It had, however, been a long standing aspiration of The Head Teacher, even when he'd been a factory worker and a nurse, to become a lecturer in a college or, better still, in a university.

At Wheatfield's, there was plenty of scope for contact with the nearby higher education colleges and to welcome students training to be teachers, later re-branded as 'trainees', in the never-ending quest for gratuitous change as an excuse for additional workload and bureaucracy. The Head Teacher made it a rule to always co-operate with the colleges and never to decline students on placements, particularly for what was then described as 'teaching practice' for, prior to the introduction of a myriad of what The Head Teacher called 'plumber's apprentice' type models of quasi-training to cheapen teacher training and demean and de-professionalise the job, that's what it actually was, the 'practice' of teaching. As a head of some notoriety he'd also been invited to help with the selection of students for the teacher training courses, when he gained some scurrility for consistently trying to reject all applicants with experience of, or an interest in private education, and to give talks about the expectations of schools when students embarked upon the various school-based observational and teaching practice placements. Thus, when the time came to relinquish his role as a primary school head, The Head Teacher contacted the placement officer, whom he knew well by then, of course, to seek some part-time employment as a lecturer or, failing that, as a supervisor for students in schools. The college needed part-time temporary help, especially during 'teaching practice' periods, so the placement officer, himself a refugee from the local LEA office, was only too willing to concur. And that was how The Head Teacher became The Lecturer.

Many years previously, as a young teacher, The Lecturer had applied for and been interviewed for a post as a lecturer of General Studies in a College of Further Education. He had no clear idea what General Studies was, so he took refuge in evasive answers and he didn't get the job but, fortunately, the post was far enough away from home and work so as not to brand him as a total educational poltroon. A second interview, this time for the post of lecturer in education at a run-of-the-mill college of higher education, merely served to expose the dearth of his knowledge of educational psychology, educational philosophy, child development and the process of teaching, all then rightly considered essential components of initial teacher training. His embarrassment became more acute when, during a break in proceedings, he encountered a rotund and narcissistic acquaintance from his own student days that treated him with dismissive contempt. He'd never been good at dealing with inferiority and left before the end of the day, thoroughly chastened and dispirited. But since these disappointments, his secondments, experience, partnership with the college and an afternoon's accreditation there found him well placed to succeed as both lecturer and supervisor, the latter being just another title for the former when performing the overseeing role.

Most of the young people who train to be teachers do so because they are idealistic, they like children and they wish to do something purposeful. A few do it because they can't think of anything else to do and a handful, like The Lecturer after graduation, either because they have relatives who are, or have been, teachers or because they just drift into it. The students that The Lecturer had seen whilst head at Wheatfield's were, almost without exception, of the first group and provided some insights into this and into the nature of teacher training. Wheatfield's was what used to be called a 'tough' school and would probably still be designated as 'challenging', so the school always stipulated that the college send only students who could cope with 'difficult' classes, were hard working, well-prepared and had that indefinable quality that all teachers should have; 'presence'. Besides, it was felt that certain classes needed an inspirational teacher from time to time as a break, either from an atmosphere resembling the 'storming of the Bastille', or from the routine boredom of the fare served up by the permanent incumbents! Notwithstanding that, it appeared that the college responded to this in a way that can best be described as random selection, most of the students turned out to be valuable assets and only a few made the lives for their mentors more difficult as the progress of the children stalled. Typically, this was because they misjudged the needs, the interests or the temperament of the children. For example, it is unwise to dish out sweets as a reward, even if your supervising class teacher was secretly doing so, when the school has a healthy eating policy and has banned sweets and crisps or to request that a child move out of your way by shouting, "Shift your ass, big ears!" or encouraging another with, "Come on, fat boy!" Nor is it a good idea to arrive dressed like a Chicago gangster or someone from the enclosure at Epsom Races or, by contrast, like a pop singer or a street child from a Dickens novel — unless a history lesson is planned. "They clearly missed the bit in my talk about sensible, serviceable, saliva-proof wear," thought The Head Teacher at the time.

Embarking upon his new, post-retirement, career, one of The Lecturer's first assignments included a visit to a disadvantaged establishment in a deprived location in a large seaside town, long since run down by the government policy to dump homeless families in redundant 'bed and breakfast' guest houses. At the end of the afternoon, the head of the school, a woman of The Lecturer's acquaintance and, therefore, familiar with him — though not overly so — intercepted The Lecturer to ask, "Are you enjoying your retirement then?" "Well," The Lecturer replied, "you remember when the caretaker came to you first thing this morning about the break-in?" "Yes," said the head, guardedly, "and you recall being called to the hall at dinner-time, when that boy had defecated under one of the tables?" The head nodded and frowned, unsure of what was coming next. "And that big man with the tattoos, who came in just now, shouting and swearing about something or other?" "Yes," smiling this time. "You had to deal with all those things, not me," said The Lecturer, with some emphasis upon the "you". "So, yes, I am enjoying my retirement!" he concluded. Indeed, the role of 'important visitor', who had to be accorded respect, was offered tea and biscuits that he didn't have to prepare himself and was treated with some deference and co-operation by the teachers, whilst having no responsibility for what went on in the school, was one that The Lecturer quickly grew to enjoy and to relish!

His personal circumstances having altered somewhat by this time, The Lecturer now dwelt in a modest flat and did not possess his own car, which meant that he had to become familiar with the timetables of the local train and bus companies. As a 'supply teacher' that he knew slightly once told him during a chance meeting on a railway platform, "You can get to nearly every school in the county by bus or train, if you get up early enough." "Not ideal," thought The Lecturer, so, although he was happy to use public transport a lot of the time, he developed considerable skill at persuading the teachers co-ordinating student placements in the schools to agree to the timetable of visits he'd prepared, as soon as he'd been given a supervision contract by the college and then to book college cars in line with these programmes. Sometimes, he'd even book the cars first and then persuade the schools to fit in with his timetable. It was tricky, but it nearly always worked out satisfactorily and even on the odd occasions that it didn't, The Lecturer could fall back upon the loan of a vehicle from one of his 'creatures' almost all of whom he was still in contact with either, as in the case of the 'black-haired girl', through an unseemly intimacy or, as with most of the others, socially through the union.

On an early assignment, The Lecturer took the first available morning train to see some students in a neglected local industrial town. Despite the train being held up by, of all things, sheep on the line, The Lecturer arrived in good time and came upon a lengthy queue, made up entirely of women, outside an enormous building in the town centre. His enquiries revealed that a quasi-opera singer was to perform there who, in the view of those in the queue, was so unbelievably handsome and a crooner of such superior quality, that it was necessary to get out of bed before it became light in order to be sure of buying tickets for his 'one night only' show in the town! On another visit, this time to a seaside town the name of which attracted far more admiration than the experience of actually being there, and again having taken care to get to his destination with time to spare, The Lecturer was leaning on the railings between the beach and the promenade, when an enormous wave rolled in and broke all over the hapless man! It's never easy to explain why your trousers are all wet, especially to young children, without arousing suspicion! Soon, however, The Lecturer was allocated his own 'patch' for the supervision of 'teaching practice' in another seaside town, more famous for fish than for sea bathing, and more famous for both of those than its contribution to education. Originally planned to be the 'Bath of the North', it had one crescent of tall stone buildings and not much else! It was, however, still renowned as a fishing port and although nearly all its boats had long since been laid up, and most of the local fish came from Scotland, it still boasted some of the finest fish and chips in the country! The Lecturer was not averse to partaking of the same as and when his commitments in the town's schools permitted.

With his own group of schools and transport arrangements pretty well sorted, short-term contracts with the college became fairly regular and The Lecturer began to enjoy himself. He always made a point of supporting the students and would offer a word of encouragement from time to time, such as, "This is hard work, you're doing really well" or "I'll sit next to Wayne and Dirk. Okay?" He also supported his schools and their staffs, often agreeing to see another student, a different student, or staying on to help out during difficult times, such as staff absence and even supervise the odd class in a crisis. The schools appreciated this level of co-operation and, indirectly, the college benefitted from it. In this way, The Lecturer acquired a reputation amongst the students for being sympathetic, even empathetic. They might laugh at his old-fashioned objection to them calling the children 'guys', insisting upon no gender discrimination in their organisation, and his astonishment at those who felt able to go out to night clubs during TP, as 'teaching practice' was commonly labelled — "You have it to do," as one young woman put it — but they were grateful for the understanding when The Lecturer assisted them in cutting through the weighty bureaucracy increasingly impinging upon their time in the form of copious record keeping and 'box-ticking', for his forbearance of those who had to work at a Tesco checkout in the evenings to make ends meet and for the little chocolate Easter eggs he invariably gave them following their de-briefing at that time of year. "Sally is off ill," said one, "but she said to be sure and get her Easter egg" as news spread of this artful munificence.

At college, The Lecturer began to be called upon to accept teaching roles, which involved teaching teachers or, at least, teaching intended teachers. The courses were devised by the college, mostly around educational issues and were highly participatory in that practical and group work was often involved and The Lecturer had a great deal of freedom to interpret the content as he saw fit and to emphasise the things that he felt were important and would be of most benefit to his young charges so that, for example, 'behaviour management' was explicitly linked to theories linking rights, rewards and responsibilities and useful strategies for involving children in devising their own systems for setting limits upon what was acceptable in their own classrooms. The Lecturer was even requested to write a format for a session on the role of classroom assistants and how they might best be employed by teachers. He took this to be a sign that he was becoming more and more a part of the establishment at the college. This was reinforced when he was approached by a colleague, senior to him as everyone was of course but rather younger and a female, with the bald statement that she needed a man! The Lecturer protested that he was happily married which, although an outright lie, lightened the exchange and it turned out that she was trying to find a suitable member-of-staff to improve the balance of the composition of a panel for an imminent set of interviews. The Lecturer was duly enrolled and took part in the selection of a 'Lecturer in Education'. It has to be acknowledged that his contribution was fairly low-key and, despite having some grave misgivings about the choice of the successful candidate, he went along with the rest of the panel — all women — in their decision to appoint another woman which, in its turn, went a small way towards addressing the preponderance of males in the college. The Lecturer's place in the college was further buttressed when someone dropped dead minutes before the start of a 'teaching practice' preparation day and he, The Lecturer that is, not the dead person, was called upon to step into the breach and take one of the seminars with a group of students. As it happens, the unfortunate deceased individual was quite well known to The Lecturer, for they had both been interviewed some time previously for a headship of a junior school that was so big that it could easily be considered more of an achievement to get that interview than the next job that was actually obtained!

The sudden demise of the colleague, who died so unexpectedly, left a largish quantity of unmarked and partly-marked student dissertations, which The Lecturer was requested to take on and complete. Given that these were three thousand word essays on esoteric subjects and in the light of his lack of experience in the field, The Lecturer was a bit reluctant to do so, but there existed a fairly clear 'marking scheme' and a reasonable allocation of paid time, so he agreed to do it. It led to more marking, for instance of exam papers or individual questions in exam papers and of 'second marking' of assignments — a form of 'moderation' or 'quality control', which was becoming more and more prevalent — during the course of which The Lecturer, several times, either resisted challenges to his evaluation and scoring or led the way in interpreting the grading schemata.

The intellectual levels of the students varied as much as any equivalent group in any other institution in any other place and they were institutionalised in much the same way. Their potential approximated to the bell-shaped 'normal curve' beloved by social scientists with not many being what The Lecturer, or anybody else for that matter, would describe as 'outstanding'. A lot were ultimately turned into very good teachers, but a handful who, although they nearly always qualified, wouldn't be able to teach a row of dead chickens; a metaphor often used by The Lecturer in his head-teacher days to depict certain colleagues. In the latter category, was the young woman who carefully explained to her six-year-old pupils how determined she was to become a teacher, a message, clearly, intended for her tutors rather than the children. The Lecturer asked her if she'd ever considered a career as a librarian. She entirely misconstrued his meaning and it was only the intervention on her behalf of teachers in her TP school that saved her from being the only student that The Lecturer ever failed. He often wondered what happened to her and what became of the student with hygiene problems who was, fortunately, female and so had to be counselled by a female colleague and the young man who always seemed to be under the influence of mysterious substances or simply still drunk from the night before but, nevertheless, was a gifted practitioner and a skilful exponent of the English language, or the gifted mature student employed by The Lecturer to demonstrate not just her abilities and some obscure educational practice, but also ,his own successful techniques in identifying and cultivating talent. And all the great majority of enthusiastic and hopeful young people at the college, "Good luck to them all," thought The Lecturer.

The students were often asked to fill in forms, giving feedback concerning the performance of their teachers. The Lecturer thought that this was a very welcome innovation, partly because he considered that it gave the youngsters a chance to pass judgement upon the quality of their experiences, but mainly, because he got good reports attesting to his recent familiarity with the 'real world' of schools and teaching and indicating that they thought that he was good humoured and 'down-to-earth'. The esteem he was held in was such that some groups even invited him to accompany them on their own raucous end-of-year outings, which usually comprised a few drinks in a local hostelry, sometimes preceded by a meal in an Indian or Chinese restaurant. The Lecturer was sufficiently astute to depart prior to the degeneration of the evening into a drunken spree. On these occasions, and in the course of the daily teaching and supervision, surrounded by eighteen to twenty-two year olds, The Lecturer marvelled that more of the male staff didn't accede to temptation and 'go astray' in the face of the sheer beauty and engaging personalities of many of the female students. He had, at times, to make a concerted and conscious effort to avert his gaze and that he succeeded was, he felt, a tribute to his restraint, wisdom and perspicacity. Besides, he was too old. Nonetheless, individual seminars were extraordinarily trying!

The Lecturer loved to go to the Senior Common Room where the coffee, supposedly to be paid for, but in practice — because no-one ever checked — was free and of excellent quality and the luxuriant armchairs made school staff-rooms look like 'cabin class'. Informal gatherings in the Senior Common Room for lunch or coffee resembled reality shows on television, with each participant vying to be the cleverest, most erudite and most whimsical of those present. The egos of these people were such that formal staff meetings were even worse. As a temporary part-time member of staff, The Lecturer felt that he was in no position to compete with the regular college staff, so he only contributed when requested to do so, which was often at the beginning of the meeting when none of the others there wanted to risk making fools of themselves or attracting opprobrium. Perversely, as far as they were concerned, this often gave The Lecturer an opportunity to demonstrate his own discernment and offer genuinely constructive ideas. As a diversion, The Lecturer gave those he encountered most often 'nicknames', normally reflecting his opinion of each of them. Thus, only he knew who the 'Meg Ryan' of higher education might be or 'The Postman', whose epitaph would read 'return to sender' or who was the ethereal 'Ballet Shoes' flippantly flitting across the 'boards' of edification, or the 'Pig in Muck', 'Catwoman', or half a dozen other such epithets.

Every so often, significant decisions in life have to be taken. Having evolved, along with the 'black-haired' girl, what might be described as a 'deny it all' philosophy which — notwithstanding any compelling circumstantial evidence — articulates that in the absence of direct eye-witness accounts, no accusation can be sustained or proven, there does comes a time when some resolution must be reached. These determinations can arise quite suddenly and unexpectedly. The Lecturer had already made several, including such momentous steps as retirement from the teaching profession, deserting the marital home and getting divorced. He now made another.

In a classroom in the erstwhile fishing port that had become his domain, and shortly following the introduction of the so-called 'joint observations' of the so-called 'trainees' — another layer of quality control and bureaucracy – The Lecturer sat listening to the droning tones and pejorative conclusions of his fellow college tutor's evaluation of the lesson, whilst glancing through the window at the children running and shouting in the playground outside. In a scene reminiscent of Orwell, he looked at the student, perplexed and tired, and from her to the class teacher, sitting impassive and patient, hoping desperately not to be asked for her opinion, and then on to the school's student tutor, eagerly awaiting an opportunity to interrupt and expound her views and, finally, back to his bombinating colleague. As he waited for a chance to defend the student, The Lecturer thought to himself, "I don't want to do this anymore." So, he didn't.

Chapter 17

THE ACCOUNTANT

Whoever said that an actuary is someone who finds accountancy too exciting may have been correct, for accountancy is more than exciting; it's exhilarating, it's provocative and it's satisfying!

When the tumbling columns of figures and the rolling rows of numbers culminate in the totals they are supposed to, when the excess of income over expenditure is equal to the assets in hand and when the whole caboodle balances, little can surpass the gratification and fulfilment to be derived therefrom! A little training in such things as the exigencies of 'double entry book-keeping' uncovers the arcane nature of it all and makes the role of an accountant a relatively straightforward one. The problem, for such organisations as trade union branches, is that everyone believes that accounts are complex enigmas, so everyone goes quiet when the election of 'the treasurer' is mooted, a treasurer being — more or less — a form of accountant. In fact, it is more of a paradox that so many people are willing to admit to being hopeless at mathematics, yet none would concede that they cannot read! Being illiterate is a taboo, but being innumerate is considered okay! This, of course, means that treasurers are rarely elected, at least not when they are present, sometimes someone volunteers and sometimes someone is coerced into the job. The third of these possibilities was the case during The Head Teacher's time in the National Union of Teachers, when he was persuaded to take the position in his local branch and, later, that of 'assistant treasurer' in the regional unit or 'Division' made up of ten or eleven branches. That is how the Head Teacher and, indeed, The Lecturer and Councillor in their turn became The Treasurer, which amounts to a modest form of accountant, serving in the first of these posts for exactly twenty-one years and in the second for rather less than that.

Being a treasurer in a 'voluntary' organisation is not a full-time proper job any more than being a referee or a waiter had been. It is an honorary occupation with, if anything, a modest annual 'honorarium'. The difference for The Treasurer was that he'd been a waiter and a referee mainly because he desperately needed the money; he became a treasurer to help out the union. It has to be owned though, that the honoraria and the occasional day's pay through a recondite agreement between unions and employers called 'trade union duties facilities time' was, as a Cockney might say, "A nice little earner!"

Now, when The Treasurer took over the branch accounts, they stood at 'minus sixty-seven pounds' and when he relinquished them two decades and one year later, they amounted to tens of thousands of pounds, a fact of which The Treasurer was justifiably proud, albeit that his judicious handling of the union's monetary affairs wasn't the only contributing factor. It is true, however, that all treasurers jealously guard their organisation's resources and he was no exception to this rule. At the outset, the job was, or appeared to be, extremely daunting. The Treasurer arranged to meet the outgoing incumbent to collect the 'books' and to get an informal seminar on how to proceed. At this point it, became clear that The Treasurer's predecessor had very little idea of what he was supposed to have been doing, or what he actually had been doing, every question raised by The Treasurer being greeted with, "Well, that's another thing," followed by a lengthy diatribe about the difficulties encountered and the lack of assistance available from anyone, anywhere. The exchanges ended with The Treasurer feeling rather more confused than he'd been at the beginning. He departed laden with two enormous volumes measuring approximately three feet by one foot — about three hundred by nine hundred centimetres in modern maths — the 'books'!

The first of these was the 'Cash Book', in which every transaction of the branch was recorded in great detail and the second was the 'Subscriptions Book', in which a record was maintained of all the members payments for their union membership fees. It was painstaking rather than complex, but The Treasurer made great play at the Annual General Meeting of bending under the considerable weight of these tomes, solemnly donning a bowler hat that he'd been given as a joke Christmas gift when it came to the presentation of the accounts and placing heavy emphasis upon the abstruseness of the intricacies involved in accounting. At the close of his address, he would, equally solemnly, say, "I will take questions on the accounts; any challenges to the accounts will be interpreted as applications for the job." There were always one or two genuine questions and these were put as meekly as the petitioner could manage. There were never any challenges and, if there was the slightest doubt that a question was bordering upon provocative, The Treasurer would immediately assert, "Are you challenging?" No-one did.

The NUT, wisely, provided some good quality training for its treasurers, often in posh hotels with superb food and refreshments, and tried hard to encourage members to pay their subscriptions by standing order or direct debit directly to headquarters. Local secretaries were entreated to persuade their membership to go over to the direct subscription process and The Treasurer's branch secretary — co-incidentally the 'black-haired girl' — proved to be one of the first to realise one hundred per cent of members paying their subs direct to the union by direct debit. It doesn't take much imagination to realise that this reduced the workload of local treasurers by a prodigious amount and, following the introduction of a computer programme to do all the calculations, more training in its use and simplification of the returns to headquarters, the job of treasurer became, to say the least, undemanding. The secret was not to let on to the membership that it was easy and to maintain the ethos of a perplexing task performed by an inscrutable necromancer. That wasn't difficult either!

Assistant Treasurer at the regional level was, at first, a sinecure. It came with representation on the divisional executive and absolutely nothing to do, a kind of 'representation without anything taxing' to misquote the eighteenth century American rallying cry. That continued until the divisional executive, following an exhausting and often ferocious debate on the issue, was determined to employ some office staff! This had the effect of transforming an avocation into an intimidating prospect of gargantuan proportions and The Treasurer was suddenly faced with learning the technicalities of calculating National Insurance and Income Tax deductions, increments and pay slips, overtime and holiday entitlement and a myriad of other things. Fortunately, training was again available — if not in such opulent circumstances — and it wasn't all that long before poring over tables of figures in the Revenue and Customs booklets was superseded by another, commensurately labour saving, computer programme, which had the effect of eliminating the drudgery and reducing the labour to a small amount of time each month. Again, to retain the mystique, the secret was not to let on!

Eventually, of course, The Treasurer surrendered both these situations. The first to avoid confrontations with other officers over his increasingly jealous protection of the branch's resources and the second because, like with so many other things in life, it seemed the right time to do so. Thus the role of accountant lapsed.

Chapter 18

THE COUNCILLOR

"Esta gran humanidad ha dicho: basta!" Ernesto (Che) Guevara.

When The Teacher joined the Labour Party as a relatively young man, so many years ago, it was because he'd also said, "Enough!" Within a very short time, he'd been approached to consider standing in the local elections for the party and was duly elected to represent a ward in the small, parochial and decaying ex-mill town where he and his family then resided. In those times, being a councillor was an entirely voluntary, unpaid activity which the Labour Party, in its wisdom, advised its followers to consider carefully before taking on because, not only was it a demanding role in terms of time and effort, but also, because career progress might be hampered by the prejudices of right-wing employers. Years later, The Councillor could recall little of these early experiences, aside from battling the noise from a sawmill, getting a concrete production works to dampen down both the dust and the racket, especially at weekends, persuading a water company, that if people paid for its product, they really ought to be getting it piped into their houses, coaxing droves of Irish students from a nearby Roman Catholic College hall of residence to come out to "fight the 'Unionists'" at election time, despairing the ruination of his prized leather coat during a particularly significant and persistently sodden campaign and watching elderly Tories sleeping through quite important council meetings in the Town Hall.

There was, however, one event – if 'event' is the right word for something so momentous and dreadful – that would be seared upon The Councillor's memory for the remainder of his life. At this stage of his life, whenever the chance occurred, The Councillor liked to take his young daughter to her day nursery. A few moments lingering to watch the children in such a setting is as great a pleasure as watching the audience from behind a Punch and Judy stall at the seaside or taking a child to a circus and as great a contrast with what The Councillor experienced on one such occasion as it is possible to imagine. Returning home on his bicycle one day from this errand The Councillor chose, almost by chance, to pass through a short street of terraced dwellings close to his home. About halfway along the street thick black smoke was issuing from the broken windows of one of the houses and flames were licking around the figure of a man at the front bedroom window. As The Councillor threw down his bike and crossed the road it became clear that the man at the window was holding in his arms a baby – the youngest of his three children – and was desperately trying to avoid the conflagration dancing around him whilst, simultaneously, attempting to get to the window sill without endangering the child. Instinctively, The Councillor rushed over to the pavement below the bedroom window and shouted, "Throw the baby to me Mario!" The man at the window hesitated for what seemed a long time but was only a few seconds before dropping the child to The Councillor who caught it and then promptly dropped it on the ground, picked it up again, turned and hurried back across the road to where a woman was standing in a doorway opposite. "Look after the baby," The Councillor ordered the woman who nodded and took the baby into her own house. It was at this point that The Councillor wondered aloud, "Where are the other children?" The man at the window had disappeared so The Councillor ran down the street and around to the back of the house where several neighbours had already erected a ladder up to a rear bedroom window from which, apparently, the stricken father had jumped only a few seconds previously. The strength of the inferno now raging inside the house was such that entry through the doors was impossible. No one seemed about to mount the ladder so The Councillor did and the heat and the smoke and the utter blackness within drove him back, defeated. The other two children were still inside.

Mario suffered quite serious burns. He recovered but life both for him and for his wife, who was at work at the time of the accident, would – of course – never be the same again. Thanks to The Councillor's clumsiness, the baby suffered a broken leg but was otherwise perfectly alright. His dad had saved his life! The Councillor, responding intuitively to the usual unrefined press intrusion, started a fund for the family beginning with a house to house collection during which the only person to question his – The Councillor's – intentions was the local vicar. In the days before 'social media' the fund nonetheless raised, in the end, quite a considerable sum. A funeral cortege doesn't normally attract much attention but when there are two coffins, one holding a six year old and the other a four year old, it does. The Councillor did not court publicity but it followed this tragedy. His response was one of his better moments.

Local government re-organisation brought this spell of public service to a close, but over twenty years later, when The Head Teacher had laid down his pen for the last time, he, too, became a councillor in the historic town in which Wheatfields was located, to represent the ward in which most of the children and parents of Wheatfield's school resided. One of the main features distinguishing this second spell was that, by the late twentieth century, being a councillor was a function which attracted remuneration! In other words, it was paid and taxed just like a job. It needed to be as well! It was a testing period that lasted for several years, coinciding almost exactly with the period as a lecturer, until the time that The Councillor, having become exasperated with the Labour Party and finding himself wishing to vote with the Greens, or even the Liberals, more times than he cared to count and occasionally actually doing so, resigned his Labour Party membership and completed his term of office as an Independent Socialist. The Councillor felt compelled to articulate his dissatisfaction in a 'letter of resignation' presented at a full meeting of the council's Labour Group of councillors! This document was a bit pompous, but it identified twenty-odd areas of policy in which The Councillor felt that the Labour Government was not living up to expectation. These included the failure to complete reform of the unelected and unrepresentative House of Lords or to deal with hyper-inflated executive incomes in corporations and, particularly, banks, the neglect of effective reform of welfare, housing and benefits to support the weakest and most vulnerable sections of society and creeping privatisation in the National Health Service. There were other contentious issues, but the one which occupied The Councillor most, not surprisingly in the light of his career history, was education which, in his resignation presentation, he summed up as an underwhelming quasi-Tory shambles! His sometime colleagues listened with polite forbearance and ignored totally all that he'd said. They did, however, because of the precarious balance of numbers representing the various groupings of political parties in the chamber at that point, exact an undertaking from The Councillor not to resign from the council until the following election was due. He agreed to this.

Elections are curious and complex procedures for political adherents and little understood by those who are not, as they say in Spain, 'al tanto de'. A thorough election campaign begins with the assembly of a team of local members and supporters, who are prepared to give up hours of their time to walking the streets, writing addresses and knocking on strangers' front doors. Ideally, several deliveries of a succession of leaflets will be made to every household in the constituency or ward when several rules apply. The first of these is the 'three second rule'. This rule stipulates that the leaflet must immediately catch the eye and then the attention of whoever picks it up first, assuming it hasn't been savaged by a dog or urinated upon by a cat, and before the elapse of the estimated three seconds it takes for the picker-up to transmit it to the nearest rubbish bin. It isn't easy to write and produce leaflets of such arresting quality and very few ever pass the 'three second rule'! The second rule for leafleting is the 'push it right into the house without getting bitten by the dog rule'. This rule is intended to reduce the number of visits to Accident and Emergency departments and to ensure that leaflets are not left sticking out of letter boxes and, therefore, easily removed by opposition party leaf-letters. The third rule follows on from the second and states that any leaflets other than those of one's own party, that are left sticking out of letter boxes, should be removed and destroyed. These rules also operate for the delivery of newsletters, which wise and hard-working councillors regularly use in the belief that they inform the voters and enhance their chances of re-election. They do neither, because of the 'three second rule' and because there exist many other sources of information available to the electorate — or not, as the case may be.

Next, copies of the Electoral Register for every ward in the constituency are obtained, cut up and pasted onto cards so that, by and large, each card has the names, addresses and 'polling numbers' of one street of voters, except in the case of very long streets or roads when two, or even several, cards may be required. A bit like 'Blue Peter for grown-ups'! The completed cards are used in something called a 'canvass', in which groups of canvassers visit all the houses listed on the cards, knock on doors or ring bells and ask the occupiers if they are likely to support the appropriate party. This process, of course, is replete with pit-falls. The house may be empty, or those within pretending that it is. There is a distinct risk of abuse, rarely anything other than verbal, and some householders may ask difficult questions or tell lies. Time consuming exchanges, debates and arguments on the doorstep should be avoided if at all possible in favour of a simple 'yes' or 'no' to identify where the favourable voters are and if they'd like a car to call to take them to the polling station on the day of the election. This latter contingency is best offered to the sick, or elderly, and those living in sheltered accommodation, or other 'old folks' homes, and care has to be taken to make sure that drivers aren't ferrying wily opposition voters to the polls, though quite how this can be totally avoided remains unclear!

The Councillor was sufficiently assiduous to have canvassed most areas in the towns where he dwelt, but an election campaign didn't end there. The information on the 'canvass cards' which, whilst never being complete, was usually largely correct, and had to be transferred onto things called 'Reading pads' several sheets thick. Legend has it that they were called 'Reading pads', either because they had been piloted first in the town of Reading or, possibly but less likely, that someone called Reading had invented them. The 'Reading pads' were assembled upon tables in the local party's election HQ, called 'Committee Rooms' for some obscure reason, presumably dating from centuries past when committees met there. The clever bit involving the 'Reading pads' was that when written upon the data was reproduced as carbon copies on all the sheets of the pad to facilitate tearing them off one at a time to pass to 'knockers up', whose task was to go around the streets and alleys knocking on the doors, where all the voters who'd promised to vote Labour resided and reminding them to go to the polling station before the appointed closing to time to register their votes. The carbon copies enabled this process to occur several times during the course of the afternoon and evening, allowing for a methodical effort to maximise the vote, whilst occasioning considerable irritation to residents!

Meanwhile, loyal members called 'snatchers' spent the day on a rota basis outside as many polling stations as there were available 'snatchers' to cover them, asking intending voters for their polling numbers on their individual polling cards. These cards were sent to all voters on the electoral register by the local council but, contrary to what many voters believe, they aren't needed for voting and many people lose or forget them anyway, so that the 'snatchers' were obliged to ask such voters to ask the Polling Clerks inside the polling station for their number and report it went they emerged. Astoundingly, the majority of voters complied with these unauthorised requests, a lot of them in the belief that the 'snatchers' outside the polling stations were election officials, so that a steady stream of lists of the polling numbers of those having voted could be collected by 'runners' operating between the polling stations and the committee rooms and passed to activists there to cross off the

'Reading pads' as the day progressed. Needless to say, voters thus crossed off would not be troubled by the 'knockers up'. Frequently, several of the principal political parties would employ 'snatchers', who would, oddly enough, co-operate with one another in the collection of the numbers. Good committee room organisers keep comfortable chairs, cups of tea and bowls of hot-pot for the workers on election days.

Finally, as many volunteers with cars who were available and were prepared to drive voters — aged, infirm or lazy — would be issued with separately prepared lists of addresses to call at and, hopefully, transmit supporters to the polling stations. Some drivers had to be reminded to wait for and return these people to their dwelling places! The Councillor believed that the Conservatives always had an inbuilt advantage at election time, in light of their greater numbers of car owners, their wealth, resources and access to media support, but, whilst this is doubtless true of General Elections, it is far less so for local elections.

This recondite election campaigning procedure persists to this day and, theoretically, it is almost perfect in that many of a party's sympathisers can be identified and cajoled into voting, but in practice, it is flawed. Not every potential supporter can be reached, some tell lies or decline to reveal their intentions with an exasperating smile and the vexatious phrase, "It's a secret ballot you know," which canvassers were told — rightly — to interpret as 'against' and there are, increasingly, limits to the numbers of people prepared to devote time and effort in working for political parties that don't seem to be much different any more within an electoral system, which results in most voters not voting for the winner! The climax of an election campaign is, of course, 'the count' and if you're ever tempted to attend the counting of the votes — don't. They are held in town halls or other large venues, are extremely boring, take ages and are attended by a handful of candidates and supporters of all those contesting the election. Once inside, it is impossible to leave, which is particularly daunting if you are associated with a party that is likely to lose, or worse by far, loses unexpectedly. This latter contingency is rare in these days of sophisticated opinion polling, in which the polls begin to form opinion rather than reflect it, but it remains an outside possibility. Either way, there are few experiences worse than having to witness the smug look on the faces of victorious Tories, whilst not even being able to slink away for a consoling pint or two! In the end, it didn't matter much for The Councillor, for he eventually concluded that a universal franchise was not worth much when the choice was limited to choosing between blue, yellow, pink and, later, purple Tories or wasting one's vote on a party, or individual with no chance of winning. Thus, voting may be seen as a bit like the elucidation offered by a minor left-wing political organisation, 'Slaves; choose your masters'!

In the course of leafleting and canvassing in his own ward and in most others, The Councillor, in common with his comrades, enjoyed a variety of experiences. Little discrimination was to be made with leaflets, except that, if there was a shortage, one should concentrate upon the most favourable streets, those likely to house sympathetic voters. The Councillor, in his early days as a relatively inexperienced campaigner, suggested that the team knock on doors and ring bells in an affluent area to enquire as to whether the householder would mind sharing their Labour Party circular with their neighbours because the local Labour Party couldn't afford to print them in sufficient numbers for every household to have their own copy! This idea was barely more enthusiastically received by his fellow members than they anticipated it would be by the well-heeled home owners, to whom it was intended to be addressed. At least, The Councillor never went as far as to offer to deliver his opponent's leaflets! This actually occurred in a small nearby town, where the mayor, an elderly and kindly Labour nominee, delivered her own and the Tory candidate's 'flyers'! "Well," she is reported to have said, "I was doing my own, so I thought I may as well do his as well." Leafleting is a boring task, one which The Councillor's daughter liked to accomplish on her roller skates and one which The Councillor often did by bicycle, propping the vehicle against the kerb, whilst going up and down each side of a street, until the day when he returned to his bike only to find that it had been stolen! Leafleting is so tedious that it is best done in teams, or at least with one other person, and with frequent breaks for refreshment. It can be enlivened when hostile recipients tear up the leaflets and toss the shredded remains into the gutter or, worse, in the face of the person doing the leafleting. Delivering with the 'black-haired girl' one evening, a well-dressed women of mature years emerged from a house and, waving the Labour Party leaflet vigorously, called out to The Councillor, "Look here! My husband is the Conservative candidate!" "Don't worry, madam," replied The Councillor, "there aren't many long words in it and he may well understand 'fairness' and 'equality' even if he doesn't care for them."

Canvassing is almost as prosaic as leafleting. It isn't often invigorated by slammed doors, oaths and threats or even by protracted discussion on the doorstep. It is rarely more than, "Hello, I am your Labour Party candidate, can I count on your vote at the election?" This, or the alternative "I represent your Labour Party candidate," may often get the response, "What election?" Getting the required "Yes" or "No" from time to time takes a bit longer than expected, or may invoke a more animated retort, in which case, a raw canvasser may need help and a practised, erudite campaigner will have to 'soldier on', whilst his supporters hide just out–of-sight around the nearest corner. The Councillor was good at such exchanges, but even he was sporadically baffled by the behaviour of some voters. People like the elderly lady, resident in a tiny terraced house in the shadow of a long defunct cotton mill, in which she'd toiled for her entire adult life, who turned out to be an implacable Tory voter, or the sartorially impeccable gentleman resident in a leafy suburb, who interrupted The Councillor's introduction with, "No problem, old boy, we're socialists here!"

As for getting things done, The Councillor quickly realised that not much of any moment was possible, given the restricted local authority financial resources and the limits this imposed upon its budgeting. Once things such as street lighting, rubbish collection, housing maintenance, parks and cemeteries had been paid for, the few thousand pounds available for grant aid to charitable and community organisations became the subject of impassioned debate in the council chamber.

People who remember when the so-called 'care in the community' strategy was introduced, ostensibly to improve the way people with serious mental health problems were treated by placing them in 'family groups' in circumstances as close to normal as possible, but in reality, to reduce its cost, will be unsurprised to learn, that when The Councillor encountered families residing on either side of what they described as "A house full of dafties who expose themselves in the back garden" the response he got from the local council was to raise the garden fences by about three feet! However, whilst the opportunities to help families were limited, if a councillor could persuade council officers to repair the odd roof, dig up some dangerous looking tree roots, or get an old lady's garden dug over, he soon acquired a reputation as one who could 'get things done'! Whilst his introduction of a 'Best Kept Garden' scheme had little impact, perhaps The Councillor's most significant, if limited, successes were in holding the line between a vociferous and often racist minority on the Wheatfield's Estate and the determined and outspoken Asian shopkeeper and taking a leading role in the residents' campaign against the redevelopment of their estate by a corporation that they felt was interested more in profit and the choicest homes overlooking the river, than it was in their well-being and the improvement of the entire area.

Most of a local council's work is done by its full-time officers and staff. In theory, they take their lead from the majority political party through the council leader, the cabinet and the committee system. The party with most elected councillors controls the leadership and most of the positions on the cabinet and places on the various committees are allocated according, firstly, to the numerical strength of each party and, secondly, according to the interests of individual members of those parties or, sometimes, groups of parties. There may be a residual of 'independents' such as The Councillor became towards the end of his time on the council, but true independents, as opposed to quasi-Tories, are rarely elected. The Councillor opted for membership of committees where he fondly imagined he might do some good such as Housing, Planning and Personnel. His experience of these soon disabused him, as he discovered the limits of the council's powers and such things as the level at which unpaid Council Tax would attract any attempt by the council officers to recover it. It became permissible for members of the public to attend planning committee meetings and to speak in support of or in opposition to items on the agenda. During a debate concerning the erection of a mobile phone mast, The Councillor approached the member of the public who'd spoken most vehemently against it and asked him if he possessed a mobile phone. "Yes, I have," he replied, "but I'm getting rid of it soon." The Councillor voted in favour of the erection of the mast. Participating in the appointment of a new Council Treasurer, a fundamental and important position, The Councillor was sorely tempted to support a colourful reprobate, whose predominant talent appeared to be derived from his previous membership of a pop group, his seemingly unlimited confidence and his sense of humour. Notwithstanding the unquestionable value of all these qualities for the post, he was not successful, and The Councillor was persuaded to vote for a more suitably qualified candidate. Much later, The Councillor felt that his initial instinct, one that he'd tried to follow many times previously, to go for the risky option, may have been the correct one after all.

Apart from being paid, another significant development over the two decades between The Councillor's two stints in office was that the time it took and the effort involved had expanded considerably and was in inverse proportion to the amount of thanks local councillors generally got, the latter mostly being precious little! A good councillor remained one who was able to devote hours and hours upon the needs of the constituents of her or his ward and one who was able to distinguish between goals that were achievable for them and for the greater good and those that were a waste of time and energy, because there was no chance whatsoever of their accomplishment! The Councillor was quite proficient at differentiating between what could and could not be achieved, the garden fences and the housing campaign being examples.

Having agreed with the local Labour Party to remain until the next electoral cycle, when the time came, The Councillor was presented with the choice of standing as something other than a Labour Party candidate or simply retiring. In the event, he was persuaded by a small army of trade unionists, teacher ex-colleagues and friends to stand again. He stood as a Socialist Alliance candidate and was soundly defeated as he expected and predicted, by the Labour Party candidate. Councillor and Accountant were the last of any paid employment. There being no other callings attracting emolument, only The Pensioner remained.

Chapter 19

THE PENSIONER

One of the criteria measuring the values of any society is how it treats its old people; others include how it treats its young and its sick — there should not be any poor — and on all of these, successive governments have failed. In fact, with the dismemberment and privatisation of the NHS and every school in the country now looking increasingly inevitable, it isn't just failure but deliberate and culpable wickedness.

Meanwhile, being a pensioner is rather like being paid not to work. The critical question, though, is whether the payments are sufficient to sustain an enjoyable existence. In many cases, they aren't! The Pensioner became fond of propounding that retirement was "not a soft option" but, of course, he knew that it was, because if you are in receipt of the Old Age Pension and an occupational pension such as half a lifetime in teaching provided and if, on top of that, you are married to the 'black-haired girl' — now 'silver-haired' and in her second headship — then, you are rich indeed.

> "Cut off even in the blossoms of my sin,
> Unhouseled, disappointed, unaneled.
> No reckoning made, but sent to my account
> With all my imperfections on my head."
> (William Shakespeare)

Or, as The Pensioner's dad would have put it, "That's it … and all about it!"